D0107718

Dear Teddi,

Congratulati...

I am grateful

in my life

love
[signature]

# UNLIMITED
# VISIBILITY

13th Ocean
11:00
1st
st mtn →
1st road on Rt →
Back Creek —
1.5 miles on right
dirt lane small
Bay Pines farm
House

— Rumi —

enneagram
9

*The space between prayers is sacred*

*power within us is always at*

# UNLIMITED
# VISIBILITY

*work, turning our thoughts into things and our words into the experiences of our life.*

*Lessons and Processes
to Improve
Your "I" Sight*

## STEPHANIE SORENSEN

**DeVorss**

Copyright © 1996 Stephanie Sorensen

ISBN: 0-87516-687-3

Library of Congress Catalog Card Number 96-83746

DeVorss & Company, *Publishers*

Box 550

Marina del Rey, CA 90294

Printed in the United States of America

This book is dedicated to the courageous ones
who are taking the spiritual journey within themselves and,
in the process, changing the only thing that can be changed:

One's thinking and point of view.

# *Acknowledgments*

My deepest gratitude to:

Laura Hart and Lilly Jessup, who first introduced me to a world beyond the physical;

Dr. Ernest Holmes, author of *The Science of Mind,* for his clear thinking and eclectic point of view;

Russell Davis, my son, for a lifetime of love and inspiration;

The Science of Mind students of the Oahu Church of Religious Science for inspiring these lessons;

Dr. Jamie Phillips for the gift of shelter and time;

Linda Holt, Religious Science Practitioner, for lovingly reading every word and doing every Process;

Gloria Phillips and the Grand Blanc Religious Science Study Group for their enthusiasm, support and valuable feedback;

Arthur Vergara, editor-in-chief, DeVorss and Company, for his wisdom, patience, and tenacity.

# Table of Contents

# Foreword

For many years I have watched people enthusiastically enter into the study and practice of Science of Mind, reach a plateau, and then struggle to realize in their lives all that the teaching seems to offer.

I noticed that at about this point some people dropped away while others sought for some magic "additive" that would make it all work, as though Science of Mind by itself were not enough.

Being fully convinced that Science of Mind *has* inherent within it the answers to help resolve every problem of life and bring us to a happy fulfilled life, I became aware that somehow we were not taking our people deep enough into Spirit, into a fuller awareness of the Oneness of All Life–our Oneness with God, if you will. Because it is here we find the faith that will bring us into the deeper consciousness, past the "parking place" syndrome and the "get rich quick" mentality. Too often when we say, "I believe..." we are really saying, "I am *trying* to believe..." But, I would remind you that it is done unto us "as we believe," not as we are *trying* to believe, and that we must *be* before we can do and have.

While I was pondering these things in my heart, wondering how best we could fill this gap, along came what I believe to be by far the best answer yet in the form of Stephanie Sorensen's book, *Unlimited Visibility.*

I was delighted when Stephanie asked me to write a foreword to this book. I have long been an admirer of hers. She is lovely to look at, of course; but to be in her presence and catch her essence is even lovelier. One immediately feels a sense of peace and quiet confidence. My plan was to scan the manuscript and write something appropriate. Instead I found myself soaking in it, devouring it. "She has done it!" I kept saying, "Stephanie has filled the void that I have been feeling so keenly for so long."

Her scholarly style makes it easy to get right to the point. She never varies from the principles of Science of Mind. Her format makes it completely practical–a quality too often missing from other metaphysical works.

The book can be used individually; it is also excellent for study groups. The processes at the end of each chapter make it usable right from the beginning by anyone seeking the better way.

If it sounds like I am high on *Unlimited Visibility*, you are right. I predict it will quickly move to the best-seller list, especially in New Thought literature. My copy will take its place right beside my *Science of Mind*. Holmes and Sorensen, what a pair!


Dr. Fred Vogt
*President Emeritus*
*United Church of Religious Science*

# Introduction

This book is inspired by the teachings of the Science of Mind by Dr. Ernest Holmes. Its intention is to assist the reader through lessons and processes in learning to use more effectively the Unlimited Power of Mind which is present within her or him. There are twenty-six Lessons, which the reader may study individually or with a group. Each Lesson is followed by a Process applicable to the Lesson for individual and group use.

The Science of Mind is a doctrine of Love rather than fear, of unity rather than dualism. It is a philosophy and a way of life based upon One All-Inclusive Divine Spirit, One Unlimited Mind, One Unified Consciousness, which is forever expressing Itself in and through all of creation, including all of humankind. No one is left out. The Truth is available to all who seek It and never fails to manifest for the one who acknowledges and calls upon It. Regardless of each individual's awareness of his or her Divine Originality, the soul of every being–individually and collectively–is inseparable from its Original Perfection and Unlimited Potential.

We must each rely upon self-knowledge–our personal awareness and inner perception of Life–or, as Dr. Holmes put it, "the direct revelation of Truth" within us. No one can step outside of his or her own consciousness for an impersonal world-view, since all that we are aware of is a composite of our beliefs, which veils our experience of life. What we hold in our mind as "true" is the basis for all that exists as real for us. Ernest Holmes wrote in *The Science of Mind:* "We can never get outside ourselves; we shall always be interior in our comprehension, we are here and It is here."[1]

All that we shall ever experience–from the beating of our own heart to the pulsating rhythms of the farthest star–we shall discover first within ourselves. Our life experience is composed solely of our awareness–the totality of our thinking.

Every soul is inherently beautiful, spiritually immortal, and potentially unlimited. By changing our thinking about ourselves and life from a purely material basis to an origin of spiritual substantiality, we begin to see value and meaning in ourselves and the world around us. "Our recognition of Truth is Its pronouncement of Itself, and when a man says 'I am,' it is God proclaiming His own Being."[2]

It may be a simple notion to believe that we can change our life experience by changing our thinking, but thoughts are powerful things, and "simple" isn't always easy when it implies altering our fixed views and cherished beliefs about ourselves and our relationship to life. It is often difficult for us to get our "bloated nothingness" out of the way, but if the reader is honest in working through the processes, he or she will find a Greater Self, one that is beautiful, capable, and free–imbued with the Nature of God, the All-Good, All-Powerful, All-Knowing, and Ever-Present Spirit. "When we see It as It is, then, we shall see ourselves as we are. We can only see It by looking at It through our own eyes."[3]

It may sound unrealistic to say that it is merely our human misconception of ourselves and life that limits our experience of boundless, harmonious, peaceful, productive, and unified living. But to the degree that each of us is able to free ourselves from the misperception of mortal frailty, human division, and spiritual severance, we will find that we are, indeed, a vital, inseparable part of a Sacred, Unified Life. Through our personal, individual realization of a Divine Inner Self and our understanding that God alone is that Self, we shall discover that all that we shall ever require for a rich, loving, peaceful, and fulfilling life experience can be found within us. And as we increase our awareness of the Truth within, we shall not only find deeper spiritual insight and greater individual possibilities and opportunities in our personal day-to-day life, but we shall experience a deeper compassion for one another and a greater desire to serve the whole of life.

There is no limit to the "I" that originates in Spirit or to what we can see "through our own eyes" when we realize that our eyes are the windows of the Unlimited Mind of God. May the lessons in this book assist you in returning to your Divine Originality–that Beautiful, Powerful Inner Self which is Altogether Good and Eternally One with Spirit.


NOTE

*References to the Holy Bible are either to the King James Version, designated (*KJV*), or to the translation by George M. Lamsa, published by Harper San Francisco, designated (*Lamsa*).*

*References to* The Science of Mind, *by Ernest Holmes, published by G.P. Putnam's Sons, are designated SOM and are given by page and paragraph. Thus SOM 413:5 designates* The Science of Mind, *page 413, paragraph 5. These references are also valid for earlier editions of* The Science of Mind *(1938) published by Robert McBride and by Dodd, Mead.*

*Quotations from* The Science of Mind *are verbatim and many contain masculine pronouns that serve as reference to both men and women. Ernest Holmes wrote "Spirit is the Father-Mother God, because It is the Principle of Unity back of all things. The masculine and the feminine principles both come from the One."* [4] *It is in this* spirit that the majority of the masculine pronouns in this book are used–inclusive of both male and female–and not intended in any way to exclude or diminish the value of the feminine.

The word prayer in this book refers solely to Affirmative Prayer or Spiritual Mind Treatment as defined by Ernest Holmes: "If when one prays his prayer is a recognition of Spirit's Omniscience, Omnipotence, and Omnipresence, and a realization of man's unity with Spirit, then his prayer is a spiritual treatment."[5]

1. SOM 173:4.    2. SOM 336:2.    3. SOM 36:3.    4. SOM 82:1.    5. SOM 149:2.

# 1      One, Not Two

Our Inseparable Oneness with God

*There is nothing
more vital for us
to understand
than our inseparable
oneness with God.*

Jesus said, "I and my Father are
one." [1] The teachings of the Science of Mind are based on
the concept of oneness. "The Ultimate Cause back of all
things must be ONE, since Life cannot be divided against
Itself. The Infinite must be One, for there *could* not be *two*
Infinite Beings." [2] "The world of *multiplicity* does not contradict the world of *Unity*, for the many live in the One." [3]

Our acceptance that all life is One Life and that we
are one with the Ultimate Cause is intrinsic to our spiritual
growth and well-being. Do we actually think of ourselves as
*one* with God, absolutely inseparable–a single entity? Or do
we speak of life as if we, and those around us, were somehow
separate from the Oneness of Life?

Do we think of ourselves as a being of *Wisdom*–or
do we speak of ourselves as forgetful, misguided, stupid, and
inept?

Do we identify ourselves as offspring of Unlimited
*Good*, heir to the fortune of the Universe–or is our conversation about our lack of prosperity and freedom?

Are we aware of the Unconditional *Love* that beats
our very heart–or do we perceive ourselves and others as
unlovable and unworthy?

Often we speak as if there were two simultaneous
but *separate* states of affairs: 1. The Spiritual Realm to which

we are *potentially* connected, a state of being where everything is bliss–complete, perfect, good, loving, harmonious, and peaceful, and 2. The material world and our life in it, where many things are miserable–fragmented, imperfect, bad, unloving, disharmonious, and chaotic. How often does it seem to us that God is off having Its whole, complete, and perfect good time, while we are left in the world trying to fix what's wrong or not working–like our messed-up psyche, imbalanced temperament, flawed past, uncertain future, dysfunctional relationships, and seriously threatened financial picture? And that's just what needs improvement with us, *personally*. Then there's the work that needs to be done on everyone else!

## A VERY PRESENT GOD

Sometimes our view is that if we pray hard enough, and say just the right words, God will zoom in from that Place where things are perfect, flow through us and our imperfections from some Higher Plane of Consciousness, and help us out of the material mess we're in. But there is no place in the Oneness of Life, in the Allness of God, for anything to be occurring outside of Life or away from God. There is no place for God to flow FROM. God is already everywhere present. God may be the wind, but God is also the stillness. God is in, through, and around everything, everywhere, all the time–not only in potential but in actuality. God is Life, and we're living *that* Life.

Right where we are, right now, within and outside each of us, the Invisible or Spiritual is *being* the visible or material. "The worlds were framed by the word of God, so that things which are seen were not made of things which do appear."[4] What we experience as ourselves, and what we believe about others and life, is our *perception* and *interpretation* of the Invisible, Spiritual Realm made visible, and not of something separate from It.

We use words to help us to get a sense of God, a feeling of Spirit, a glimpse of Truth; but words can confuse us because we are attempting to use them to describe That which cannot be described at all. Joseph Campbell wrote: "There is no way you can use the word *reality* without quotation marks around it." Often when a certain metaphor is used to assist us in a greater awareness of Spirit, it can also give us a *mis*perception of Spirit as well. For instance, to give a sense of the abstract, fluid nature of Spirit, we might say that Spirit "flows" through us and out into our lives. Thinking of spiritual flow can give us a beautiful sense of movement and change in our own life when things seem to be stagnant and stuck. But if we're not careful, thinking of Spirit as flowing can give us a subtle sense of separation from Spirit.

A woman who was seeking to improve her financial situation using the Science of Mind Principle "God is Source" told me that nothing seemed to be happening to improve her financial picture even though she was "open to her good." She said that she was fully expecting God to flow into her life and was wondering why the flow hadn't started yet. I asked her where she thought God would be flowing *from*. As we talked, she discovered that she had actually been separating herself from the good she desired by thinking of her Spiritual Good as being *somewhere else* and needing to flow *to* her, rather than experiencing Spirit, Abundant Good, and Unlimited Source as already present within, around, through, and *as* her.

## WE ARE THE EMBODIMENT OF GOD

*Wherever we are, God is*–because we are the embodiment of God.

3

We are spiritual beings. When we think of Spirit as simply flowing, we might feel more like a tube than a spiritual being–a material hollowness through which the spiritual substance flows; a human being waiting on the Spiritual Being to flow through us. But there is not God *and* materiality. There is God *as* materiality–yet not really materiality, but the *appearance* of materiality or what we call material. "God is not conscious of matter as we know it."[5] "Matter" is our limited interpretation and *mis*interpretation of Spirit. If we were like a tube, the tube would also have to be made of Spirit, since *"things which are seen were not made of things which do appear."*

God creates out of Itself. There isn't some substance that we are made of or that we use called matter, and another substance that God is made of and uses called Spirit. "There is one nature diffused throughout all nature; One God incarnated in all peoples…'Whose Center is everywhere and Whose Circumference is nowhere.' "[6] The Infinite has no boundaries and therefore could have no circumference. And, if the Center of God is everywhere, it means that God is at the Center of each of us.

If you have been waiting for God to show up in your life, it is time for you to go look in the mirror. If you are alive, God is already Present. You won't see all that you truly are or were created to be, but you can catch a glimpse. The Light of Life that is at the Center of our being emanates from our eyes. To believe that God is not Present in our life when we are alive is to believe that there is a life apart from God. But this cannot be, for Life must be One–because Life cannot be divided against Itself.

There is nothing that we cannot know, or do, or create in our life as a being of God. But we must cultivate an attitude of spiritual confidence, and we must experience ourselves as the unlimited, creative being of Spirit that we are. "Prove me now in this, says the Lord of hosts, and I will open the windows of heaven for you and pour out blessings for you until you shall say, It is enough."[7] When we speak of ourselves and others as limited or valueless, we limit the boundless blessings that could be ours. When we don't love ourselves and others, we are saying, "Enough!" to Unlimited Love's expression in us. Each of us must ask: "As a seeker of Truth, do I seek to prove the presence of Spirit in my life day-to-day, moment-to-moment?"

What we focus on in mind becomes an unceasing prayer–a heavenly petition which will manifest as our reality. Our prayers are composed of beliefs that will be answered as the experiences in our life. Our *thoughts* become *things* (or a lack of things)–things we want and things we don't want. When we condemn ourselves and others to a solely material existence, we put a cap on our experience of the Infinite Qualities of Goodness that are right where we are as the Substance of all that we see.

## "ONE, ONE, ONE...NEVER TWO"[8]

When we are steadfast in our acknowledgment of oneness with God, we do not look to the world as the source of our joy, happiness, love, and peace. We look *within* to that Eternal Wellspring of Life that is always pouring forth the aliveness we seek. Then we bring joy, happiness, love, and peace to our world. At the Center of our being we find that we *already are* that Life for which we are looking. Rather than looking for something to make us happy, we bring our happiness to everything we do. When we know that we are love, we no longer wait to be loved, we bring love to all of our relationships. And when we know that we are intrinsically good– because God is good and we are one with Goodness–we cease to allow feelings of unworthiness to block the blessings of heaven in our life.

We are created to move in perfect harmony, live in total unity, and love unconditionally. It is unnatural for us to run up against Life or away from each other. We are *one* body and *one* life. It is our perception that we and others are separate from Spirit and that there is a life other than God which creates fear and conflict with one another. "Ignorance stays with us until the day of enlightenment, until our vision toward the Spirit broadens and casts out the image of a no longer useful littleness."[9]

The practice of the Science of Mind is a conscious commitment by the practitioner to mentally reveal and express the Truth of Being which is that God lives not only *in* us, but *as* us. All that we shall ever know of God we must experience within ourselves, and when we discover the God within, we shall see God in the world everywhere we look.

From *The Vedic Upanishads* come these beautiful words of oneness:

> *O Lord,*
> *Thou hast woven the web of the*
> *world from Thyself,*
> *as a spider spins its threads...*
> *Thou art the one God, hidden in all.*
> *Thou art everywhere, the inner Self of all...*
> *Remaining still, Thou movest all that moves.*
> *Thou art the Eternal among eternals,*
> *the consciousness within all minds,*
> *the unity in the diversity.*

Thou art One, not two.

# One, Not Two

## *INDIVIDUAL*

Write ten affirmations about yourself that identify your oneness with Spirit. (Example: *"I dwell eternally in the Heart of Love and I express love in all that I do."*)

1. _____

2. _____

3. _____

4. _____

5. _____

6. _____

7. _____

8. _____

9. _____

10. _____

Write ten affirmations that identify your spiritual oneness with others. (Example: *"The Heart of Love beats in me and I feel Its Resounding Pulse in all that I see."*)

1.

2.

3.

4.

5.

6.

7.

8.

9.

10.

## GROUP
Discussion of Lesson.

**Activity:** Same as for Individual.

**Meditation:** One, Not Two

*(Facilitator: read slowly with restful music in background, if desired. Begin with one of the Relaxation Techniques on pages 299-300.)*
        Imagine now a ball of White Light within you right where your heart is…a Light that is beautiful and pure in Its Radiance…a Light that is peaceful and loving in Its Presence…see and feel this Light expand until it fills your entire body…see and feel the Light as It radiates out beyond the boundary of your physical body…as if It were emanating from every pore of your body…see and feel the Light now as It radiates from you and touches and embraces those on either side of you…see and feel them in the Light…sense them seeing and feeling the Light…see them seeing the Beauty and feeling Its Peace and Love…now see and feel the Light as It touches everyone else in the room…sense all those in the room seeing and feeling the Light…seeing the same Beauty and feeling the same Peace and Love…see and feel the Love as It fills the entire room…until all that you can see and feel in the room is Light…Its Beauty, Peace, and Love…now see and feel the Light as It emanates and radiates from the room and on out into the neighborhood, and sense all those in the neighborhood seeing and feeling the Light…seeing the same Beauty and feeling the same Peace and Love…imagine that the Light is filling the entire city…and now the whole state…and sense everyone in the whole state seeing the same Beauty and feeling the same Peace and Love…see and feel the Light moving across the country, flowing in every direction, filling the continent…moving across the oceans…see and feel the Light filling every country… every town…every city, permeating every field…every battleground…every heart…every soul…every leader…every soldier… every refugee…everyone…every place…see and feel the Light

radiating around the Earth...sense everyone of Earth seeing the same Beauty and feeling the same Peace and Love...now imagine the Light radiating from Earth and filling the entire Universe so that all that you can see or feel is the Light...and sense that the entire Universe is seeing the same Beauty and feeling the same Peace and Love...all Life is One Life...the people of the Earth are One...the Earth is One with the Universe...the Universe is One with Spirit...and Spirit is all there is...One, not two...not Spirit *and* you...not you *and* something else...One Life...One Beauty...One Peace...One Love...and nothing else...see and feel the Oneness of Life...all beings of Life...one with each other... one with the One...and bask in the glow of the All-Embracing Light...(*Facilitator: allow a minute or two*)...now bring your focus back into the room with your eyes still closed...and continue to be aware of the Unifying Light which unites everyone here, and everyone here with the Universe...and on the count of three, open your eyes.

---

1. John 10:30, King James Version (hereafter shown as KJV).   2. *The Science of Mind* (hereafter SOM), p. 68, par. 3 (hereafter e.g. 68:3).   3. SOM 69:2.   4. Hebrews 11:3 (KJV).   5. SOM 208:5. 6. SOM 42:2, 330:2.   7. Malachi 3:10, George M. Lamsa translation (hereafter shown as Lamsa). 8. SOM 493:6.   9. SOM 418:4.

The Mind/Body Connection:
Learning to Perceive Ourselves as Whole

*Is there someone who really "irritates" you? Did the outcome of a certain situation leave a "bad taste in your mouth"?*

Is there something that is "eating away" at you? Do you know someone who's "a pain in the neck" or a pain somewhat lower? Do you find a particular excuse "hard to swallow"? Are you "pissed-off," "broken-hearted," or just plain "sick and tired"? If so, you may be setting up a mental atmosphere for the physical manifestation of pain, discomfort, fatigue, and disease in your body.

There is an inseparable mind/body connection, and there is no division between what we think and what is "out-pictured" in our body, even when we are not consciously associating our thoughts with our body. "The simplest way to think of body is to realize that it is the objective manifestation of a subjective mind and consciousness; and if we are to be well and happy…the mind must be peaceful and harmonious."[1] How we think and feel about the world can be (and often is) *recreated* in our physical body.

The Science of Mind gives the term "body language" a more expanded meaning than the analysis of crossed legs, folded arms, or other gestures of attitude. How we *talk* about our life is also body language. The word *body* as used in Science of Mind means all objective manifestations of invisible thought. Our body extends beyond our physical self and includes our body of finances, our body of relationships, our body of activities, and the body of ideas behind *all* that we outpicture in our life. And it is all interrelated, interconnected, and inseparable from our individual health and wholeness. "We would not say that consciousness is in the body, but rather that *body is in consciousness!* " [2]

We speak as though we know the association between what we think about our life and the state of our physical body. Look at how we talk about events and relate them to functions and dysfunctions in our body: We try to "digest information" or "swallow our pride." *Body language can turn into body problems.* That "pain in the neck" in our life can easily turn into a chronic stiff neck. Something that is "hard to swallow" could become an incessant sore throat or, in time, an esophageal tumor.

When we focus on negativity and constantly affirm it in our life, and when our thoughts are angry, judgmental, and condemning, our problems are likely to be reproduced in our body. Anger can manifest as boils. Our being "pissed-off" can lead to a bladder infection. Irritation can create a rash or sinus problems. If we let things eat away at us long enough, we could develop cancer. And being sick and tired in our mind can make us sick and tired in our body.

I'm not saying that a particular mental attitude absolutely has to lead to one particular physical problem. What I am saying is this: We can't truly practice the art and science of mental healing, believe that thoughts become things (and that *our* thoughts become things), accept that we can change things with our thinking, *and then assume that our body has a mind of its own!*

## "EVERYTHING IS A THING OF THOUGHT"[3]

We cannot be effective mental practitioners if we believe that our body is outside the realm of thought and that it is in a world of infectious germs and allergens all on its own. We talk about germs and viruses as though they were separate from ourselves and Spirit, as if they lived *between* people and *on* people, and as though they could be given and caught. Even on a Sunday morning, after we've talked about (and sung about and prayed about) the allness of Spirit, someone will inevitably say to me at the door, "I don't want to hug you because I don't want to give you my cold."

Some people make a *career* out of being sick. If they didn't get sick, they would have nothing else going on in their lives. Did you ever ask someone you haven't talked to in a while how they have been, and you were told about all their aches and pains? I always get a few Christmas letters at the end of the year, and often they include a year's worth of ailments. "We caught the flu from Aunt Lucy and we were down for three weeks with it," or "My bursitis was acting up this winter so we didn't travel, but (praise the Lord!) I didn't get the hives again this spring." It is a sad commentary on our life when the highlights are pain and sickness.

If we want to experience health and wholeness, *we must think of ourselves as healthy and whole.* We must dwell in a healthy place in consciousness if we want health to dwell in our body. "Turn entirely from the condition, or limited situation, to its opposite, to the realization of health, happiness and harmony."[4] We cannot outpicture health, happiness, and harmony while our mind and our words are portraying disease, discord, and disharmony.

It helps me to think of the physical body, and all material form, as *congealed* subjectivity or jelled consciousness. "The Subconscious (or Subjective) state of mind–sometimes called the unconscious state–is that part of mind which is set in motion as a creative thing by the conscious state....It will do for us whatever we wish It to do provided we first create the thought mold."[5] We could say that our body is like molded "Jell-O." Our thoughts create the mold and the Substance of Life pours into it, filling every "nook and cranny," and forming every cell, tissue, and organ according to the thought that is sending it forth. Just as there is no separation between the water, sugar, and flavoring that make up Jell-O and the form it takes as it congeals in a mold, so there is no separation between the contents of our thoughts, the beliefs we accept, and the form we call our physical body.

Our individual subjective consciousness contains not only our personally gathered thoughts, conclusions, and values, but the inherited beliefs of our parents and ancestors, and the collective concepts of the entire human race. These are the ingredients of our mental "Jell-O." We are a blend of all of these; and unless we consciously choose to change the thoughts that create our subjective molds, our body will automatically take on the shape of our subconscious mind: We shall start aging according to the collective time-frame of the race; we shall develop unwanted traits and the inherited diseases of our family tree; and, unless we change our thinking, we shall re-create in our physical body the disease, discomfort, and dysfunction we focus on in our world–even if our thoughts are not directly related to a *specific* disease.

A particular disease is "representative" of the idea behind it. It may depict festering resentment, inflamed anger, painful guilt, congested and confused decisions, etc. "Destructive emotions, desires or ideas, unless neutralized, will grow into some bodily condition, and may produce disease. *Disease without thought could not manifest, no matter what the disease may be.*"[6]

## "THOUGHT CONTROLS THE BODY"[7]

Often we treat our body, the very thing that is closest to us–the
form we walk around in, the vehicle we take with us everywhere
we go–as if it weren't connected to our thinking. We numb,
ignore, or talk about the pain in our body while making affirmations for increases in our bank account! How can we believe that
our thoughts are affecting our prosperity but not our body? Either
all things are thought or no things are thought. If we believe that
thoughts are things, then we cannot separate the *thought* from
the *thing* that is formed, including our body. *Our body–healthy
or unhealthy–is the effect of the healthy or unhealthy thoughts
projecting it.*

      Some of us may believe that we have "matured" beyond
believing that a draft causes a cold. Perhaps, we've even stopped
decorating for the flu season, and no longer deck the halls with
boughs of Kleenex and bottles of Nyquil! But how much power
do we give to *food* to keep us well or to make us sick? Do we rely
on *caffeine* to wake us up and *alcohol* to calm us down? Do we
"stay away from dairy," wear garlic around our necks, and ingest
megadoses of bran? We are not what we eat. We are what we
*think* about what we eat–as well as what we *think* about ourselves
and the world around us.

      This doesn't mean that we shouldn't take care of our body
and view it as a holy temple expressing the purity of our soul. But
we can't eat our way into health or Heaven without a healthy
mind to go along with our food. Legend has it that Dr. Ernest
Holmes ate thick slabs of bacon for breakfast each day, yet he
sustained excellent health throughout his life. Jesus reminded his
disciples that "It is not what enters into the mouth which defiles
a man; but what comes out of the mouth, that is what defiles a

man."[8] We have not taken responsibility for our thoughts, owned our mental power, nor internalized and spiritualized our health and wholeness if we are giving chocolate, cheese, carrots, or cauliflower the power to make us sick or keep us well.

## THE PATTERN IS PERFECT

God is Eternal Wellness and God is all there is. We are made in the image and likeness of God. There is nothing inside of God to create disease, discomfort, or disharmony, and there is nothing outside of God (period!). Because we live within God, there can be nothing (outside of our thinking) to harm or affect our wellness in any way. The Divine Pattern residing at the core of our being cannot be affected by climate or food and is unaffected by distress or disease. It is our misperception–not Spirit's Conception–that outpictures imperfection in our body. The perfect idea of body exists in the Mind of God. Healing takes place in our physical body as the Truth within our body is revealed.

Behind the outpicture of our body is our own individual thinking–true and false–which is projecting it. And behind those thoughts, no matter what seems to be manifesting at any moment, is the Divine Pattern of body (your body and my body) which is changeless, flawless, and eternal. "The Divine Ideas stand back of all human thought, seeking admittance through the doorway of the mind."[9] We have a body not made with hands, eternal in the heavens. As our thought reaches up and on to that greater Truth, we more perfectly pattern the Divine.

One of the wonderful things about the Science of Mind is that it can be used in conjunction with medical doctors and alternative healthcare practitioners. There are no dogmas, creeds, rules or restrictions that make one out to be less spiritual because he or she seeks physical assistance. But the study of mental healing also informs us that cases of chronic discomfort and disease require a change in the mind before permanent healing can take place in the body. Certainly in an emergency situation under physically urgent circumstances it would be ludicrous for us to attempt to discover the "mental cause" for a physical crisis without first seeking first aid. Equally certain it would be foolish for us to endure chronic illness without seeking to discover the chronic mental condition behind it.

We change the pattern of our health, just as we change the pattern of anything else in our life–by changing our thinking and attitudes. If we want to experience health in our body, we must consciously strive to maintain a healthy point of view. The definition of health is not merely freedom from disease or abnormality. It is also "Soundness, especially of body or mind; and a condition of optimal well-being."[10] True health is our being filled and overflowing with life, energy, vitality, enthusiasm, joy, and happiness. More important than worrying about what food we eat, we should concern ourselves with *food for thought*. We need to give ourselves *mind* medicine and *spiritual* supplements.

The Bible suggests a great mental menu: *Whatever is true, whatever is honest, whatever is just, whatever is pure, whatever is lovely, whatever is of good report; if there is any virtue and if there is any praise, think about these things.*[11]

Here's to Your Health!

*Process Sheet Two*

# The Whole Story

### INDIVIDUAL

Think about your mental attitudes and daily conversations concerning other people and events in your life. Write down any "body language" you discover.

_____

_____

_____

_____

_____

Knowing that "thoughts become things" and that the language of the mind manifests as the form of the body, what changes will you make in your mental attitudes and daily conversations?

_____

_____

_____

_____

_____

_____

### GROUP

Discussion of Lesson.

**Activity:** Same as for Individual.

**Meditation:** Washed in the River of Love

*(Facilitator: read slowly with restful music in background, if desired.*
*Begin with one of the Relaxation Techniques on pages 299-300.)*
Imagine that you are walking along a path in a forest...all
around you are large, stately trees...sunlight is filtering through
the leaves and falling in round drops on your path...as you walk
you hear the gentle sound of water moving down a river...as you
come closer to the river, you hear the muted sounds of happy
people...and in the clearing just up ahead, you see several smiling
people wading into the river...you come to the clearing and the
river is before you–but this river is like none you have ever
seen...the water is like crystal, and the sunlight glistening on it
creates a myriad of dancing colors...along the banks of the river
there is soft grass greener than any green you have seen before...
and at various intervals there are stones shaped like steps leading
down into the crystal waters...you are told by one of the people
that this river has healing power...this river can wash away irritat-
ing notions, festering concepts, and sickly beliefs...are you ready
to wash away those notions, concepts, and beliefs that have the
potential to create discord, discomfort, and disease in your body
and in your world of affairs?...if so, walk now into the healing
waters and feel yourself being cleansed...the temperature is perfect...feel the crystal waters cleansing you inside and out...
washing your consciousness clean, so that all that is left when the
lies are washed away is the Truth–the Presence of Perfection,
Wholeness, Health, Peace, and Contentment...immerse yourself
in the waters...(*Facilitator: allow one or two minutes*)...take a
moment now to come out of the river and lie along the bank on
the soft green grass and allow the sunlight to warm you...as you
rest in the warmth of the sun, you feel a peace that you have never

experienced before...a peace beyond understanding...an unspeakable peace...(*Facilitator: allow one or two minutes*)...slowly rise and walk back through the forest and into the room...still feeling peace...now, open your eyes and take a few moments to feel the same peace with your eyes open.

1. SOM 99:4.   2. SOM 99:2.   3. SOM 224:3.   4. SOM 186:1.   5. SOM 29:1, 397:1.
6. SOM 234:4.   7. SOM 256:2.   8. Matthew 15:11 (Lamsa).   9. SOM 491:3.   10. *Webster's New Collegiate Dictionary* (G. & C. Merriam, 1977).   11. Philippians 4:8 (Lamsa).

# 3     G-O-D, Not J-O-B

Trusting God as Our Source and Supply

*It is amazing what
some people will do
for money, isn't it?
Some will lie, cheat,
steal, or sell drugs.*
Others will pollute the environment, endanger lives, make ineffective or defective products and then make false claims about their reliability. All this for financial profit, monetary gain, and material wealth. We live in a world where business and industry often put creativity, morality, humanity, and integrity *below* the proverbial "bottom line." For some, the main commercial objective seems to be to accumulate money *at any cost*. To look around, it would certainly seem that "money makes the world go 'round." If that is the case, then our world is in danger of spinning out of control, because money in and of itself can never take us where we truly desire to go.

"For the love of money is the root of all evil"[1] the Scriptures tell us. Note that it is not money, but the *love* of money, that is at the root of the problem. Money is neither bad nor good. It is what money means to us that motivates our positive or negative responses to it: how we feel when we have it and when we don't, and what we're willing to do to get it and keep it.

## LIVING IN REVERSE

Oddly enough, "evil" is the verb "live" spelled *backwards*. If we think about it, our focus on money not only can prevent us from moving forward, it often keeps us living in *reverse*. What we are willing to do for money (or what we feel we must do) keeps us from experiencing the joy, happiness, peace of mind, creativity, energy, and fulfillment that make us feel truly alive–those qualities that are naturally ours as free, spiritual beings. When *getting* money is our first priority, we often neglect our inner cravings–our health, our family, and the beauty of the world around us. We become tired or sick (or sick and tired); and because we are so busy doing what we believe we need to do to get money, we don't take the time to stop and consider what we really want to do with our life. In our earn-a-living day-to-day activities, we have forgotten to actually live a life worth living. We are so preoccupied with, and exhausted from, our job, or our search for a job, that we don't take the time for God.

Money cannot buy what Spirit is already providing for us. We can never earn on the outside what is already ours on the inside. Still, we focus our attention on getting from the outer world–seeking to procure our wealth from *people* and *jobs*. We become worldly "yes-men" trying to please and placate others– often at the expense of our own happiness and integrity–because we think they have what we need: money and security. Rather than turning within ourselves and claiming our spiritual inheritance, which provides for us moment to moment, we look to the world to see how much we can make by the hour.

"Never depend upon people or say that things must come from this or that source....SAY THAT THEY ARE, and let them come from where they may...."[2] Everything comes from the same Source. Things come into our life by the activity of our thought, and we have been limited only by our lack of knowledge. We have thought that outside things controlled us when all the time we have had That within which could have changed everything and given us freedom from bondage.

When we focus on the world and believe that it is the source of our supply, we are controlled by the world. We become the captive of the person or the place that we believe holds the key to our monetary comfort and security. We turn away from our True Source, and we don't seek to know ourselves as much as we seek to know *what others expect from us.*

"Evil" is also the reverse of the adjective "live." Evil is the deadness we feel when we forget the Truth of who we are. We must remember that we are the living embodiment of Unlimited Goodness. Just by *being*, we are supplied. Then by *giving* (not by getting) we receive even more because through our giving we stimulate the flow of Good into our life.

We are sustained by the Unlimited Imagination of God. Are you living the life that God is imagining for you? What most of us wanted to be when we were children and thinking about growing up didn't have anything to do with money. It had to do with self-expression—with color, creativity, excitement and adventure. As adults, our desire for self-expression has been overruled by our fear of monetary limitation. It seems that our human "maturity" is leading us to spiritual *obscurity*.

Ask yourself: "Do I honestly put *myself* into what I do each day? Do I use my creativity and express my uniqueness? Does my life have color and vitality? Am I excited about what I get paid to do? Is it an adventure to get up in the morning? Or do I merely tolerate the day, waiting for the evening; the weekdays, waiting for the week-end; and fifty weeks of workdays just for two weeks of vacation a year? Am I waiting for the day when I don't *have* to work any more so that I can do what I *really* want to do?"–when all the time you have That within you which can change everything and give you freedom from bondage.

We've all heard a story about someone who has kept something valuable hidden away. And because that person could always sell whatever it was if things got rough, he or she took more risks, lived more freely, and ended up wealthy without ever having to part with the valuable object–like the couple who had inherited a ruby ring and kept it in a safe deposit box. They borrowed money to start a business because they knew that if their new venture did not succeed, they could repay the loan by selling the ring.

However, their business prospered. They invested money in stocks, art, and new inventions, feeling confident that if any one of their investments failed, they could always convert the ring into cash. They lived freely, raising three children and sending them to college. They provided a lavish wedding for their only daughter and set up college funds for their grandchildren as they came into the world.

Eventually the couple happily retired. When they died many years later, their daughter discovered the ruby ring beneath valuable papers in the safe deposit box. She decided to keep the ring and have it appraised so that she could insure it. The appraiser found that the "ruby" ring was made of glass. Throughout her parents' lifetime, however, it had been to them as precious as a genuine ruby.

## "HIDDEN IN THE INNERMOST RECESSES OF OUR NATURE"[3]

As children of the living God, each of us has the *Real Thing* hidden away within us. The Bible tells us, "Blessed is the man who finds wisdom, and the son of the man who gets understanding. For the merchandise of it is better than the merchandise of

silver, and its gains than fine gold."[4] We are immersed in the Mind
of the Living Spirit–imbued with the Wisdom of the Universe.
All that we will ever need to know or utilize can be found within
us. Why do we sacrifice the richness of our inner Resource and
keep ourselves small and shackled doing the mundane tasks of the
world when all has already been freely given to us by Spirit? If
we believed that we could always *fall back* on Spirit the way the
couple believed that they could fall back on the ruby ring, we
would *step forth* into life unafraid of failure. We would choose
self-expression and soul-fulfillment over unimpassioned and
unfulfilling employment.

There are unlimited ways and means for Spirit to supply
our needs. However, we usually limit the ways to just a few: job,
winning a sweepstakes or lottery, getting it left to us in a will.
When we choose an occupation because it is a means of self-expression and because it is a joy to do (in addition to getting paid), we
are aligning ourselves with something greater than the finite concept of money. Because we are focusing on self-expression–and the
self that we are expressing is Unlimited Spirit–more abundant good
expresses in our life.

The avenues through which our good can come surround
us like countless stars twinkling in a boundless universe. Yet we
limit ourselves because we force the Unlimited Source to squeeze
our good through the tiny openings of our acceptance. We accept
our boundless supply through a pinpoint of light in the heavens
when Spirit would pour forth our goodness through celestial
quasars and supernovas. We don't need the Publishers' Clearing
House Sweepstakes to set us free. Yet so many people are waiting to
be saved by Ed McMahon that he should be elevated to sainthood!

"And be not conformed to this world; but be ye transformed by the renewing of your mind."[5] When we're "conformed"

to the world, we try to mold and shape ourselves into something we're not, so that we can have what we want. We are *transformed* when we know that we work for God. *The job we do for God is to be the unique, spiritual expression we were created to be.* There's good money in it! In fact, the entire Spiritual Universe supports our self-expression by manifesting joy, peace, and prosperity in our life.

God has no hands but our hands, no tongue but our tongue. If we don't express the nature of God, who will? If our hands are not reaching out in love in whatever we do, if our tongue does not speak the words of love in whatever we do, we are not working for God. When God is not fully expressed in our life to the highest level of our understanding, we limit the very thing we are working for: abundant good, prosperity, and success.

## "SAY THAT THEY ARE"

The details of our success and happiness unfold when we step out in faith, when we allow ourselves to be guided and directed by the inspiration of our inner nature, and when we understand that we are supplied by the One Source. We don't have to know "how" the good things are going to happen in our life. All we need to do is "SAY THAT THEY ARE, and let them come from where they may." All that is required of us is an openness to, and belief in, the existence of the unlimited avenues of Spirit. In this way we do not limit the ways in which we can prosper.

If we affirm aloud that we are a rich, radiant expression of Spirit, but silently we are still believing that our prosperity is limited to our job or a lottery ticket or a sweepstakes or some-one's last will and testament, the countless stars twinkling in a boundless universe of Unlimited Spirit that would shine for us and enrich our life instead die to us and fade away.

"In demonstrating over conditions, the only inquiries we need to make are: 'Do the things we want lend themselves to a constructive program? Do they express a more abundant life, rob no one, create no delusion, and express a greater degree of living-ness?' If we are able to answer these questions affirmatively, *then all the power in the Universe is back of our program!* If it is money, houses, automobiles, lands, stocks, bonds, dresses, shirts or shoe-strings–all of which come from the same source–there can be nothing, either in the Law or in the Spirit back of the Law, to deny us the right to the greatest possible expression of life."[6]

It is important for us to ask: "What would I be doing right now with my life if money were not an issue?" Then, eyes closed, imagine living that life and doing what we would do if we didn't believe that we had to earn money doing it. We must envision our ideal life until we feel something stirring within us–because that feeling, that stirring, is the Spirit within us desiring fuller expression in our life. It is the very Presence of the Power of the Universe looking for a greater outlet through us. How often do we ignore that feeling or say, "Not today; I have to go to work." Or "I already gave all I had at the office and I'm too tired to think about anything new or anything else."

Most of us were taught, even though we may be trying to convince ourselves otherwise, that we deserve to get money only through hard work; by keeping our nose to the grindstone. When I was in elementary school, a boy in my second-grade class drew all over his nice, clean desk with an ink pen. When the teacher discovered what the boy had done, she shouted at him to drag his desk to the back of the room, next to the sink, and to scrub the desk until it was completely free of graffiti. She concluded with, "And use some elbow grease!" Several minutes later she stopped the lesson again and stared incredulously at the boy, who was sobbing as he frantically pulled out the contents of the cabinet under the sink. The teacher shouted, "*Now* what are you doing?!" Through his sobs the boy replied that he was looking for the elbow grease.

## "THE DOOR THAT YOU ALONE CAN OPEN"[7]

He was looking for the very thing that only he could provide. Many of us are looking for the elbow grease when all that we require to do the work before us is *within* us. We are all employees of the Kingdom of Heaven. Before we were set upon this earth to do our job, our ability to perform was pronounced "very, very good" by our Employer. We can't shirk our responsibility and expect to benefit from the Divine Payroll. All that is required of us is to be our *authentic, God-created* self. We work for God wherever we are, whether we are self-employed, employed by others, or standing in the employment line. Every day we are getting on-the-job training so that we can perform at higher levels. We can't wait for outer circumstances to change before we begin our holy occupation. If we want to be a part of the Universal Bonus Plan, if we want a promotion to higher levels of consciousness, we must let the Presence of Spirit bless our environment *right where we stand.*

Edward Bok–journalist, editor, and founder of Bok Syndicate Press–wrote: "Find your place and hold it; find your work and do it. And put everything you've got into it." Our place is in the realm of Spirit. Our work is to express our spiritual nature. If we put everything we have into that, we will never be out of work or underpaid again!

# G-O-D, Not J-O-B

## *INDIVIDUAL*

The avenues through which our abundant good can come
surround us like countless stars twinkling in a boundless universe.
On a separate sheet of paper list as many ways as you can think
of for money to "come" to you.

Close your eyes for a moment and "dig deeper," finding a few
more ways for money to come to you, and add them to your list.

If "money were no object," what would you be doing with your
life and what qualities of Spirit would you be experiencing?

_____

_____

_____

Write an affirmation celebrating the Spiritual Truth that you
are supplied in *Unlimited* ways. (Example: *"I express the richness
of Spirit in all that I do, and all that I do reflects my spiritual
richness."*)

_____

_____

## *GROUP*

Discussion of Lesson.

**Activity:** Same as for Individual.

**Meditation:** The Heavenly "Want Ads"

(*Facilitator: read slowly with restful music in background, if desired. Begin with one of the Relaxation Techniques on pages 299-300.*)

Imagine that you are in a lovely den...the room temperature is perfect...there is a fireplace with a gently burning log...the walls are lined with wonderful books...and, in front of the fireplace, is a big, inviting chair with a comfortable footstool...you are compelled to sit down...relax...put your feet up...you feel peaceful as you watch the fire...then you notice that there is a newspaper on the end-table next to the chair...you pick up the newspaper and find that it is the *Celestial Chronicle*...as you browse through it, you note that it contains only good news...towards the end, you discover the Want Ads and you see the column heading "Opportunities for Self-Expression"...look slowly down the column because there is the most heavenly position just for you...as you find it, it stands out from all the rest...what does it say?...what is the current position open for your perfect self-expression?...there is a telephone number in the ad, and a telephone is on the end-table...place the call, and be sure to end with the "star" button...on the other end a wonderful, wise, gentle, soothing voice answers...tell the one who has answered that you are more than willing to take the position... Now, listen as you are told what is required of you in order for you to take the position, perhaps some beliefs you may need to change ...listen carefully to what you are being told...(*Facilitator: allow several minutes...*are you willing to start today?...look again at the position...consider what is required of you...now find yourself back in the room...take a few deep breaths...open your eyes and write a letter of acceptance.

1. 1 Timothy 6:10 (Lamsa).   2. SOM 304:4.   3. SOM 503:3.   4. Proverbs 3:13-14 (Lamsa).   5. Romans 12:2 (KJV).   6. SOM 188:4.   7. Ernest Holmes, *Living the Science of Mind* (DeVorss), p. 178.

# 4 "Because He First Loved Us"

## The Ever-Presence of Our Boundless Potential

*When I was a child I attended a Southern Baptist Sunday School where each Bible verse I memorized*

earned for me a shiny gold star next to my name on the class roster. One of the verses I committed to memory was 1 John 4:19: "We love him, because he first loved us."

I had been taught in Sunday School that God was separate from the world (and the people in it). He was up in heaven and far away from me. I was told that my quest in life should be to try to be as good as I could be, considering that I was "born in sin." I assumed that part of my being good included loving God—even though, to me, the vengeful God I'd learned about didn't seem very lovable. But, according to 1 John, I was *supposed* to love Him because He loved me first. It was my duty and obligation, and hopefully, my salvation. After all, a person would not be considered good if she didn't love someone who loved her first—especially God.

I pondered that particular verse all the way into adulthood. It wasn't until I began studying the Science of Mind that I understood it to be a powerful statement of my spiritual endowment. I was, I discovered, not *required* to love God because He loved me first, but rather that I was *able* to love God because He first loved me; that I was *imbued* with His Love—a Love without beginning—and a Love that was metaphorically *first*..."It is written that God is Love, and that we are His expressed likeness, the image of the Eternal Being. Love is self-givingness through creation, the impartation of the Divine through the human."[1] Being created in the image and likeness of God meant that I was created in the image and likeness of Love. I was actually formed out of Love. The substance of my very being was the Substance of Love. And I was free to use that love to love God and everyone else.

Often we think that we personally possess love–that it belongs to us like our money or other personal possessions, and that it is ours to give or withhold according to our judgment as to who deserves it and who doesn't. But, we don't *possess* love. We *are* love. We are formed out of that Holy Substance which contains the Unconditional Love of the Creator for Its Creation. Love dwells within everyone, equally. Some people don't have more of It, others less. We are all able to express as much Love as we choose to express because Unlimited, Unconditional Love Itself– eternally loving all of creation–is the Core of our being.

## GOD'S LOVE EXPRESSED–NOT POSSESSED– BY US

"It is impossible to plumb the depths of the individual mind, because it is not really *individual* but *individualized.* Behind or within the individualized point is the Universal, which has no limits."[2] There is no limit to how much love we can experience except the limitation we place upon Its expression through us as we individualize It. When we withhold love from someone, we lose the experience of God's Love for that person in us. But God's Love for the person is not lost. We have the capacity to love anyone, anytime, because the Creator's Love within us is already loving everyone, everywhere, all of the time–and we can "tap into" that Love.

We experience Love as we allow the Indwelling, Impersonal, Unconditional Love within us to emerge into our awareness. This often happens when we think of our family, our friends, or when we meet someone new who stimulates feelings of love within us. But the love we call our own was God's Love "first." We can never personally possess Love; however, we can individually express It. When we think that we are giving love to someone, in Truth, *we are expressing God's Love for that person*, which already exists in us! When someone loves us, they are expressing God's Love for us within themselves. When we choose not to love someone, it doesn't prevent God from loving them. It prevents God from loving them *through us*.

The Love within us preexists our desire to express It. So does every other Quality of Spirit. "Your Father knows what you need, before you ask him."[3] The Presence of Wisdom, Peace, Joy, and creativity–all that we could ever desire or require for a successful, fulfilling life–dwells within us already. Our "asking" activates that which is Present in us all the time.

The Science of Mind speaks of God as Infinite Mind, Unlimited Consciousness, and Unconditional Love. The manifest universe is what Infinite Mind is thinking about. It is what Infinite Consciousness is conscious of. And it is what Unconditional Love is loving. Since each of us is a unique creation in the manifest universe, then Infinite Mind is thinking of us; Unlimited Consciousness is conscious of us; and Unconditional Love is loving us. We and the entire Universe–both visible and invisible–are ideas of Mind, forms of Consciousness, and objects of Love. We are important to God because without Creation, the Creator would be unexpressed. Without ideas, Infinite Mind would be blank. Without forms, Eternal Consciousness would be empty. And without something to love, Unconditional Love would have no meaning. "An eternal creation is proved by the fact that we must suppose Spirit to be Conscious Intelligence, and *there can be no*

*Conscious Intelligence unless It is conscious of something!"* [4]

## "IN THE BEGINNING, GOD" [5]

As an idea, a form, or an object of love–as creation–we do not in actuality have a mind of our own, a consciousness of our own, or love of our own. We use the Mind of God to think with and the Consciousness of Spirit for awareness. And every time we love, we use the Love of the Divine. Not only are we able to love because God first loved us; we are able to think because God is Mind first. We are conscious because Consciousness preexisted our individual awareness. Jesus said, "Truly, truly, I say to you that the Son can do nothing of his own accord, except what he sees the Father doing." [6] Paul reminds us in 1 Corinthians: "And if any man thinks that, of himself, he knows any thing, he knows nothing yet as he ought to know it." [7] We can know nothing, of ourselves; instead, we perceive what the Father knows.

It is easy to forget that we are one with God and to believe, instead, that we are living a separate life. We go along thinking that we are in control, making things happen, planning and reaching our goals. It is usually when we want something that we're having trouble getting "on our own," when things don't seem to be going our way, or when we have gotten our life so tangled up that we don't know where to begin to unravel it that we consciously include God in our life through affirmative prayer or Spiritual Mind Treatment. But the Power is always Present even when we're not calling upon It, just as Love is there even when we are choosing not to express It. Where could the Infinite go? Where outside of Allness, where outside of everywhere, could Boundless Spirit disappear into? Where do we think we would be if the Infinite disappeared? If God were not Present *in* our life, *as* our life, we wouldn't merely have a miserable existence–we would cease to exist at all.

We are *spiritual beings* having a *human experience*, but our human experience can never exclude God. There is no other life, movement, or existence outside of the Infinite, Boundless Life that is Spirit. Within the Christ Consciousness (the Entire Manifestation of God) is "all that the Father has," every quality of Spirit and every idea of Mind. "This One Father, conceiving within Himself, gives birth to all the Divine ideas. The sum-total of all these ideas constitutes the Mystic Christ."[8] The Christ Consciousness belongs to each of us because, in Truth, it is the only Consciousness that exists. "To be filled with the fullness of God is to manifest our true nature, which is Christ, the Son of God."[9] Through it we can partake of the infinite ideas of Divine Mind. We can become aware of what Cosmic Consciousness is conscious of. And we can experience the Unconditional Love of the Divine. It is in, around, and through us–the very substance of our soul and the very fiber of our form. It is the living force within our mind and in every cell of our being.

We shall find that the qualities of Spirit more clearly emerge in us as we identify ourselves with the Christ Consciousness–as we see ourselves as Jesus saw himself, as the Buddha saw himself: One with the Father. If we are ever to experience the Love they knew–the Love that is God–if we are ever to manifest the life that we are created to live, we must first *cease* to think, speak, and act as though we were from another Universe in which God has taken a leave of absence.

It takes tremendous humility for us to accept that we are created by that which is Holy, Perfect, and Pure, and to believe that we are born out of and live within an Infinite, Unerring, and Magnificent Being. But it takes an incredible ego to believe that we could have created ourselves out of something else besides Spirit and that we can live, at all, without God.

When we understand that *God* has made us, and not we ourselves, such humility brings with it a clearer receptivity within us to the good that is ours already–the good that preexists our desire for it, the good that has always been Present since the beginning. "Say not ye, There are yet four months, and then cometh harvest? behold, I say unto you, Lift up your eyes, and look on the fields; for they are white already to harvest."[10]

We can experience our good, *here and now.* It is ready and waiting for our acceptance–because He *first* loved us.

*Process Sheet Four*

# "Because He First Loved Us"

## *INDIVIDUAL*

When we understand that God has made us and not we ourselves, that humility brings with it a clearer receptivity within us to the qualities that are ours already. In what areas of your life have you been "waiting" for inspiration and motivation to "show up"?

_____

_____

_____

_____

Write affirmations in the "NOW," in the Present Tense, confirming that the spiritual qualities you are awaiting are yours already. (Example: *"I am imbued with the Spirit of Love, therefore I express love in all of my relationships NOW!"*)

_____

_____

_____

_____

## *GROUP*

Discussion of Lesson.

**Activity:** (*Materials: "seed packet"-size squares of white paper; crayons or colored pencils.*)

Have each person make "spiritual" seed-packet covers. These seed packets represent the qualities of Spirit that each person desires to grow stronger in his or her life. Each may create as many covers as desired. Each cover should indicate what particular "seeds of Spirit" are inside the packet. A picture can be drawn on each cover to reflect what the seeds will "look like" when they grow into fruition. For example, a seed packet may have "Love" written on it, with a picture of a heart or a radiant sun. When everyone has completed their packets, have them look at each packet thoroughly, place them in their laps, and begin the following meditation.

**Meditation:** The Fields Are Already Ripe for the Harvest

*(Facilitator: read slowly with restful music in background, if desired. Begin with one of the Relaxation Techniques on pages 299-300.)*
 Imagine now that there is a small field of fertile soil before you...the field has been plowed, the rows are dug, and the soil is ready for you to plant the seeds from the packets that you have made...scatter the seeds or drop them one by one until all of the seeds are planted and covered with soil...*(Facilitator: allow a few minutes)*...when you are complete, a warm, gentle mist begins to fall...although you remain dry, the soil becomes fully moist and you inhale the wonderful, earthy fragrance of damp ground... slowly, almost as if one ray at a time, the sun begins to shine on the soil...you feel the warmth of the sun on your face and body... and as you look at the field you have planted, you see green sprouts everywhere...the sprouts continue to grow...and grow... until they fully blossom into all of the images that reflect the qualities of Spirit you have planted...look at the field...look at the shape...color...inhale the fragrance...your inner field of Spirit is ripe for the harvest...these qualities are yours now...you don't need to wait to express all that is planted within you, all the qualities of Spirit that have been nurtured within you...there is

more than enough Love...more than enough Peace...more than enough Happiness...more than enough Self-Worth...more than enough Richness...more than enough Prosperity...more than enough Health...more than enough Success...look up into your inner field and know that all this, and more, is ready for your use and expression...now...in this moment...there is no more waiting...not years or months or days or hours need pass for the qualities of Spirit to be ripe within you...now is the time...right where you are is the place...you are a fully flourishing being of Spirit...(*Facilitator: allow a minute*)...know that as you come back to the room, these qualities remain abundant within you...and when you are ready, open your eyes.

1. SOM 478:3.    2. SOM 93:4,5.    3. Matthew 6:8 (Lamsa).    4. SOM 67:2.    5. Genesis 1:1 (KJV).
6. John 5:19 (Lamsa).    7. 1 Corinthians 8:2 (Lamsa).    8. SOM 422:3.    9. SOM 492:6.
10. John 4:35 (KJV).

# Why NOT You?

Recognizing and Utilizing Spiritual Power

*When some unexpected problem has come up in your life, or a personal catastrophe has occurred, how often have you found yourself asking "Why me?"*
Doesn't it feel at times as if you were indiscriminately targeted for disaster by some dark universal force that doesn't have your best interests in mind?

Several years ago I underwent minor surgery. I was told by the doctor that the odds of my developing a blood clot in my leg from such a surgery were around 1 percent. This meant, of course, that 99 percent of those people who had undergone the same surgery had not developed a blood clot in their legs. Afterward, when I experienced severe cramping in my legs and several blood clots were discovered, I was shocked. When I began to have difficulty breathing and the doctors found that a large clot had dislodged from the mass in my leg, broken into smaller clots, and sprayed my lungs, I was horrified to find myself in an even smaller percentage than the original 1 percent risk group: I was in a fractional percentile group that had developed *pulmonary emboli* from such surgery, and in a smaller group still–those who had survived such a condition.

It looked like a great case for "Why me?" In fact, I tried it on for size! "*Why me*?!" There had been such a small chance that someone would find themselves in such a predicament; "why me" when others–many, many others–

had not? As I lay in the hospital trying to find something good in what had happened, my first "positive" thought was that since I was temporarily inhabiting the rarified realm of odds that most people did not enter, it might be a good time for me to play the lottery in all of the states that had one. One-in-a-million was looking like odds at which I could succeed!

I had to remind myself that the success or failure of my life–my health, my wealth, and my happiness–had nothing to do with percentages, odds, or chance; that my life and everything in it had to do with my relationship to Spirit. The odds of my being whole, complete, and perfect hadn't changed. They were still one in One. I was *still* 100 percent whole. "The spiritual man needs no healing, health is an omnipresent reality, and when the obstructions that hinder healing are removed, *it will be found that health was there all the time.*"[1]

Even though it looked like it, physically, the odds really weren't against me. Something hadn't happened *to* me. It had happened *through* me. And I knew that I needed to change the thinking that had created the opportunity for such an event to take place in my life. I also needed to remove any fear that I was now, somehow, separate from the Wholeness of Spirit. I began by refusing to see myself as the "odd-man-out" and affirmed, instead, that being one in a million meant that I was a unique creation, not a separate one, and that I belonged to Spirit 100 percent.

Throughout my stay in the hospital I felt calm even though I was in the Intensive Care Unit. With my heart hooked up to a screen monitored around the clock by nurses, IV needles in my arm, and a pan in my bed, I meditated upon my unchanged spiritual perfection, until that perfection manifested as healing in my physical body.

## WHY *NOT* ME?

The question "Why me?", however, is not the only question that can make us feel separate from our good. "Why NOT me?" works the same way. How often do we look around us with envy when we see others experiencing prosperity and the financial freedom we desire? How many times do we covet the deep and enduring love relationships other people seem to have? When we look at the rewarding and fulfilling self-expression in other people's lives, how routinely do we think, "Why not *me?*" and assume that the incredible adventures, the unexpected windfalls, and the great successes happen to everyone but *us.*

Often, we not only view others as luckier or more fortunate than we are, but also as somehow better equipped for life than we are–smarter, more easy-going, more coordinated, more talented, more attractive, more confident. When we look at people who seem to have a deeper spiritual understanding than we do, or see others who appear to have actually obtained peace of mind, we assume that it has been easier for them than it has been for us; that they haven't been through what we've been through, or they haven't been faced with the same kinds of challenges we have.

The realm of Infinite Possibility belongs to all of us. Ernest Holmes wrote in his *Declaration of Science of Mind Principles*: "We believe in the incarnation (or Presence) of the Spirit in all life, and that all beings are incarnations of the One Spirit. We believe in the direct revelation of Truth through the intuitive and spiritual nature of every being, and that anyone may become a revealer of Truth who lives in close contact with the Indwelling God."[2] So, why NOT you?

*Each* of us can be a revealer of the Truth of Spirit. *Each* of us can impart perfect health, unlimited wealth, constant joy, enduring love, boundless creativity, and richly rewarding activities. There is no spiritual reason why anyone cannot live the life of his or her dreams. There is no *spiritual* precedent for anyone to be sick, poor, lonely, or unfulfilled. There is no reason in heaven. So, what reason on earth are we letting get in our way? If *all* are permitted to use the Power and Creativity of the Universe, if *everyone* has the potential to live his or her dreams, why NOT you?

## "A POWER THAT CAN OVERCOME EVERY OBSTACLE"[3]

I read a book not too long ago that was filled with stories of incredible human achievement seemingly accomplished against all odds. The book was loaded with tales of individuals who had overcome horrendous poverty and deprivation to become multi-millionaires. It was packed with heart-wrenching stories of people who had been born with debilitating deformities or who had been crippled through horrible accidents and devastating injury, and yet had overcome the obstacles and succeeded in sports, business, love relationships, and every other area of their lives. They were tough stories of faith, determination, and unbeatable dreams.

We are astounded and moved by such stories of courage and spirit. However, what should really amaze us is not that the Spirit is alive and active in human beings, and that It always comes through when called upon, but *how few call upon Spirit at all!* What *should* astonish us is how "wimpy" most of us are about our spiritual potential, and how uncommitted we are to our spiritual path. What *should* bewilder us is how many people give up on themselves and their potential in life when they have far fewer obstacles to overcome than those who are crippled and maimed.

And what also should perplex and startle us is how many of us spend our lives pouring water on the fire in our souls because we are not willing, with our fully functioning bodies, to move through our challenges and fears so that we can be all that we were created to be!

A man without the use of his legs becomes a millionaire while some of us are still walking with both of our legs into yet another Prosperity Workshop when the principles we heard in the first one would have worked for us if we had put them to use! A man with a totally disfigured face falls in love and happily marries. Yet, some of us are still worried that we're not attractive enough, young enough, firm enough, buffed enough, or good enough to find true love and happiness in a relationship! A woman without the total use of her body takes up white-water rafting and flies an airplane while many of us are afraid to try anything new because we might fail or look awkward! A woman who can't stand at a podium because her legs do not function is a successful public speaker, while most of us are too frightened to even sign up for Toastmasters, much less speak up for ourselves!

Why should it be "extraordinary" for people to overcome their challenges through faith, belief, and determination? Don Juan said: "The basic difference between an ordinary man and a warrior is that a warrior takes everything as a challenge, while an ordinary man takes everything either as a blessing or a curse." It takes a life of faith, determination, and willingness to be successful. Pain can turn our lack of commitment into determination. Personal catastrophe can turn our spiritual apathy into willingness. Physical debilitation can turn our doubt into faith. But we don't need to wait to be forced into a spiritual corner by circumstances to begin to really live, do we?

## "CHOOSE YOU THIS DAY"[4]

We can make a conscious decision to search our soul, examine our life, and become real and honest with ourselves while we are in a healthy body. We can choose to discover and rid ourselves of the beliefs and fears that are keeping us from living fully. Some of us are much more crippled within ourselves than a person in a wheel chair, and some of our views of ourselves are much more disfigured than someone with burns or scars. If we don't consciously and actively seek our true spiritual nature, and if we allow our negative hidden beliefs to go unchanged, eventually the thoughts of the inner self will become the outer circumstances of our life. We may find ourselves asking "Why me?" when disaster happens, and "Why not me?" when the good passes us by.

It is easier to change a crippling thought than it is to live with the challenges of a crippled body. It is less complex to change a distorted thought than to overcome the pain of a disfigured body. And it is far more simple to overcome limited thinking than to rise above the devastating hardships of poverty. But so often we are waiting to be *pushed* into change by "extenuating circumstances." All most of us would have to do to vastly improve our life is change our thinking. We make our life hard, and keep ourselves limited, by holding onto the lies that imprison us, when we have the choice to embrace the Truth that would set us free.

We are created in the Image and Likeness of an Unlimited and Powerful Creator. As each of us consciously chooses to seek the Power within us *and to live fully without excuses*, perhaps the day will come when another "astounding" book about "unusual" people will be written—only *this* one will be about people who live *without* accomplishment because they think that they are merely feeble humans–victims of circumstance, powerless beyond material parameters, and separate from God. It will tell of *limited* lives–impoverished, diseased, lonely, and unfulfilled. And we shall shake our heads in amazement because to us that kind of thinking will be *astounding!*

The Spirit within us can do all things. It can overcome any obstacle in our mind, in our body, and in our affairs. It is the Infinite Power that creates riches, bestows love, gives peace, inspires purpose. It gives to all equally and boundlessly. Everyone can live the life of their dreams through recognizing and utilizing spiritual power.

So...why NOT you?

*Process Sheet Five*

# Why NOT You?

### INDIVIDUAL

Do you feel envious when you see others experiencing prosperity and the financial freedom you desire? Do you covet the deep and enduring love relationships other people seem to have? When you look at the rewarding and fulfilling self-expression in other people's lives, do you think, "Why not me?" Write down any areas of your life where you feel that you are being "overlooked" by the Universe of Good.

_____

_____

_____


It is important to remind yourself, daily, that no one is luckier or more fortunate than you are; no one is better equipped for life than you are. "The realm of Infinite Possibility belongs to all of us." You have been given all that you require to fully express your magnificence. Write spiritually affirmative statements regarding the above issues that will assist you in claiming your "place" in the realm of Infinite Possibility.

_____

_____


### GROUP
Discussion of Lesson.

**Activity:** *(Materials: paper; pencils or pens; chalk board or dry erase board; chalk or pens.)*
Each member of the group (anonymously) writes on a slip of paper some goal that he or she would like to achieve or experience

in life but which it is felt that "something" is preventing. (Example: "I want to quit my current job and enter another field of work.") On a separate slip of paper each person writes down the "something"(= excuse) that is preventing him or her from achieving the desired goal. The "excuse" should be general rather than specific. (Example: The general excuse for not quitting a job to take another could be "I am afraid of what other people might think of me," rather than the specific discussion of "job.") The facilitator collects the slips of paper, keeping the *goals* separate from the *excuses*, then lists all of the goals on the board. When the list is complete, the facilitator draws a slip from the excuse pile and the group attempts to match the excuse with the goal. The one whose goal and excuse are being discussed remains silent.

The purpose of this exercise is to make the students become aware that ALL excuses are really THE SAME excuse. For example, the excuse for *not* changing careers could be the same as for *not* entering into a new relationship, *not* moving from a familiar city, etc. The students may discover that all excuses are based upon *outer concerns* rather than *inner inspiration*.

The students should have pencil/pen and paper ready for the completion of the following meditation.

**Meditation:** Why NOT You?

*(Facilitator: read slowly with restful music in background, if desired. Begin with one of the Relaxation Techniques on pages 299-300.)*
Imagine now that you are walking down a road that leads to a gate...as you reach the gate you see a sign on it that says, "Beyond this point is the Land of Opportunity"...the gate is made of heavy black wrought-iron posts...there are spaces wide enough between the posts for you to see beyond the gate...you peek

through the gate and you see that everything you have ever desired…everything that you desire in this moment…lies beyond the gate–in the Land of Opportunity…but the gate is locked… the lock is a big black square box secured to the gate by a thick metal chain…you notice that written on the box are the words "Your Excuses"…although the box and chain cannot be removed from the gate without a key, the box can be opened…if you open it, you will find all of your "excuses" for not entering into the Land of Opportunity and living the life of your dreams…take a few moments, now, to open the box and read your excuses… (*Facilitator: allow one to two minutes*)…if you let them do so, these excuses will keep you out of the Land of Opportunity–the Land where others choose to live successfully…"Why not you?"… you have the permission of your Heavenly Father to live, move, and have your being in the Land of Opportunity…only your excuses can keep you from experiencing the Unlimited life of a Child of God…inherent within you are all of the qualities, all of the knowledge, all of the creativity, all of the energy, all that you will ever need, to do whatever you desire to do, and to live the life you desire to live…but at the moment, your excuses are keeping you from living in the Land of Opportunity…however, there is a solution that belongs solely to you…a custom-made key that will unlock the gateway to the Land of Opportunity…look down at your feet and notice that there is a golden box…bend over and pick it up, and you will see that engraved in gold upon it is written "Your key to the Land of Opportunity"…if you open the box you will find a key inside that is also made of gold, but you cannot remove it from the box because it is under a piece of glass that you must first break or otherwise remove…also in the box is a folded piece of parchment paper…on this piece of paper is written what you must do to extract the key to the Land of

Opportunity...something you must do, or *something of which you must be certain*, in order for you to move past your excuses... unfold the paper and read the message–the message that is especially for you...(*Facilitator: allow a full minute*)...are you willing to take action to seize your key to the Land of Opportunity?...are you willing to do what is written on the paper?...are you willing to meditate upon that of which you must become certain?...for now, though, fold up the piece of paper and put it back in the golden box...for now, it is time for you to leave the gate to the Land of Opportunity...but, remember...the Land of Opportunity still dwells within you...it is your inheritance as a Child of God... as the Offspring of Spirit...bring the golden box with you as you find yourself back in the room with your eyes still closed...consider the key inside the box that you hold in your hands...it is yours alone given to you by your Creator...if you do whatever you need to do...if you seek to know whatever it is that you need to know...you can seize the key that will open for you a Land of Unlimited Opportunity...a Realm of Boundless Good...it is up to you...take a moment now to consider what steps you will take to unlock the gate to your success...(*Facilitator: allow a full minute*)...and now, open your eyes and silently write about your meditation experience.

---

1. SOM 203:1.   2. Ernest Holmes, *What We Believe* (first issue of *Science of Mind Magazine*, October 1927).   3. SOM 146:2.   4. Joshua 24:15  (KJV).

# 6

# Front and Center

Consciously Living Our Spiritual Identity

*In the military when
a superior wants a recruit
to identify himself or
herself, the officer will
call that person by name
and issue the command,
"Front and Center!"*

The individual knows that he or
she must step forward and acknowledge who they are. But
even though we may recognize our name, and step forward
when our name is called, do we really *know* ourself? A
Proverb tells us: "With all thy getting get understanding."[1]
Socrates counseled "Know thyself." And Lao-tsu proposed
that "He who knows others is clever; he who knows himself
is enlightened."

Are you enlightened? Do you know your inner self?
And do you live with your true identity "front and center" in
your life? The knowledge of self can only be found within
the self. No one can tell us who we are. No one can find the
self for us that is within us. We must issue the command
from within for the real self to step forward in our consciousness. We may search out a philosophical ideology or a
religious discipline that can assist us along the spiritual path
of self-discovery. But it is only through our individual
*contemplation* of an ideology or our *practice* of a discipline
that we can move forward on our journey; it is not accomplished through a philosophy or the religion of itself.

There are many paths that lead to self-discovery.
The contemplation and practice of the Science of Mind are

one. Anyone who practices its principles will find greater self-knowledge. Its teachings can assist those who follow them to turn within, find out what makes them tick, and discover how they might tick more in rhythm with the Perfect Syncopation of the Universe.

## A PRACTICAL PHILOSOPHY

However, for it to be useful, the Science of Mind requires an active moment-to-moment practice. It is not a doctrine or creed that one adopts blindly so that one is guaranteed superiority here on earth and a better spot in the hereafter. No one is "saved" or freed from the constraints of limited human concepts merely by listening to its Principles, but rather by practicing them.

The Science of Mind is a living philosophy that, when embodied and practiced day by day, can transform anyone from a powerless victim living as the effect of the world into a powerful co-creator capable of effectively changing every area of his or her life through conscious unity with, and active use of, the Universal Power of Spirit. "Behind the individual is the Universal, which has no limits. In this concept alone lies the possibility of eternal and endless expansion."[2]

The Science of Mind is practical because anyone can practice it and use it effectively, no matter where the individual is in his or her conscious evolution and spiritual understanding. If we feel like a victim in life, and if it seems like things are being done *to* us rather than occurring *through* us, the philosophy of the Science of Mind can teach us how to change our thinking from helplessness and hopelessness to empowerment and confidence. Through the understanding that our own thoughts are creative, and that we are capable of making powerful and effective choices and changes, we learn to take charge of our life and responsibility for our circumstances.

It is important for us to remember that no one can lead us where we do not want to go. Most of what goes "wrong" in our life really does look as though it were other people's fault. *They* did it to us either intentionally, inadvertently, or through bad genes. But until we own our problems, they are not ours to solve. We may have a great attachment to our "poor me" stories and "they did me wrong" songs. After all, the detailed chronicle of our life does give us an identity; and when those details are told vividly and intensely, they can get us a whole lot of attention too. However, our problems will not go away, and our pain will not be healed, until we stop identifying ourselves as victims of the outer world, and until we are willing to put aside our colorful past and live with our spiritual identity "front and center" in our mind, our actions, and our stories.

We wouldn't feel miserable about our misfortunes unless we sensed deep within us that our "rightful" state is one of harmony—because we cannot miss what we do not know exists. Our *bad* times would not feel unnatural unless we had an innate sense that we were missing *good* times. The knowledge that dwells at the core of our being—the intrinsic recognition that the Creator's intention for creation is one of Joy—causes us to strive for joy and to feel miserable without it! But when we reach for that joy in the outer world, we often come up empty-handed. In order for us to experience true and lasting happiness, we must stop depending upon the outer, changing world for it and trust the Unchanging Joy at the core of our own being. Victor Frankel, the Austrian psychiatrist imprisoned in a concentration camp, wrote: "Freedom is not a condition of the environment; freedom is a condition of the person. Liberty means that you have many options to choose among in your environment. Freedom means that you have the internal power to exercise those options."

The Science of Mind teaches that changing our thinking changes our life. This also means that our life *doesn't* change if we don't change our thinking. Often we would like to believe otherwise. We look for a *miracle* or a "*break*" to circumvent the Creative Law of cause and effect that we have set in motion by our thinking. However, the only miracle or "break" we shall find begins in our mind.

We can become a master of our fate instead of a victim of circumstance by shifting our thinking from dependency on the outer world to trust in the inner world, and by keeping our true, spiritual identity "front and center" in our mind no matter what is happening in the outer world. As we turn within ourselves, we find the Power of Spirit waiting to bring about all that we seek in the outer world. We realize that no one can keep us from our good because *no one can reach inside us and separate us from it.* We create our good *from the inside out* as the Creative Medium of Spirit is activated by our thinking and beliefs.

Everything in the outer world–money, a mountain, a baby–are all made from the Unseen Substance of Spirit. "The worlds were framed by the word of God, so that the things which are seen came to be from those which are not seen."[3] Our world is framed by our thought. If we want that which appears in our life to change, we must change that which has created the appearance: *our thinking.*

We can keep trying to physically alter our environment by getting a new job, moving to a new house, or finding a new relationship. We can continue to attempt to control and manipulate the people and conditions around us, but if we don't change the thinking that created what we don't want, we'll just create more of it. Unless we rely on the condition of our mind to bring about better experiences, we shall find that we do not have enough hands or plans to make everything in our life behave the way we want it to.

## "THE UNIVERSE IS FOR US AND NOT AGAINST US"[4]

When we discover that we can manifest, or create, all that we want and desire, we no longer feel like a powerless victim dodging the "fickle finger of fate." We find that "it" really is done to us as we believe and comes to us through the forms of our beliefs. Through changing our thinking, and experiencing our changed thought in physical form, we no longer doubt that we really are connected to an Invisible, Creative Power that denies us nothing that we are willing to accept. We become empowered by the knowledge of the creativity of our thoughts and that there *is* a Power that responds to our thinking. *We have tangible evidence that the universe is good and that it is on our side.*

This is a vitally important step along the path of the Science of Mind because we cannot fully surrender to a Power that we do not trust–and our surrender to the Power that is greater than we are is vital to our spiritual progress and growth. Within us is the untapped, Unlimited Resource of Universal Mind. "The Universal Mind contains all knowledge. It is the potential ultimate of all things. To It, all things are possible."[5] When we are caught up in a one-sided relationship with Spirit, *always* telling God what to do for us, rather than listening to the Voice within for inspiration, we fail to see what God *could* do for us without our *constant* human demands. If we want to see more of the Unlimited Spiritual Plan, we must be willing to surrender our limited wisdom of what we want and need and allow the Greater Wisdom of the Spirit to lead us. "The Spirit within man is God, and only to the degree that we listen to and seek to obey this Spirit shall we really succeed."[6] "An attitude of quietness and confidence, a listening attitude of: 'Speak, Lord, for thy servant heareth,' will open the way for the voice of Spirit to speak to the inner ear."[7]

If we are feeling like a victim of circumstance, if our life is in total chaos, and we are convinced that it is being done to us by the vacillating forces of the material world, or by a God Whose actions bring as much suffering as joy, we may be unable to "rest in the Lord and wait patiently for him."[8] When one surrenders to a Higher Power while still maintaining a victim's consciousness, that person feels like a "victim" of God. This is the one who often experiences catastrophes and believes that it is "the will of God."

## "IT IS YOUR FATHER'S GOOD PLEASURE TO GIVE YOU THE KINGDOM"[9]

Unless we have had a personal experience of Spirit's goodness and love for us through the direct manifestion of our affirmative prayers or Spiritual Mind Treatments, we won't trust that whatever appears in our life is being governed by the Love of that which is Unseen.

We can't actually surrender control of our life if we've never experienced control of it to begin with–nor can we trust the goodness of a God we have not come to know personally as good. It is crucial that we understand that the Universe is Good and that we are loved with an everlasting love by a Creator whose good pleasure rests eternally in giving us "the kingdom." Otherwise, our spiritual quest for answers begins and ends with

"Why me, Lord?" when things fall apart; and the Power that would create only good for us through our understanding becomes, in our ignorance, as fickle to us as the pseudo forces of the world we fear.

The teaching of the Science of Mind is a step-by-step progression up the ladder of spiritual understanding. If we try to skip a rung and race ahead, we could fall backwards, rather than moving forward. We must learn to take responsibility for the condition of our life. We must have a personal experience that our thoughts are creative and learn to use the power of our own thinking to create what we desire. *Then*, when we've got our life in order the way our (limited) perspective believes that it should be, is when surrender to God is a life-transforming action. *Then* is when we are not afraid to momentarily cease our demands and listen to the "Inner Voice, that speaks supremely,"[10] and inspires us to greater action and expression.

If we focus only on creating more and more of what we see in the world, we cannot discover what "eye hath not seen, nor ear heard...the things which God hath prepared for them that love him."[11] Our inner resources are unlimited. There is infinitely more than we are conscious of, or that we can imagine or wish for at this moment. We experience more spiritual depth and inspiration by turning within to Spirit and allowing God to "use" us–inspire, guide, and direct us–so that our use of the Creative Medium of Spirit brings about greater good.

If we want to know the Unlimited, we must silence our limited thoughts and let that Boundless Nature reveal Itself to us. We can't get to know someone if we are always talking about ourself. In the same way, if our relationship with God consists of our constantly specifying our need, we cannot see beyond our small sense of self to the magnificence Spirit has created. If we want to experience the greater, we must give up the lesser no matter how good the lesser seems to be. If we want Life to reveal Itself to us, it is necessary for us to give up our small, contracted, limited idea about what Life is. "Since we cannot contract the Absolute we shall have to expand the relative."[12] We must close our eyes, still our lips, and empty our mind of pompous nothingness, and allow Spirit to emerge "front and center."

## "WE SHALL BE MET WITH A SMILE FROM THE UNIVERSE"

When we trust that there is a "highest and best" in every situation because God is at the center of every situation, and when we're willing to do our part (which might be for us to do nothing at all), our individual experiences unfold in harmony with the rest of Life. When we surrender to Spirit we are able to maintain a calm trust in the middle of chaos because we understand that a Divine Plan is unfolding even if we personally have not seen the blueprints. When we are convinced that Life is for us and not against us, then, should things seem to fall apart, we don't have to feel victimized. Rather, we can feel vitalized, because we trust that the smallness of our life is breaking open so that the greatness of God can manifest, "front and center."

As we practice the Science of Mind in our day-to-day lives, as we learn more and more about ourselves, who we are and why we're here, we may find that occasionally we feel like a victim, but more and more often we take charge of life–by praying for what we believe that we need and by seeking Divine Inspiration. The Allness of God, and our eternal oneness with All that is, never changes, but our experience of It may. In one situation we might feel like a victim and need to remind ourself that we are a

powerful being in charge of our own life. In another instance
we might be tempted to control and manipulate a situation whose
solution requires more knowledge than we *consciously* have, and
we'll need to remind ourself to turn within and listen for
Inspiration and Guidance.

The Science of Mind can also lead us to the mystical
experience of total, undifferentiated immersion in Spirit. As we
meditate upon the vastness of the Inner Life and surrender the
personal to the greater possibilities of the Universal, we find a Self
far beyond our every day experience. "There is a place in the mentality–in the heights of its greatest realizations–where it throws
itself with complete abandonment into the very center of the
Universe. There is a point in the supreme moment of realization
where the individual merges with the Universe, but not to the loss
of his individuality; where a sense of the Oneness of all Life so
enters his being that there is no sense of otherness."[13]

In that resplendent occasion of "complete abandonment"
the Allness steps forward "front and center," and there is nothing
else. We no longer feel that Spirit is moving through us because
there is no sense of a separate person through which Spirit must
move. All boundaries end in that mystical moment when one
experiences God as all, realizes Life as One–fluid and whole–and
the "I" transcends the personal and becomes the trees, the moun-
tains, the planets, the stars, and all people.

"GOD IS MORE THAN LAW OR PRINCIPLE. God is
the Infinite Spirit, the Limitless Conscious Life of the Universe;
the One Infinite Person, within whom all people live…the One
Indivisible Whole."[14] There is One Life behind all that lives–One
Spirit behind all that moves–One Being behind all that is, was, or
ever will be. The Spirit of Unity descends into our minds as we
listen for Its Voice–as we contemplate, and meditate upon the

Allness–needing nothing, wanting nothing, demanding nothing.

As we listen with our heart–mind and soul open to the Infinite–we will hear the Voice of Creation eternally proclaiming: "This is my beloved child in whom I am well pleased." And we will be compelled to identify ourself by stepping forward "front and center."

*Process Sheet Six*

# Front and Center

## *INDIVIDUAL*
In which areas of your life do you feel powerless or victimized?

_____

_____

_____

_____

You can become a master of your fate instead of a victim of circumstance by shifting your thinking from fear of, and dependency on, the outer world to trust in the inner world of Spirit. Keeping your true identity "front and center" in mind, write affirmations proclaiming the spiritual power within you as "master" in each circumstance above. (Example: *"Wisdom guides and directs my decision in this matter, and I calmly await the joyous outcome."*)

_____

_____

_____

_____

## *GROUP*
Discussion of Lesson.

**Activity:** (*Materials: Chalk board or dry erase board; marker for board; drawing paper; pen or pencil.*)
The facilitator lists the following five words on the board: *Health, Relationships, Finances, Career, Goals*. Each person draws a ladder. At the bottom of the ladder, each person writes the word *victim*;

one-third of the way up the ladder, the words *responsibly creating*;
two-thirds of the way up the ladder, the words *being used by God.*
Then each person places on the appropriate rung of the ladder
where they feel they are in the five areas listed on the board.

**Meditation:** Entering the Allness

(*Facilitator: do not use music for this meditation. Use Relaxation
Technique 2 on page 299 and darken the room, if possible.*)
  Now, listen with your heart–mind and soul open...
surrender the personal and open to the greater possibilities of the
Universal...let any worldly thoughts drift away or settle like
falling leaves in your mind...relax...you have plenty of time *right
now* to hear the Inner Voice of Truth...the Voice of the Spirit of
Unity...throw yourself *with complete abandonment into the very
center of the Universe* and listen...(*Facilitator: allow five minutes
and then very quietly bring the group back into the room and have
them open their eyes*)

1. Proverbs 4:7 (KJV). 2. SOM 30:2. 3. Hebrews 11:3 (Lamsa). 4. SOM 109:4. 5. SOM 44:5.
6. SOM 275:3. 7. SOM 258:1. 8. Psalms 37:7 (KJV). 9. Luke 12:32 (KJV). 10. SOM 366:1.
11. 1 Corinthians 2:9 (KJV). 12. SOM 405:3. 13. SOM 358:3. 14. SOM 365:3.

# 7    Write Your Own Song

*Mystics throughout the ages have talked about the Music of Life and of the euphonious tone and melody of colors, flowers, rocks, and trees.*

Lao-tsu spoke of the Great Tone that is "the tone that goes beyond all usual imagination." The Hindus talk of *Nada Brahma*, "the tone from which God made the world, which continues to sound at the bottom of creation, and which sounds through everything." Ernest Holmes says: "The Original Spirit is Harmony."[1]

Using the concept of "Nature as Melody," a geneticist took strands of DNA and assigned musical notes to the various "nucleotides" which make up DNA. After designating "do, re, mi," etc., the scientist chose a particular key and time signature, and the duration of each note. The result was a melodic composition. His musician wife "fleshed out" the melodies with harmonies. When the completely transcribed scores were performed by professional musicians, the result was compositions that sounded like the music of Bach, Brahms, Chopin and other great composers. The melodies were majestic. Many people who heard the songs were moved to tears. They could not believe that their bodies contained such uplifting, inspiring harmonies.

Science is proving through extensive research what mystics and philosophers have always intuitively known. Einstein proclaimed: "Science without religion is lame, religion without science is blind."[2] Ernest Holmes looked "forward to the day when science and religion shall walk hand in hand through the visible to the invisible."[3] We are living in an age where these hands are closer than ever before. Science is beginning to show us physically what mystics have seen metaphysically: that each of us is a beautiful song in Harmony with the Perfection of the One Metrical Poem, One Song, the Uni-verse. The music of the spheres pulsates in our soul, and each of us is a vital part of the Celestial Choir or the Spiritual Symphony.

Why, then, does there seem to be so much discord in our world? Why do we sometimes feel so out of step with Life? Often it is because we are not listening to our own inner song. We are disregarding the rhythm of our own nature and ignoring our interior harmony in favor of "fitting in." In order for us to be in harmony with life, we must be in harmony with who we are, so that we can discover our part in the One Song of Life. We need to look within, or rather to *listen* within, to the Magnificent Music of the Uni-verse, which includes our own unique tone and melody.

## HEARING OUR OWN SONG

We must get to know our own sound. We all need to ask ourselves Olivia Newton-John's musical question, "Have you ever been mellow, have you ever tried to hear something deep inside you? Have you ever been happy just to hear your song?"[4] With all of the clatter of the material world, it is difficult for us to hear our song, to know who we are, how we sound, and where our music harmonizes best in life. It is important for us to take the time to turn within, to get "mellow," and to meditate upon the One Tone until we feel the harmony within us. "We can so train our ears to listen to the Divine Harmony within, that we shall reproduce Its melody, rhythm and beauty in all our ways."[5]

When we think of our life metaphorically as a song, it becomes easier for us to see where we may need to make changes so that our outer life is as harmonious as our true inner state. If our life were a song, it could be divided into four parts: Rhythm, Melody, Harmony, and Words.

## "I'VE GOT RHYTHM"–BUT IS IT MY OWN?

Although we are capable of relating to a variety of *rhythms* because we are one with the Rhythmic Nature of the Whole, each of us has a particular rhythm, an individual pace that allows us to express who we are easily and effortlessly. Our body reflects "the perfect motion, the rhythmic ease of Mind in action."[6] Some people move at a fast pace in life like a hummingbird or a road-runner. They work well under pressure; stress is a stimulus. These people move best along lifelines that are tightly-tuned like the strings on a guitar, banjo, or ukulele.

When we see people who are successful living in "the fast lane," we think that we must emulate them in order to be success-ful too. But our natural rhythm may not be as fast. Perhaps our timing in the One Song is slower. We need to acknowledge our own rhythm and know that we can be successful at our own pace. Most people who develop stress-related physical and emotional problems are those who are trying to live their life at a faster rhythm than what is natural for them.

On the other hand, people who race around are often told to "slow down, take it easy, don't try to do so much." If those whose natural rhythm is fast force themselves to slow down mere-ly to please others, they often develop physical and emotional problems just as those who are trying to speed up often do. These people are usually the ones who die six months after retirement, not because they are old, but because they are not living at their natural rhythm.

In order for us to live a healthy life *it is essential for us to discover the pulse at the core of our being, honor our individual rhythm, and not compare ourselves to others* moving faster or slower. Have you ever been out on a dance floor and moving really great to the music until you noticed someone else dancing differently than you? The steps may have been faster or slower than yours, or just so different from what you were doing that you tripped over your own feet. Because you were focusing on the rhythm of the other dancer, you lost your own timing. When we concentrate on the outer world with its twists, turns, and arrhythmia and don't listen to our inner pulse or check our personal pace, we can get tripped up and out of step with our own purpose in life.

However, even though our individual life has its own particular rhythm, it doesn't mean that we are traveling to the beat of a "different drummer" (even though at times we may feel that we are). *There is only One Divine Drummer beating out the Rhythm of Life.* Just as in an orchestra when one instrument is playing a slow, steady rhythm and another is playing a faster one, each instrument in the orchestra is playing its part within the one overall tempo of the music. When we move to our natural rhythm, we feel more in tempo with all of Life. And, as we live at our own pace, we find that everything else in our world works in cadence with us.

## NAME THAT TUNE!

Our *melody* is like our personality: our unique, individual expression of the One Life. How many notes of your melody would someone need to hear in order to claim: "I know that person!"

Can someone name your "tune" in, say, two notes? Three notes? Has anyone even *heard* your melody before? Are you living out loud in the world, playing each note of your unique expression fully and clearly? Do you "sing unto him a new song,"[7] the one put into your heart since the beginning? Or do you have your volume turned down so low that no one even notices that you are "on" at all?

Sometimes we hide who we really are and what we honestly think and feel because we're afraid of our own sound. We've been told so often to be quiet, or to sound the way someone else wants us to sound, that we don't think our song is *good enough for anyone else to hear*. So we turn ourselves way down in order to fit in, or we try to hum something else. *But we shall never be happy singing someone else's song.* Every sound of Life is important. Each of us helps to "flesh out" the musical score and enrich the performance of Life with our unique sound. We are a part of the Universal Symphony and, within It, there is no one tone that is more important than another, no matter how simple or complex the individual sound might be.

Some people are like a light little tune, repetitive and easy to catch on to. They are easy to get to know, dependable, often predictable. They are like the simple songs that everyone loves to sing, like "Row, row, row your boat," or play, like "Chopsticks." The individual range in a *simple* song is small; just so, someone with a "light" melody does not have an emotional range that runs extremely high or low. They are easy to be around because there are no difficult or extreme characteristics that challenge anyone.

Then there are the more *complex* melodies, with lots of highs and lows. Someone with a more "heavy" melody might have mood swings from *adagio* to *allegro*, the very solemn to the extremely animated. Mozart heard the *Requiem* within himself as well as *The Marriage of Figaro*. All is Spirit.

Finally, there are the "drama queens" (and kings), whose entire lives sound like: "Da, da, da, *dummmm!*" or "*Dum*, da, *dum, dum!*"

We cannot live our melody fully and beautifully unless we are willing to take the time to listen to the song within us and then give to it everything we've got. As we listen to our melody, we begin to appreciate the uniqueness of our song. We give ourselves permission to express our song, whether our melody is simple, complex, or downright dramatic. If we are singing our song in earnest, we are guided to that place in Life where our melody fits in.

## IN HARMONY–OR INHARMONY?

*Harmony* in our lives is how we interact with others. As we begin to sing our song, it is easier for us to discover with whom we harmonize and where the discords are. If we are experiencing inharmony and discord in our lives, it could be because we are selling out on ourselves and not singing the song of who we are and how we feel. *When we are not being honest, we attract people and experiences that are as confused and discordant as we are.* When we are playing our melody loud and clear and there still is no harmony in our relationships, then we're probably in the wrong section of the orchestra and we need to move. The song in our soul, whether fast or slow, long or short, soft or loud, is always a Love Song. As we sing our song of love, we automatically move into right relationship with others and harmonize with life. "Out of any chaos we can produce harmony.[8] Infinite Love harmonizes man's entire being."[9]

## WORDS

Last of all our song includes *words*. These are the words we say every day. Are the lyrics of your song happy–about life and its possibilities–or do you sing the blues?

When I was a teenager my girlfriend and I would sit around reading Rod McKuen's poems and crying. Then we'd turn on the radio and listen to the Country & Western songs, the ones that I now call "razor blade music." They were songs about lost love and broken hearts. My favorite one was "I've Got Tears in My Ears from Lying on My Back Crying over You."

*New York Magazine* ran a competition several years ago in which readers were asked to invent a title for a Country & Western song. If you were to title your song of life, would it resemble "He Put a Ring on Her Finger and a Dagger in My Heart" or "He Left Me Flat in Texas and Didn't Leave a Spare"? It is important for us to watch what we say and to listen to the lyrics of our life, because our words have power. "We speak into our words the intelligence which we are, and backed by that greater Intelligence of the Universal Mind, our word becomes a law unto the thing for which it is spoken."[10]

What words are you writing for your song of life? What are you affirming with your daily words? Are they clear, positive and to the point–or are they filled with clutter and disarray, muddled by added verses of indecision, doubt, and fear? The most memorable songs are made up of simple, affirmative statements: "You Are My Sunshine." Positive, affirmative statements give the Creative Medium a clearer message of what we want to create in our world because *we* are clear about what we want to create. Then we don't confuse the message with "what ifs," "yeah buts," or fear and anxiety.

Would we enjoy singing "Here comes Peter Cottontail" if it were not such a positive song? What if it were written with the words of doubt and fear that often accompany our daily song: "Here comes Peter Cottontail," *if he doesn't change his mind or find someone else to give his candy to.* "Coming down the bunny trail," *if the trail isn't blocked and he has to take a detour and gets lost.* "Hippity, Hoppity," *if he doesn't hurt himself.* "Easter's on its way," *if I truly deserve to experience it.*

Our words create the images that become our reality, and so we must sing our song *individually*, if we want to participate in the Harmony of the Whole. If we are to ever experience the fullness of life and tap into our hidden potential, we must listen to the heartbeat of our soul, then stand up, move our feet, open our mouths, and sing The Hallelujah Chorus! In the Inner Kingdom where our true nature resides, no one is tone deaf or uncoordinated. Because we are one with the Uni-verse, because we are harmonious, melodic beings of God, we can all write our own song: We have rhythm, we have music, we are Spirit...who could ask for anything more?

*Process Sheet Seven*

# Write Your Own Song

## *INDIVIDUAL AND GROUP*

Write your own song.

Include your individual *Rhythm*: What is your natural pace in life?

*Melody*: What are the qualities of your personality?

*Harmony*: Where do you "fit in"?

*Words*: What are the words you would like to speak about yourself and life? Be sure to give your song a title.

If this is a group activity, share your song with a partner or the group.

**Meditation:** The Uni-verse

*(Facilitator: read slowly without music. Begin with one of the Relaxation Techniques on pages 299-300.)*

Imagine that you are standing in a beautiful, flower-covered meadow...you are wearing a white satin choir robe...there are hundreds of people, also wearing white robes, standing around you, but the meadow is large and you do not feel crowded...in fact, you feel happy to be with all of the people and, even though you may not have met all of them, you feel as if they are all your friends...you hear the sound of a baton being tapped on a wooden podium, and as you look up you see the choir director– a cheerful old man, in a white robe with a deep purple cord around his waist. He has a long white beard and twinkling eyes... you understand that he is signaling for everyone present to take their choir positions...take your place now...as you stand in place ready to sing, you hear music...the music seems to be coming from the trees that border the meadow...you listen for a moment to the music of the trees...beautiful music...the most glorious melody you have ever heard...then the flowers in the meadow join in...and the music is even more beautiful–the most perfect sound you have ever heard...listen to the music...feel it in your heart...feel it in your soul...(*Facilitator: allow one minute*)...now the Choir Director is raising His baton, and it is time for you and the other members of the choir to join in–to sing your individual parts...begin to sing your part, and listen to the Inner Harmony of your soul...listen to your own voice...hear how your voice harmonizes with those around you...with the entire choir...with the music of the trees and flowers...One Song in Perfect Harmony...a Perfect Sound filling the air...you are adding to the melodious sound...you are an integral part of the One Song–the Uni-verse...continue to sing, feeling the music in your heart and in your soul...(*Facilitator: allow two to three minutes*)... now it is time to end this particular performance, but know that the One Song continues to play in your soul even as you open your eyes...even as you go about your daily life...and when you are ready, open your eyes.

1. SOM 53:3.  2. Albert Einstein, *Out of My Later Years* (Citadel Press), p. 26.  3. SOM 25:1.
4. Olivia Newton-John: *Have You Ever Been Mellow?*  5. SOM 258:1.  6. SOM 242:3.
7. Psalms 33:3 (KJV).  8. SOM 187:3.  9. SOM 219:1  10. SOM 304:1.

Thinking and Speaking in the Affirmative

*Do you know someone
who just isn't happy
unless he or she has
the final say? Whether
it is a simple discussion
on a subject they are
unfamiliar with,*
or it is a heated debate about their
favorite topic, they just have to get in the last word. Perhaps
they have gone so far as to call you up, tell you their opinion, then hang up the phone before you could speak just so
that they could have the last word. The last word would
seem to hang in the air as though it were the reigning
authority, the final verdict, the irrevocable Truth. The last
word suggests that there is nothing further to be said on the
subject. *That's the way it is–and so it is...amen.*

The phrase "and so it is" or the word *amen* is
often used at the end of an affirmative prayer or Spiritual
Mind Treatment. These last words indicate that the one
praying is convinced in his or her own mind and heart that
what was spoken in prayerful voice and affirmed within the
realm of the Divine Listener is the reigning authority, the
final verdict, the irrevocable Truth. There is nothing further
to be said on the subject. *That's the way it is–and, so it
is...amen.*

Unfortunately, most of us just can't seem to leave
well enough alone. The last word in our prayers is not always
the last word we have to say about the problem for which we
have prayed. Often, when our prayers are complete, we con-

tinue to give the problem more power than our prayer. The "facts" which we want to heal through Treatment remain more real to us than the Truth we have called upon through prayer.

For instance, after we've prayed about our health, we continue to graphically talk about our disease and our aches and pains. After we've prayed for prosperity, we continue to speak fearfully of our financial problems, e.g. how broke we are, what we can't afford, or how we just can't seem to make ends meet; after we've prayed to experience love in our life, we continue our forlorn discourse about our relationships, and how we just can't seem to meet the right person, or we whine about the relationship we're in. We moan and groan, judge and condemn, and validate our lack, limitation, and separateness from Universal Good. We speak as though *that's the way it is–and so it is…amen.* "The objective form to which we give our attention is created from the very attention which we give to it."[1]

## WHICH WAY ARE WE LOOKING?

There is always physical evidence to validate our problems. But healing takes place through "affirmative" or "scientific" prayer only as we turn away from that evidence to that which is unseen–the Perfection of Spirit behind the seen. "A scientific treatment cannot be conditioned upon anything that now exists, upon any experience less than perfection. In treatment, we turn entirely away from the relative–entirely away from that which appears to be."[2]

It is the recognition of the Ever-Presence of Wholeness that brings about wholeness. When we continue to look at, think of, and talk about the evidence of our five senses, our last words validate the very thing we wanted changed through prayer. Then, rather than speaking our words of healing Truth and finding that

"It is so" in our life, we speak our accustomed words and find that our life is still "so-so."

When our prayers don't manifest according to the words we've spoken in prayer, when our life doesn't change no matter how many affirmations we've been speaking, it isn't that Spirit isn't listening or that our thoughts really don't become things. It isn't that changing our thinking doesn't change our life or that mental healing doesn't work. The fact is, our life is reflecting back to us in glorious color and perfect detail exactly what we are focusing on: the "facts" we *really* believe about ourselves and life.

There isn't anything wrong with us, our creative ability or the healing Laws we are using. Spirit is creating powerfully and perfectly–through the conviction of our spoken words and the action of our silent thoughts–exactly what we don't want in our life. Why? Because that is where our focus is and our conversation fixates. Our last words are on the problem, and the problem continues to be validated by more physical evidence created by our thought. For instance, when we are having financial problems, and we are praying for an increase in our finances, lack of money usually is not the problem even though we think that more money would be the solution. *The problem is our limited thinking and impoverished conversation.* As Coco Chanel said, "There are people that have money and people who are rich." There are many beliefs that we hold that don't enrich our life, and, there are many concepts we hold that indirectly limit our monetary income but don't appear to be associated with money itself. All of them have to do with the *words* we speak in our head and out loud–words that separate us, in concept, from the Abundance of the Universe.

We think that we can hold onto our self-condemnation and our judgments of others, that we can continue to speak of ourselves and others as limited, material beings existing separate from God, and then somehow increase our prosperity through prayer and affirmation by tapping into a Divine Inheritance that we have spent all day denying is ours. We can't effectively borrow a little bit of God's "attention" for a specific thing and believe that the rest of life is separate from God. This is duality.

Spiritual healing occurs when we have a singleness of mind focused on the allness of Spiritual Perfection. Spiritual Truth is an all-or-nothing proposition. We can never fragment the Omnipresent Spirit. Either Spirit is everywhere or It is nowhere. Spiritual healing takes place as we move our thoughts (and our last words) to a high place within us, where Divine Wholeness is everything and there is no sickness to be cured, no poverty to be eliminated, and no loneliness to be rectified; where there is only the Pure Essence of Spirit moving in, through, around, and as all. "There is no one to be healed in the Truth and we must think in the Truth if we expect to heal."[3]

## SHE AFFIRMS INJUSTICE

There is a woman who calls me on the telephone from time to time who is a staunch feminist. However, in her conversation she seems to be more anti-male than pro-female. She seems to see herself, and women in general, as victims of a male-dominated society where females always get the short end of things and men are tyrants who never support or defend feminine issues. When someone mentions an injustice against a man, she has ten about women to top it. She has accumulated more than enough material evidence to prove her position, and she isn't happy unless she has the last word on the subject.

This same woman has been working on increasing her financial prosperity through "mind power" for years. She is an extremely creative and articulate person who is quite aggressive in business. There seems to be no outer reason at all for her limited success; but no matter how good her ideas are, no matter how well her presentations are put together, they don't sell.

She claims, emphatically, that she is doing "all the right things" to increase her prosperity. (She has taken dozens of prosperity workshops, gone to numerous lectures, and read scores of self-help books on the subject.) Still, financial success eludes her. She swears that her affirmative statements declare her oneness with the Source. In fact, on the surface, it sounds like she *is* doing "all the right things." But as the creative energy of life moves through her thought forms, It creates out of her *total* belief system. God as the Creator of prosperity cannot be separated from God as the Creator of man, God the Creator of woman, and God the Creator of all that is in her life.

## "HOW LONG WILL YOU HALT BETWEEN TWO OPINIONS?"[4]

While praying for prosperity her daily conversation is about the lack of support she receives from her husband and the failure of the male-dominated business world to recognize her creative ideas. Even though she affirms her success in business, she also declares herself to be a victimized female. The concept of victim constricts the Nature of Freedom, and her beliefs about her status limit her experience of the Abundance of the Universe. If all day long she is talking about the blocks to her success put up by men, then the impressionable and always agreeable Creative Medium must concur with her. Therefore she cannot experience the Omnipotent Allness of God's Creation in her life—as everything, everyone and everywhere—as the very Power which would increase her prosperity when she continues to perceive, focus on and speak about so many unloving beings who have power over her life.

We are always thinking and speaking into the realm of Mind, every moment of every day. *We get away with nothing.* "It is as though there were a Universal Ear, listening to and hearing everything that we say, feel or think, and reacting to it."[5] Every thought is a prayer. That is why it is vital for us to watch our thinking. The Creative Nature of Spirit is to listen and act. It is listening to what we *believe* about life, not what we *wish* for, and It creates out of what we think and what we speak of as fact in our conversation. "Whatever we think, act, believe in, feel, visualize, vision, image, read and talk about–in fact all processes which affect or impress us at all–are going into the subjective state of our thought…[and] tend to return again as some condition. So we, and we alone, control our destiny."[6]

## "EVERY DAY, EVERY MOMENT, EVERY SECOND, THERE IS CHOICE"[7]

The power of creation moves through our "last words"–what we say *is so*–the words that hang in the air and dwell in our mind as the reigning authority, the final verdict, and the irrevocable truth. We are at choice: either we can believe in the evidence of the outer world–think of it and talk about it as though it were hard and true–or we can place our faith in the Unseen Power of Spirit and with unshakable conviction accept as unalterable Truth that no matter what is going on around us, our good is unfolding every moment of every day. This kind of conviction, with no opposing belief to hamper or block it, will produce the results we desire.

Our ignorance is not so much in what we treat about.

*It is what we think about and talk about between treatments that negates everything we've said in treatment.* If we don't back up our prayers with our thinking, then our prayers don't stand a chance in hell—or heaven—of manifesting. It is like our planting a flower seed in the soil and then pouring weed seeds on top of it. The flower seed may try to grow into a flower, but it is outnumbered. As the weeds grow, they will choke the root of the budding plant and draw away all of its nourishment. Because of their sheer number, the weeds will succeed in growing healthy and strong. If our life looks like a crop of weeds, then we might want to look at the bulk of thoughts that we've been planting in mind.

If I close my eyes in prayer and affirm the allness of God's Goodness and then open my eyes (and my mouth) and speak words of separateness—condemning words of judgment against myself and others—and then justify all of my words with external evidence, *that* will be my experience in life. "When [one] thinks, or gives a treatment, or makes a prayer, he is dealing with involution—the first step of the creative order. This is what the Bible calls the Word. That which follows is evolution, or the unfoldment of the word, or concept, into objective existence....Ignorance of the Law excuses no one from its effects."[8]

The last word of the prayers of Jesus was *amen*. His prayers became manifested Truth in the moment they were spoken. He had nothing else to add to the Truth he spoke, and he expected immediate response from the Heavenly Father to Whom he spoke. He entertained no doubt and no other reality than the Allness of God. There was nothing else to say, *and so it was*—and so it shall be for us when we understand that all is said and *done* once we have uttered our *amen*.

The standard definition for the word *amen* is: "used at the end of a prayer or a statement to express assent or approval."[9] It is important for us to ask ourselves if we are placing our *amen* where it doesn't belong. To what are we giving our assent and approval: the high cost of living? the increase in crime and violence? the scarcity of jobs? How often when we hear gossip, or a racial or gender slur, do we say, "Amen" through our silence? How many times do we say, "Ain't that the Truth!" when in fact, it isn't the Truth at all?

We shall never really know "the Truth" by looking at the world and agreeing with it. There is much in this world that seems to hang in the air as the reigning authority, the final verdict, the undebatable Truth, that is anything *but* the Truth. If we want Spirit to move through our life and create our dreams, then we must turn away from, and cease to agree with, the limited evidence of the senses. We must disclaim solid fact and give our assent to the unseen Spiritual Truth. When we have called upon, recognized, and accepted the Truth in any situation and have refused to give lip service to any other power or force, the Truth will manifest in our life.

*That's the way It is—and so It is...amen!*

*Process Sheet Eight*

# The Last Word

## INDIVIDUAL

"We shall never really know 'the Truth' by looking at the world and agreeing with it. There is much in this world that seems to hang in the air as the reigning authority, the final verdict, the undebatable Truth, that is anything *but* the Truth." Are there some things that you have been saying *amen* to in your life that have no Spiritual basis?

_____

_____

_____

_____

Write an affirmative statement of Spiritual Truth for each of the above items. End the affirmation with "and so it is" or "amen" or both "and so it is, amen." (Example: *"Spirit is the Creator of every being, therefore all humankind is created equal, and so it is, amen."*)

_____

_____

_____

_____

Write a Spiritual Mind Treatment about a specific issue that you want to change in your life, a prayer which you can say every day. An "affirmative" or "scientific" prayer can be effective daily prayer. It begins with the Allness of Spirit, everywhere, all of the time, and includes the Qualities of Spirit which you want to recognize as ever-present in your life. For example: If you want to experience more loving relationships in your life, begin your prayer by recognizing and stating the Allness of Love everywhere, all of the time. Then recognize and state that because Love is everywhere, all of the time, Love must be right where you are— in fact, you must be Love because Love must be you. Then recognize and state that because Love is everywhere, all of the time, not only are you Love, but everyone else is Love too. Your prayer for loving relationships can now include all of your relationships, because Love is present in all of your relationships. An acceptance of affirmative or scientific prayer includes gratitude for the Truth of our prayer and the manifestation or material proof in our life. Finally, an affirmative or scientific prayer ends with the last words "and so it is" or "amen," indicating that the words you have spoken within the Realm of Divine Creative Action are the reigning authority, the final verdict, the irrevocable Truth. The last words indicate that there is nothing further to be said on the subject. Spend the week supporting your prayer with thoughts and actions, and guarding against any other words that would negate it.

### *GROUP*
Discussion of Lesson.

**Activity:** After completing the *Individual* exercise, the group may want to write a group Spiritual Mind Treatment about a specific issue. When the wording for the treatment has been agreed upon, the evening could end with everyone closing their eyes, and the facilitator reading the group treatment. The treatment could be preceeded by one of the Relaxation Techniques on pages 299-300, and music could be played as well, if desired. When all but the *last words* of the treatment are complete, the whole group may want to join in with *and so it is, amen.* (The group should be reminded to support the treatment all week with their thoughts and actions.)

1. SOM 412:2.   2. SOM 169:3.   3. SOM 408:5.   4. 1 Kings 18:21 (Lamsa).
5. SOM 170:3.   6. SOM 126:2.   7. SOM 143:3.   8. SOM 38:2, 4.
9. *American Heritage Dictionary, Standard Edition,* 1992.

# Godspeed

### Unblocking the Abundant Good Within

*I used to believe that Godspeed
meant "faster than the speed
of light" or "at the speed of Spirit."
I had heard the word used
many times at funerals* when the minister would
conclude the service by wishing the newly departed
"Godspeed." I assumed that the pastor was asking God to
rush that soul on to its next plane of existence as quickly as
possible! However, while looking for another word under "g"
in the dictionary, I happened to run across *Godspeed.* I discovered that the word originated in Middle English and was
taken from the three-word phrase: "God speid you [which
meant] God prosper you."[1] A farewell salute of "Godspeed"
was actually a wish for the soul to have a spiritually
prosperous journey.

Of course, most of us would prefer to begin our
journey of prosperity right here on earth rather than waiting
until we get to destinations unknown beyond "the Pearly
Gates." We want an abundance of good in our life, here
and now: lots of money, a great career, a terrific relationship,
and plenty of physical comforts. We are ready right where we
are to let God prosper us. After all, if it is the Father's good
pleasure to give us the Kingdom, we'd be pretty foolish not
to take it and improve our material life.

NOT A "GET-RICH-QUICK" SCHEME

There is nothing wrong with our desiring to improve our

worldly existence. However, there are those who believe that the ultimate purpose of the teachings of the Science of Mind is to show us how to obtain a comfortable material lifestyle, and that the ultimate goal of spiritual enlightenment is earthly luxury. This is not the case. "Lessons on *prosperity* and mental control of conditions can be dangerous because of the misunderstanding of this subject. Science of Mind is not a 'get-rich-quick' scheme, neither does it promise something for nothing. It does, however, promise the one who will comply with its teachings that he shall be able to bring greater possibilities and happier conditions into his experience."[2] Often, we are looking for "something for nothing." We're looking to get-rich-quick, get-love-quick, or get-healed-quick. We don't want to learn a new way of being. We just want the *results* that come from one!

A friend of mine who is a doctor believes that true wellness for her patients occurs as they take responsibility for the health of their bodies. She often suggests to them changes in diet, more exercise, and other activities that will not only help them with their current physical challenge but will have long-term benefits to their health. She told me the other day that after giving advice to a patient who was suffering from a painful problem brought on by years of unhealthy living, the patient asked, "Isn't there just a pill I can take for this?"

Many of us approach our mental-emotional-spiritual health the same way. We want pain relief, not permanent relief. "Can't I just pray to win the lottery or that my bills will disappear?" Certainly; but the results of such prayers are temporary, not permanent. Nothing in our life changes permanently until *we* do. There is not enough money in all the lotteries combined to buy one bit of spiritual knowledge or transform our soul. Affirmative prayer can be useful in improving our physical situation. But when improvement occurs, it can be fleeting if it is not accompanied by a permanent change in our thinking–by an alteration in the way we see ourselves and our relation to Spirit.

## "NOT SOMETHING FOR NOTHING"[3]

Only God can truly prosper us, and the riches "prepared for them that love him"[4] are not found in games of chance. We can't expect to get something for nothing. Change comes with a price tag. Impoverished thinking that leaves us spiritually bankrupt–intolerance, judgment, guilt, greed, and selfishness–must be relinquished. In order to grow in spiritual richness, in order for God to prosper us, we must understand our inseparable relationship to the Source and cease to look at the world as even *capable* of fulfilling our true needs. What we genuinely require for full self-expression and fulfillment can only be supplied by Spirit. If we desire true prosperity, we must give up our limited ideas about ourselves and others, and surrender our petty grievances, grudges, victimized thinking, excuses, and blame–because this is the poverty we carry with us.

We aren't "creating" prosperity when we let go of limiting thoughts. We are moving the junk out of the way so that we can experience the Presence of Abundant Good already existing within us and ready to express through us if given a clear passage. The teachings of the Science of Mind with which we must comply if we want to "bring greater possibilities and happier conditions into our experience" are founded upon the Oneness of God and humankind and the Fullness of a Creation that is imbued with the qualities of its Creator. We don't need to ask God to give us *things* to make us happy. God knows precisely what we require for full self-expression, because we were God's idea in the first place! We come "fully loaded" with all of the accessories that make us a "luxury model"! We are rich by birth, and a wellspring of Joy forever bursts forth from the center of our soul and nourishes every area of our life. As we recognize our spiritual inheritance, this wealth of understanding takes form in our life.

There is a Still Small Voice of Unlimited Wisdom within us that is constantly revealing our preexisting, God-Ordained Abundant Good. "We do well to listen to this Inner Voice, for it tells us of a life wonderful in its scope; of a love beyond our fondest dreams; of a freedom which the soul craves."[5] The purpose of the teachings of the Science of Mind is to show us how to find ourselves in the Abundance of Creation where we eternally exist, not how to bum another dollar off the Universe.

Often, rather than listening for our Inner Voice, we are busy looking for the Inner Pocketbook. We often pray merely for more and better *things* rather than for the spiritual awareness of our Divinity which, by Its Presence, brings about more and better things by revealing Itself to us in form. When our life is lacking materially, it is because our life is lacking spiritually. We cannot build a stairway to heaven by piling up earthly possessions. We don't need more stuff. We need more Truth. Our outward life will always personify our inward life. The mirror of the world will invariably reflect the one who is looking into it. The unrestricted Presence of God in our conscious awareness provides the perfect material form to balance the outer with the inner.

When we're missing something *outside* of us, it is because we have yet to find it *inside* of us. Richness ought to be viewed as a spiritual condition, not a material goal. When we understand that true wealth must be a *heavenly* statement of prosperity *before* it touches the ground, our earthly experience improves from the inside out as the treasures we have discovered in Mind manifest in form. When we embody the richness of the Spirit, the goodies of

the world pale in comparison. *Material things* become a byproduct
of our realization of the Kingdom of Heaven rather than the
motivating force behind our *spiritual quest.*

When we express more spiritual qualities–gentleness,
peacefulness, loving-kindness, thoughtfulness, generosity, happiness, creativeness, and aliveness–the material world around us
"impersonates" our inner wealth in physical form. We "bring
greater possibilities and happier conditions into our experience."
Our relationships are happier and more harmonious. Our activities
are more rewarding and fulfilling. Our bodies are healthier and
more energetic. When we are prospered by the God *within,* our
prosperity increases in the world *without* because we are living at a
higher, less inhibited level of awareness, and we are allowing more
of Life to flow through us.

Our improved material life, our earthly inheritance,
should be thought of as the residual effect of our spiritual enrichment, growth, self-discovery, and self-expression, and not the ultimate aim. "For what is a man profited if he shall gain the whole
world, and lose his own soul?"[6] When our whole purpose for
praying is merely to *get something* from God, because we believe
that we are *missing something,* what we are really missing is the
point of Treatment. The Bible reminds us, "With all of thy getting
get understanding."[7] When we understand that Unlimited Spirit is
All–in all and through all, including ourselves–we realize the
inevitability of our own abundant nature. The outer manifestation
must and will reflect this inner realization. "Could we conceive of
Spirit as being incarnate in us–while at the same time being ever
*more* than that which is incarnated–would we not expand spiritually and intellectually? Would not our prayers be answered before
they were uttered?"[8]

There was a time when I thought that I was progressing

spiritually when my idea of prosperity shifted from seeing Divine Supply as a Celestial Sears Catalog to seeing it as a Celestial Neiman-Marcus Catalog! Asking God for better stuff (and getting it) is not necessarily spiritual progress. Our spiritual progress cannot be determined *simply* by how many goodies we can pop out of the ethers. Spiritual richness should not be measured *solely* by an outer assessment of material wealth–for there are many who are *rich in things* and *poor in Spirit.* True Prosperity begins with our recognition of the Omnipresence of Abundant Good within us, and flows from the Heart of God into our outer experience.

## FROM THINGS TO THOUGHT

In order to "comply with the teachings of the Science of Mind" and "bring greater opportunities and happier conditions into our experience," we must reverse our focus from things to thought and understand that all is Mind and all comes from Mind. The thought "I need," if not neutralized by the spiritual realization "I have," can keep away from us the very thing we want because the world will reflect back to us the emptiness we feel. Since we cannot *need* what we already have, the statement "I need" may create a barrier to our having, and we shall not, because we cannot, experience the wealth we desire. Instead, we continue to "need" no matter how much we have. Mind creates through thought, and It creates for *us* through *our* thinking. Our outer conditions match, precisely, our inner statements. "We live in Mind and It can return to us only what we think into it....If we are thinking of ourselves as poor and needy, then Mind has no choice but to return what we have thought into It."[9]

If Spirit is our Source and we are forever inseparable from our Good, how could we be needy? If the Unlimited Life of

Spirit is at the core of our being (knowing what we require *before* we ask) then Spirit doesn't need to be alerted every time a new product comes on the market! The Creative, Unified Presence of Unconditional Love, Unfathomable Peace, and Unlimited Joy forever moves into form. It takes shape as *all* life, and It takes shape as *our* life. The material forms around us merely reflect our wholeness. They don't make us whole!

We are promised that if we seek *first* the Kingdom of Heaven, "that good, and acceptable, and perfect, will of God,"[10] all else will be added to us. We won't have to go around collecting it. When we walk through our life consciously aware of the Presence of the Sufficiency of Spirit within us, that Presence manifests as the cornucopia of our life.

Everything material stays on the planet when we leave the earth–for all earthly manifestations are temporary forms for a temporary journey. The Transcending and Everlasting is that good, acceptable, and perfect will of God. We are born into this world with empty hands and an unlimited mind. We take with us only what we carry in our consciousness. The spiritual journey is a journey without distance. Godspeed!

*Process Sheet Nine*

# Godspeed

### INDIVIDUAL

"We need to reverse our focus from things to thought, and to understand that all is Mind and all comes from Mind. The thought 'I need,' if not neutralized by the spiritual realization 'I have,' can keep away from us the very thing we want because the world will reflect back to us the emptiness we feel." Write ten "I need" statements that represent areas of lack and limitation in your life. (Example: *"I need a new car," "I need a job," "I need a friend," "I need discipline."* )

1. _____

2. _____

3. _____

4. _____

5. _____

6. _____

7. _____

8. _____

9. _____

10. _____

"When we express more spiritual qualities–gentleness, peacefulness, loving-kindness, thoughtfulness, generosity, happiness, creativeness, and aliveness–the material world around us 'impersonates' our inner wealth in physical form." Study the ten statements above and write down what quality or qualities of Spirit the outer form would "impersonate." (Example: The qualities of Spirit that a new car might represent are Freedom and Unlimited Mobility; a job might represent the Self-Expression, Creativity, and Abundant Supply of Spirit; a friend might represent the Love, Support, Unity, Intimacy and Loyalty of Spirit; discipline might represent the Dependability, Persistence, and "Art" of Spirit.)

1._____

2._____

3._____

4._____

5._____

6._____

7._____

8._____

9._____

10._____

Write ten "I am" statements to assist you in knowing that the above qualities of Spirit are in you, *as* you. (Example: *"I am free and I experience unlimited mobility in my life"; "The Universe of Spirit supports my full self-expression"; "I express and recognize Love in all of my relationships"; "The Changeless Nature of Spirit dwells at the core of my being; I trust and believe in myself."*)

1._____

2._____

3._____

4._____

5._____

6._____

7._____

8._____

9._____

10._____

## GROUP
Discussion of Lesson.

**Activity:** Same as for Individual.

**Meditation:**  Perpetuating the Presence

*(Facilitator: read slowly with restful music in background, if desired. Begin with one of the Relaxation Techniques on pages 299-300.)*
 The unrestricted Creative Medium within us always provides the perfect material form to balance the outer with the inner...the Substance of all that you desire and all that you require is within you at this very moment...Divine Mind holds within Itself the true idea of you complete with every detail for your happiness and full self-expression...you do well to listen to this Inner Voice...for It will tell you of a life wonderful in its scope...of a love beyond your fondest dreams...of a freedom which your soul craves...it is within this inner place that your soul is fed and nourished with Love...Peace...Joy...it is within this place that all outer form originates...extending out from the center of your consciousness like beams of light...shining here...and there...and everywhere in your life...the All-Sufficiency of Spirit gives to all alike...within the Realm of Eternal Richness and Glory there is no neediness, for all are enriched alike...allow this Presence to enter your conscious awareness...greet the Presence with the recognition that this "I am" is who you are...say within yourself... "I am Love...I am Peace...I am Joy...I am Rich and Radiant Self-Expression...I am Free...I am Fulfilled...I welcome and accept this Presence in me as me...there is no other self but the Self of Love, Peace, Joy, and Free and Fulfilled Self-Expression... this is God in me...this is me in God"...open to your greater experience of the Presence...*(Facilitator: allow one or two minutes)*...still feeling the Presence within you, move your awareness back into your body with your eyes still closed...feeling Love, Peace, Joy, and Freedom, knowing that as you move forward in your life, every step is a movement in Self-Fulfillment...breathe

deeply, feeling the Presence, knowing there is no separation from this Presence as you open your eyes.

1. *Webster's New Collegiate Dictionary,* G. & C. Merriam Co., 1977.   2. SOM 266:1.
3. SOM 266:1.   4. 1 Corinthians 2:9 (KJV).   5. SOM 26:1.   6. Matthew 16:26 (KJV).
7. Proverbs 4:7 (KJV).   8. SOM 150:5.   9. SOM 301:3.   10. Romans 12:2 (KJV).

# Hell, No!

Creating a Heavenly Consciousness on Earth

*"That which we look upon is real while we look at it....Hell is the phantom abode of our morbid imaginations. Heaven and Hell are states of consciousness."* [1]

Everything that we see, hear, feel, and touch–everything we experience and everything that occurs in our life–takes place within our own consciousness. We cannot think outside of our own mind nor stand outside of our own perceptions. Hell is not a place where we go when we die if we've been bad here on earth, any more than heaven is a place reserved for those who have earned some special status through good deeds on the planet. What we are conscious of becomes our personal heaven or hell.

Heaven and hell are "planes" of consciousness, "levels" of awareness which can be either beautiful, harmonious, loving, and peaceful, or ugly, discordant, hateful, and chaotic. Heaven is the Great Reality, while hell is the Grand Illusion. We are capable of living in both states of consciousness, but not at the same time. What we experience of either is in direct relationship to what we believe is true about life, where we focus our thought, and where we point our view.

We could say that heaven and hell are inner convictions rather than outer destinations. "The greatest good that can come to anyone is the forming within him of an absolute certainty of himself, and of his relationship to the Universe, forever removing the sense of heaven as being outside himself."[2] We must also remove the sense of hell as being outside of ourselves as well.

## "TRUTH KNOWS NO OPPOSITE"[3]

Most of us have probably experienced a day when it seemed that every little detail of it was influenced by some evil force that wanted to make sure that we were miserable: everything that could go wrong did go wrong. Everyone and everything we came in contact with either had a problem or was a problem. But even though it may seem so at times, there is no opposing force out there, somewhere, that is out to get us or that can actually get to us. There isn't a configuration of stars that has power over us or a host of demons preparing our fate. Our thoughts are the only power creating or opposing our success and happiness. "Freedom and bondage, sickness and health, poverty and riches, heaven and hell, good and bad, happiness and misery, peace and confusion, faith and fear, and all conditions which *appear* to be opposites, are not really a result of the operation of *opposing powers*, but ARE THE WAY THE ONE POWER IS USED."[4]

    The One Power is the Universal Creative Medium in, around, and through us. We can use It to create heaven and we can inadvertently use It to create hell in our life. If we allow a bad mood or bad attitude to linger; if we can't seem to "get off" some negative event that has happened; if we are filled with guilt, regret, and resentment; we can create an atmosphere around us that attracts to us more and more of the same. When we're in a "bad space" it is amazing what we find in that space–hellish configurations of everything we don't want in our life. Our accumulated thoughts are powerful. When they are concentrated on lack, limitation, fear, and frustration, our messes get messier.

Things just seem to go from bad to worse, and the only "stroke" of fortune we experience seems to be a long stroke of bad luck.

Our mental space (or subjective atmosphere) determines what we see, attract, and experience. If we believe that nothing goes our way, it won't. If we believe that we always choose relationships that are bad for us, we shall. If we believe that good money always follows bad, it will. If we allow the past to color our present, then today becomes just a darker shade of yesterday and a paler shade of tomorrow.

It is vital for us to change negative thinking as quickly as possible. When we dwell upon problems without seeking solutions and beat the evidence into the ground to justify our misery, we perpetuate our agony. It is difficult for us to see the "angel of His Presence" when we continue to dwell in dark despair where even "angels fear to tread." However, the Spirit of Goodness is a constant Presence and awaits only our acknowledgment of It–and steadfast faith in It–to come forth in every situation no matter what seems to be going on: like when my father suffered a stroke twelve years ago. His lifestyle up to that point would probably not be considered healthy by anyone's standards. He had not eaten nutritiously and had begun to smoke cigarettes incessantly after my mother died ten years earlier.

At first, the stroke appeared to be catastrophic. The doctors believed that my formerly active and loquacious father would never regain the use of his right arm and leg, or much of his ability to speak. This man who could "never sit still" and whose stories made him the "life of the party" truly seemed to be experiencing "hell on earth." The prognosis looked so dim that my father's concerned doctor prescribed a psychiatric visitation for him each day to counteract any suicidal tendencies.

## HE HAD "FELT LIKE HELL"

However, it didn't take a professional for my father to realize that he had literally "felt like hell" since the death of his wife of thirty years. He knew that his hellish state of mind had manifested a disabled body. He also knew that if his physical condition was ever to improve, his mental atmosphere needed some heavenly inspiration. We recited together the words from one of his favorite Psalms which said in part, "if I make my bed in hell, behold, thou art there."[5] He tearfully reminded himself that even in his darkest hour the Spirit of Good was Present, and he had, indeed, reached that hour. He realized that even though his life had taken a turn for the worse and led to the black fissure in which he found himself, he didn't have to stay hell-bound. Spirit and the Kingdom of Heaven were still available to him.

Early the next morning the doctor came into my father's room and told him that he was "lucky" that he'd had a stroke, because when he was admitted to the hospital, routine examination had also revealed congestion in his lungs. The X-rays that followed confirmed numerous spots on his lungs that certainly would have developed into lung cancer before long if not treated. My father knew that his stroke had also given him an opportunity to clear up more than just his unhealthy physical habits. He was able to clear up the misguided thinking that had led him to believe that heaven had forsaken him.

Three months later when he was finally released from the hospital–determined to keep both his mind and body free from "pollutants"–his lungs were completely clear. He had fully regained his speech, and the prognosis for the healthy return of the function of both his arm and leg was excellent.

When we change our mental focus, we change the

direction in which the events in our life are going. A new thought sets a new cause in motion. When we refuse to be defeated by hellish circumstances because we know that heaven is available to us, and when we are convinced that Spirit has something wonderful in store for us in spite of appearances, we succeed in overcoming adversity.

## "...HEAVEN IS LIKE LEAVEN"[6]

Our good cannot vanish, because our good resides in the Kingdom of Heaven. That kingdom is everywhere present. It is always right where we are because heaven is a state of consciousness. In the midst of hell, we can turn to find heaven. Right where chaos seems be, right where that painful relationship appears most active, right where there seem to be symptoms of sickness, there is a blessing, a gift, a shining dividend from the Heavenly Realm of Goodness.

Every time it rains, it may rain "pennies from heaven," but it is up to us to turn our mental umbrellas upside down during the storms of our life. When all is well, it is easy for us to walk outside and feel the sunshine and know that "God's in His Heaven, all's right with the world!" But it is even more vital for us to know that when we are out on the storm-tossed sea of adversity, with thunder crashing and lightning flashing all around us, heaven is right there, too.

Most of us are happy to know that hell is not a place of eternal damnation for *ourselves*, but it is harder for us to let go of the hope that there is a place of punishment for those who sin and seem to get away with it. It is comforting for us to think that there is *somewhere* where "certain people" will go and get what's coming to them, since they often don't seem to be reaping any ill effects on earth from their behavior! But even though it appears as if some people can lie, cheat, steal, and make life miserable for others (and get rich in the process), the Law of the Universe is always just. No one escapes the hell of his or her own creation without first embracing heaven within his or her own consciousness. We can't judge from outer appearances what another may be experiencing in consciousness. Hell is a matter of interpretation, and punishment can often be hard to recognize on the surface of another's life.

It is also interesting how many people are willing to accept that hell is not a place but still want to believe that heaven *is* a place. They have the idea that when they leave the planet, they will "automatically" go to a more peaceful place where they will suddenly "know the Truth" no matter how ignorant of It they were at the time of their departure. But heaven and the wisdom to perceive it is not suddenly thrust upon us because we die. Heaven must be discovered in our consciousness. Any time we are willing to turn our focus away from the outer world–with its appearances of lack, limitation, responsibilities, debts, rejections, and losses– and turn our focus upon the eternal Reality of the Allness of God and our Oneness with Universal Spirit, we are automatically heaven-bound. We enter the Inner Kingdom to the degree that we turn inward towards that Kingdom…"for behold, the kingdom of God is within you."[7]

If we don't believe that we are loved by Everlasting Love, here and now; if we do not believe that we are sustained by the Unlimited Spirit of Creation in this moment: how do we expect to "suddenly" believe these things immediately hereafter? It has been said that the experience of death, itself, can motivate us towards introspection. We could say that when we die to this world, we make a "permanent turn" toward the inner world. Devoid of material expression, we have a wonderful opportunity to ponder the Great Vastness of Subconscious Life which is ruled by thought, awareness, and imagination.

Leaving our material body may remove many of the obstacles to our spiritual growth that having a material body placed there. We may feel our oneness with Spirit more clearly when we feel more spiritual. However, mystics tell us that we also take with us all that we believed when we left planet earth. If we believe in the reality of hate, greed, lack, limitation, and evil at the very moment of our death, we will take those beliefs with us. And, just as those beliefs created hell for us on earth, they have the potential to create hell for us wherever we are.

It is important for us to develop our spiritual conscious-ness here on earth and to begin to experience our oneness with Spirit "in the flesh." We are spiritual beings *now*. Divine Love is loving us *here* and will continue to love us in the *hereafter*. It is vital that we seek to fill our consciousness with the Beauty of Spirit on "earth as it is in heaven." For if we are not interested in finding the "kingdom of God" within us while we here, we shall probably have a difficult time finding It in the hereafter. We shall never know more of heaven than we can perceive within ourselves. "The only news we have of Heaven has come through the con-sciousness of men....anyone who wills to know Truth may know it."[8] Unless it is our will to know Truth, we shall not experience it within our consciousness.

Heaven is not a place just over the horizon where we have earned the privilege of going just because we left earth. It is a Holy, Whole, and Perfect State of Consciousness–the Kingdom of God–where Love, Peace, Joy, and Good reign supreme. We shall find it in the *hereafter* the same way we find it *here*: by saying "no" to hell and "yes" to heaven, and by turning to the Kingdom within with all of our heart, soul, and mind. Then, when death comes, as we leap into "eternity," we will land on Holy Ground.

# Hell, No!

## *INDIVIDUAL*

What are your personal beliefs about "heaven" and "hell"?

_____

_____

_____

_____

Describe a "hellish" event and a "heavenly" occurrence in your life.

_____

_____

_____

_____

List all of the heavenly "qualities" of Life (such as Love, Peace, etc.) that you can think of, and then focus on those qualities throughout the week.

_____

_____

_____

_____

_____

## *GROUP*

Discussion of Lesson.

**Activity:** (*Materials: drawing paper, colored pencils, pens, or crayons.*)
Have each person draw a picture of heaven and a picture of hell.

**Meditation:** Door Number One or Door Number Two?

*(Facilitator: read slowly with restful music in background, if desired. Being with one of the Relaxation Techniques on pages 299-300.)*

Imagine now that you are walking down a long hall...just up ahead, at the end of the hall, two doors are visible...as you come to the doors, you see that one of the doors is marked *Heaven* and the other is marked *Hell*...on the door marked *Hell* is a list that reads: *guilt, anger, resentment, grudges, judgment, intolerance*...beneath the list is this invitation: "Please enter all victims, tyrants, and bigots, all those filled with self-righteousness, self-loathing, and self-condemnation"...on the other door, beneath the word *Heaven*, is the simple phrase "Enter in Peace"...you, of course, would love to enter the door marked *Heaven*, but as you attempt to turn the handle, it feels locked...you notice that between the two doors is a receptacle...it reads: "Deposit all hellish thoughts here before entering heaven, or relinquish all peace before entering hell"...is there a deposit or two that you need to make before the door of heaven will open for you?...consider for a moment your concepts of yourself and others...your beliefs about life...there is no peace of mind when our mind is filled with hellish beliefs...you are free to relinquish all you may hold... notice what they are, and deposit them now...*(Facilitator: allow a few minutes)*...you will know when you have deposited all that you have because you will feel light, and free, and at peace... when you feel peaceful, try the door to heaven again...when it opens, walk within and experience It...*(Facilitator: allow a minute or two)*...now it is time to come back to the room, but as you do, remember that the Kingdom of Heaven is always within you, and you can enter It any time you choose, as long as you are willing to let go of all else.

1. SOM 124:2   2. SOM 180:3.   3. SOM 189:3.   4. SOM 133:5.   5. Psalms 139:8 (KJV).
6. Matthew 13:33 (KJV).   7. Luke 17:21 (Lamsa).   8. SOM 452:3.

Discovering the Gifts of Good in Every Situation

*Healing in mind science*
*is based upon three assumptions:*
*1. Spirit is Whole, Complete*
*and Perfect. Spirit is everywhere,*
*in everything, all of the time;*
*2. The Universe is an orderly,*
*harmonious system; and*
*3. Spirit is the Creator of all,*
and our human
experiences, no matter how they appear to be, occur within
Order and Harmony.

It is difficult for us to rationalize our earthly existence and connect our worldly experiences with the concept
of the Allness of Perfection and the Ever-Presence of Order
and Harmony because much of what occurs in our life seems
to be far less than good and far from what is orderly and harmonious. Discovering the Presence of Perfection right where
imperfection seems to be is like being given a gift when it's
not our birthday.

How do we discover this gift of good that is ever-
present in our life, and how do we experience order and harmony in situations that seem to fall *very* short of the *glory of*
*God*? The Bible and the teachings of the Science of Mind
inform us that in order for us to experience Good in the
midst of that which doesn't look so good, we are to *judge not*
*according to the appearance.*[1] "If we believe that the Spirit,
incarnated in us, can demonstrate, shall we be disturbed at
what *appears* to contradict this? We shall often need to *know*

that the Truth which we announce is superior to the condition we are to change."[2]

Spirit is multidimensional reality. It is far greater than the three dimensions we see and much more than the three-dimensional experience that we appear to be having. God is the Invisible Presence that, even though unseen, is right where we are. We do not see Spirit; but we can see the *results* of Spirit–the forms of Good which originate in the invisible realm of the All-Good. We can experience the gifts which are created by the Mind of Intelligence and appear as material form. However, we cannot experience the perfection of forms which emanate from the inner world of Creative Good, the realm of Order and Harmony, if we allow the outer world of appearances to talk us out of them.

## "WE MUST TRANSCEND THE APPEARANCE"[3]

No matter what is going on in our three-dimensional experience– whether it is discomfort or disease in our body, lack of financial abundance, disharmony in our relationships, or confusion in our decision making–God is right where the problem appears to be. We must "know that the Truth which we announce is superior to the condition we are to change" if we want to experience the healing that will unfailingly occur as the Invisible Truth becomes visible form and result. Our spiritual knowledge and commitment to the Truth, coupled with our mental focus upon It, reveals the Truth, the Good, the Gift in every situation. There is a gift for us perfectly crafted in the heavens that can and will manifest for us even in those circumstances that seem totally devoid of good, completely barren of purpose, and absolutely empty of meaning. But, we must call forth the Invisible into tangible form by our insistence that Good is present in spite of appearances.

Everywhere around us we have examples that there is more than meets the eye and that many things are not as they appear to be. For instance, there are posters, postcards, greeting cards, and books currently out on the market depicting "3-D illusion." What first appears to the eye is usually a colorful, abstract, random pattern, or a two-dimensional repetition of a recognizable image, such as tropical fish, flowers, or butterflies. However, with a little relaxation of the eyes, a lot of patience, and a shift in focus, like magic a three-dimensional image suddenly emerges from the two-dimensional pattern.

Our three-dimensional life, from a spiritual perspective, is like the two-dimensional pattern. There is an unseen dimension in every condition or situation, and it can be seen when we look for it with a little relaxation, a lot of patience, and a shift in focus. At first, we often do not see the Dimension of Spirit that is present in what appears to be a disharmonious, unhappy, or unhealthy situation. Just as we would not take the time or have the patience to image-view the 3-D illusions unless we believed something else would appear, we first must *believe* that the dimension of Spirit is there, or else we will not take the time or be patient enough to look beyond the obvious to see the Invisible Truth emerge into form. "Healing is not accomplished through will power but by knowing the Truth. This Truth is that the Spiritual Man is already Perfect, no matter what the appearance may be."[4]

I took up scuba diving about eleven years ago because my *Pisces* husband (who swam like a fish) wanted to learn the sport. Being a newlywed, I wanted to share in this important experience with him...even though I could not swim. However, it had not occurred to me that I'd actually have to go scuba diving *after* completing the classes. I had not considered that we were taking the course in order to take up a lifetime sport rather than just learning how to do it!

One evening several weeks after becoming "certified" scuba divers, my husband wanted us to join a chartered dive boat that was scheduled to depart for the Channel Islands at three the following morning. A trip to the islands just off the coast of Southern California takes about three hours across a sea that is often choppy and always unpredictable. Even on a sunny day or clear night, the conditions can change dangerously and without warning.

We joined the charter, and by six the next morning, after a somewhat uneventful boat ride, the captain anchored just off Anacapa Island. Most of the divers were going to dive for abalone since the area was well known for its rich supply of black abalone, the most common type found at a shallow diving depth of thirty to forty feet. I emerged, groggy and slightly seasick, from the shipboard bunks where we had spent the night. I was greeted by a day that was cold, overcast, and dreary. The water was slate gray and several large kelp beds rose and sank silently with the morning's ocean swell. The thought of jumping into the cold wetness increased my nausea, but I said nothing to my husband as I pulled on my uncooperative rubber wetsuit.

Within fifteen minutes we were in the water with the other divers. As we dove toward the sea floor forty feet below, the natural heat of my body slowly began to warm the frigid water that had seeped into my wetsuit. "Why couldn't we have taken up tennis?" kept coming to mind as my husband and I searched the murky water for abalone. Since this was our first hunting expedition, we had a difficult time distinguishing between rocks, coral, and abalone.

After a fruitless half-hour of searching, and with air tanks near empty, we started back in the direction of the boat's anchor line. As we slowly moved our stiff, rubber fins through the currents, I began to think about what I had learned as a new student of the Science of Mind: "The Eternal Gift is always made"[5] and "To each is given what he needs and the gifts of heaven come alike to all."[6] I knew that there must be a gift of the Spirit in every situation, including the one I found myself in at the moment. I affirmed that even though the surroundings seemed dismal, the beauty of God was there in the midst. I closed my eyes for a moment and asked the Spirit within for the gift I knew was present. "Ask, and it shall be given to you."[7] As I opened my eyes, the murky water cleared. It was almost like the parting of the Red Sea for Moses! A ray of light shone through the clearing and illuminated something that looked possibly like an abalone. My husband looked at me, his eyes wide beneath his mask, as he swam over and easily popped the abalone off the rock. We headed quickly for the surface.

## "I HAVE CALLED THEE BY THY NAME"[8]

The dive master looked surprised as we handed him our catch. It wasn't until later that we were told that our abalone was quite unusual. We had brought to the surface not the black abalone ordinarily found in such shallow depths, but a rare white abalone usually discovered in waters of seventy feet or deeper. And even though "the gifts of heaven come alike to all," I discovered that the gifts also come *specifically* to each. In fact, *my gift had my name on it.* The white abalone, we were told, is also known as the *sorensini* abalone–a slight variation of my new last name!

"God cannot help making the gift, because GOD IS THE GIFT…There can be no gift without a receiver."[9] If we want to receive the gift, we must first affirm that there *is* a gift for us no matter what the situation. Then we must wait with heart, mind, and hands open for the gift to appear. Many of our spiritual gifts are lost to us because we stare into the pain, negativity, chaos, and gloom in a situation, instead of patiently waiting for the Spirit of Good to become visible to us. Many of our gifts are lost to us because we turn our backs and walk away (or swim away) from events in our life without asking for the gift that was there all the time.

It has been said that "problems are God in disguise." Too often we fall for the disguise, and we don't seek to reveal the Holy One behind the mask. When we know that there is a gift in every circumstance, we are more patient and more composed no matter what is going on around us. When we believe and trust that the outcome for us in a situation cannot help but to be a gift and a blessing, we are poised and expectant. It is as though we've seen the script of our life and we know that everything turns out okay in the end–like the young starlet who was filming an adventure movie: at one point, lions were released from cages offscreen so that they could rush at her while she was fastened to a stake in the Roman Coliseum. A reporter watching the scene being filmed asked the budding thespian, "Weren't you frightened when the lions rushed out at you and you couldn't get away?" She replied, "No, I wasn't afraid. I'd read the script and I knew that the leading man would save me." It never occurred to her that something might go wrong or that the lions hadn't read the script! We, too, can know that no matter how trapped we seem to be in a situa-tion–even when our hands appear to be tied, even when the"oppo-sition" seems powerful and dangerous–Spirit, the Presence of Good, is right there to bring about a safe and successful outcome.

## LOOKING FOR TROUBLE?

We sabotage ourselves when we predict the worst, and predicting the worst can be habitual. For instance, what is the first thing you think about when a "Special News Bulletin" interrupts a TV program you're watching? Do you think, "Uh-oh!" and assume that some disaster has struck? What are your first thoughts when the telephone rings in the middle of the night? Do you automatically assume that it must be a wrong number or are you certain that some horrible thing has happened to someone you love? Does your stomach jump when you receive an envelope addressed to you with a return address showing IRS or FBI? When we are in the habit of assuming the worst, we become an unconscious cynic. Someone once said that "a cynic is someone who, when he smells flowers, looks around for a coffin."

When we believe in the positive outcome of events in our life, our mind is open to inner guidance. We are inspired to do whatever it is necessary for us to do, including simply staying calm, centered, and silent. When we believe that there is a gift of Spirit for us in the events of our life, we see every event as a holy experience. We are not willing to settle for a superficial solution. "If it is God's pleasure to give us the Kingdom then it should be our privilege to accept the gift,"[10] and "It is the nature of the Universe to give us what we are able to take. It cannot give us more. It has given all, we have not yet accepted the greater gift."[11]

Whatever the event, whatever the circumstance, whatever the relationship, whatever the experience, Spirit–Good, Wisdom, Joy, and Fulfillment–is at the core of our life and at the center of everything happening in our life. We can be assured of a positive result, a life-enriching answer, and the manifestation of good in our life any time and any place, no matter what. *With a little relaxation of the eyes, a lot of patience, and a shift in focus, we will always find the gift.*

*Process Sheet Eleven*

# Where's the Gift?

## *INDIVIDUAL*

"If we want to receive the gift, we must first affirm that there is a gift for us no matter what the situation, and then wait with heart, mind, and hands open for the gift to appear." Is there a situation in your life which seems totally devoid of good, completely barren of purpose, and absolutely empty of meaning?

_____

_____

We must call forth the invisible into tangible form by our insistence that Good is present despite appearances. Begin to cultivate a sense of relaxation and patience towards the situation above. Shift your focus from the obvious and material, and moment to moment look beyond to the Unseen Spirit with expectation–and "the gift" will appear. When it does, write what it was:

_____

_____

Write a spiritual statement affirming the presence of a gift in this situation:

_____

_____

## *GROUP*
Discussion of Lesson.

**Activity:** This is an opportunity for the members of the group to share an experience in which a gift emerged for them from circumstances that seemed "totally devoid of good, completely barren of purpose, and absolutely empty of meaning."

**Meditation:** There's the Gift!

(*Facilitator: read slowly with restful music in background, if desired. Begin with one of the Relaxation Techniques on pages 299-300.*)
Imagine now that you are swimming under water...you are comfortable with whatever breathing apparatus you are wearing...you are an excellent swimmer and you are calm as you swim...however, all around you is murky water...you cannot see ahead of you, in back of you, or on either side of you...the water is cold, and for just a moment you are feeling lost and alone...and this feeling–the feeling of being cold, lost and alone–reminds you of a current situation in your life...one in which you cannot see a solution or resolution...a situation that appears to be "devoid of good, barren of purpose, and empty of meaning"...as you swim in the cold, murky water you consider this situation...but you know that there is a gift of Spirit for you in every event of your life, and you know that the situation you are thinking about can be for you a holy experience *if you are not willing to settle for a superficial solution*...you accept that it is God's pleasure to give you the Kingdom, and it is your privilege to accept the gift...you know that God cannot help making the gift, because GOD IS THE GIFT, but there can be no gift without a receiver...YOU are ready for your gift in this situation..."The Eternal Gift is always made...to each is given what he or she needs, and "the gifts of heaven come alike to all"...there is a gift of the Spirit in every moment, in every situation...the beauty of God is here in the midst...is there in the midst...relax now and shift your focus from the situation to the Spiritual Truth back of it..."Ask, and it

shall be given to you"...see before you, like the parting of the Red Sea for Moses...the murky water clearing before your eyes...a ray of light shining through the clearing and illuminating something that is a gift for you...a gift that is within the very situation you had been considering...go to it...look at it...take it...bring it back into this room with your eyes still closed...consider the meaning of the gift...take a few deep breaths...open your eyes... and find a partner whom you can tell about the gift.

1. John 7:24 (KJV).   2. SOM 159:5.   3. SOM 213:3.   4. SOM 320:2.   5. SOM 280:1.
6. SOM 423:2.   7. Matthew 7:7 (Lamsa).   8. Isaiah 43:1 (KJV).   9. SOM 280:1, 3.
10. SOM 405:1.   11. SOM 42:4.

# 12   It's a Matter of Opinion

Learning to Appreciate the Variety in the One

*Have you ever wondered what the world would look like if everything was exactly the way you thought it ought to be and if everyone was* being, doing, and acting as you believed they should? Think about it. For instance, if you were in charge of all artistic expression, what would be considered "art"? If every author were required to write just what you liked to read, how big would the libraries be and what categories would be available? Would every painting be "sensible" and all abstract art banned? Would anyone ever see, again, a fountain with recycled water arching from the sculpted appendage of a naked little boy? Would rap music or opera vanish from the airwaves? What would happen if you alone decided which flowers and vegetables should grow? Would dandelions, eggplant, or brussels sprouts even stand a chance?

Often we mistakenly assume that *our* way is the *only* way. We have been taught that there is only One Mind, but sometimes it seems we mistake our little point of view for the One Mind, overlooking the *Infinite* Mind of Spirit, which expresses Itself in endless form and variety. It is obvious even to the casual observer that the Nature of the Universe is not one of duplication, sameness, or monotony. "The Universe is not...an endless and monotonous repetition of the same old thing."[1] If there are no two snowflakes alike, when absolutely no one would notice or care if there were; if Nature doesn't

ration Her creativity where rationing would be subtle or go unde-
tected; then why do we look for sameness in the more obvious
forms of Creation, such as each other?

Rather than celebrating the beauty of diversity among us,
we are often intolerant of the differences of others. We disapprove
of those things and those people who are not like us. We catego-
rize variety and diversity into *right* and *wrong*. Of course, what is
*right* goes in the column with our name at the top.

## "OPINION IS OUR *ESTIMATE...*"[2]

We choose to forget that our personal view of anything is merely
an opinion. Opinion, according to the dictionary, is "a view, a
judgment, a belief stronger than impression and less strong than
positive knowledge."[3] An opinion is not actual knowledge. It is a
point of view or a judgment. Yet we often treat our opinions, and
the opinions of others, as though they were "Gospel." We mistake
opinion for Divine Wisdom and we confuse our tiny, limited view
of life with the Universal Vista–the vast realm of Unlimited
Knowledge and Infinite Variety and Diversity.

Mark Twain wrote: "Its name is Public Opinion. It is held
in reverence. It settles everything. Some think it is the voice of
God."[4] Today's world seems to revolve more and more around
opinions that are less than Godlike and that settle nothing at
all. People on talk shows tell about the intimacies or peculiarities
of their life and then everyone in the audience has an opportunity
to give their opinion about that life. They agree or disagree with
each other, support or condemn. They argue and out-and-out
fight about who is right, and all the time they seem to be forget-
ting that what they are fighting about on either side is just an
opinion, a view, a judgment. American playwright Lillian Hellman

wrote, "Nobody outside of a baby carriage or a judge's chamber believes in an unprejudiced point of view." Positive Knowledge–that which is beyond a prejudiced point of view–is only able to permeate a mind that is willing to look beyond personal opinion and center itself in Love, Compassion, and Tolerance.

Remember when the New Age came of age and everyone began "telling the truth"? Being truthful about our thoughts and feelings was meant to assist us in releasing our personal inhibitions; to keep us from "stuffing our stuff" deep into our psyches and denying its existence. We were encouraged to "Speak up! Tell it like you see it, and create it the way you want it!!"

For most us coming from repressive religious and social backgrounds, being given permission to "tell the truth"–to finally admit what we thought and to actually say it out loud–opened up a brand new world of personal freedom. We started going around "telling the truth" to our parents, our mate, our boss, our friends, and our peers, despite the fact that no one had asked to hear it, and even though "the truth" was often hurtful and tactless. It was then that the phrase "Thank you for sharing" became so popular!

## TRUTHFUL TRUTH-TELLING

But our telling the truth is not about telling each other what to do or how to live. It is about being honest with ourselves and letting our attitudes, values, and points of view surface in our conscious mind so that we can take a look at who we are being. Then we can choose what beliefs we want to keep, expand on, or toss out completely. Our truth-telling is not an exercise in comparing ourselves with others and what they may think, but in comparing our mind to the Mind of God and the Ideas of Spirit. The Creator sees all of creation as beautiful and perfect and has pronounced it "very, very good." *God's eternal proclamation transcends everyone's opinion.* When we are not seeing the "very, very good" around us, or when It is not being seen in us, it is important for us to remember that what is being seen is merely an opinion, a judgment, that which is less than positive knowledge, and not the *Truth* about anything at all.

We shall not find ourselves in the opinions of others. Emmet Fox wrote: "Do not let anyone else tell you what sort of mind you have, because they do not know. People who like you will think your mentality is better than it is; those who do not like you will think it is worse. Just examine your conditions and see what you are demonstrating. This method is scientific and infallible."[5] We cannot demonstrate a life that is greater than our thinking. The world around us reflects back to us the consequences of our viewpoints.

Many people spend their time critiquing the actions of others so that they won't have to look at their own self-expression. They live in fear that if they stop working on changing the world, they might have to start working on themselves. As each of us examines our own "conditions" to see what we are demonstrating, we can improve our demonstrations by telling the truth to ourselves and changing the thinking that is creating limited self-expression. As we expand our mind to include more ideas and greater creativity, we shall no longer desire to mold the outer world to our tiny specifications, because we shall realize that Life is Infinite. We shall begin to see the variations of life as Divine diversity and not negative complicity.

Intolerance is born of the fear that Divine Intelligence is not in charge of the Universe. It springs forth from a mistrust that there is another power opposed to Good that is at work within those different from ourselves. "Each individual...is a unique

variation in the Universe; no two people are alike, and yet all people are rooted in that which is identical."[6] The snowflakes don't
fight with each other as they fall to the ground. Each snowflake in
its unique way falls gently to earth and joins with the rest.
Together, they cover the land with a seamless blanket of silence
and peace, and diversity manifests unity.

## WE SEE AS WE ARE

We can't see the world *as it is* because we can only see the world *as
we are*. What we see is always colored by our opinions. The more
dense our opinions, the less we can see of the lightness of Spirit's
creation, which is unified and whole. As we let go of our hardened
views, as our thinking changes and flows more easily with Truth,
what we experience in the world around us changes too.

A friend of mine was a highway patrolman in Thousand
Oaks, California, for eight years. He spent the majority of his
time issuing warnings and citations to frightened and often angry
motorists. He told me that he liked his job. He said he enjoyed
seeing the red brake-lights flash on the rows of fast-moving cars as
he scooted up the freeway on-ramps, and that he felt a sense of
power as he watched the effect a speeding ticket had on the
emotions of the people he pulled over.

When he became a student of the Science of Mind, however, his view of a world separate from himself changed. He began
to understand the Unity of all of Creation and his oneness with
Life. He confessed that the thrill was soon gone from his work as
he began to identify with the people he had once seen as different
and separate from himself.

One day he stopped a motorist for speeding. As the man
got out of his car, my friend noticed that he looked haggard and

worried, almost defeated by yet another setback. He said to the man sympathetically, "You look like you've had a hard day." The man gave an emotional testament as to just what a difficult day it had been. When he was finished, my friend gave him a hug. When he related the story to me later he said that he knew then and there, as he embraced his fellow-journeyer, that he needed to find another line of work!

Each of us must interpret Life for ourselves. In all the world there is no one else exactly like us. There are people who have some parts of us, but no one adds up exactly like we do. Diversity is integral to the wholeness of Creation, and our unique self-expression is vital to the whole. We must discover who we are, and what life is, in the solitude of our own being, alone with God, engulfed in our oneness with our Creator. In that Holy Place we are free from the assessment of the outside world. In that Holy Place we find that we are one with Positive Knowledge. And, in that Holy Place...our true identity is NOT a matter of opinion.

*Process Sheet Twelve*

# It's a Matter of Opinion

## INDIVIDUAL

What are some opinions you have about yourself based on your heritage, physical appearance, education, financial condition, job or career, etc.?

_____

_____

_____

_____

Do you compare yourself to others? In what way?

_____

_____

_____

The diversity of life is rooted in the Oneness of Spirit. Write an affirmation celebrating the unity of Life:

_____

_____

## GROUP

Discussion of Lesson.

**Activity:** (*Materials: pencil and paper.*)
The purpose of this activity is to learn tolerance of opinions that are in opposition to one's own view. Begin by having one-half of the students in the group (every *other* person) write down an issue about which he or she has a strong opinion. Then each person *with an opinion* (A) chooses a partner *without an opinion* (B). *A* gives the opinion he or she has written down to *B*. *B* now holds

*A* 's opinion–as if it were his or her own. For the purpose of this process *A* now holds the *opposite* view from his or her *original* opinion. For example: *A* writes down his or her strong opinion *against* smoking. After *A* has given this opinion to *B*, *B* now holds *A*'s *orginal* opinion *against* smoking, and *A* must now defend a view *for* smoking. The ensuing debates between partners may be performed in front of the rest of the group if time permits.

**Meditation:** Embracing Seeming Opposites, Seeing Life's Unity

*(Facilitator: read slowly with restful music in background, if desired. Begin with one of the Relaxation Techniques on pages 299-300.)*
        You are a unique variation in the Universe...no two people are alike...therefore no one is quite like you...and yet all people are rooted in that which is identical...the Spirit of Life... you are immersed in the perfection of Spirit...imagine that some- one is walking toward you...someone whom you have viewed as "separate" or "alien" from you...perhaps someone of another race, social or economic status, or religion...you know why you have believed that you are different from this person...remembering now that you are immersed in the perfection of Spirit, know this one is rooted in that which is identical to you...as the person comes closer, feel your own features changing as you take on the identical characteristics of the person...the same coloring...the same clothing...feel in this moment what it may feel like to be like this person...*(Facilitator: allow two minutes)*...now, look into the person's face and see it changing...until the face becomes your own face...see yourself in the other person...look with loving eyes...see this person as yourself...and now see the features changing back...feel your features changing back...until you are you...and the other is the other...look again with loving eyes...

know this person continues to be a part of you...feel the Love within you...feel it emanating from the other...know that this Love connects and unites you with all others...with all Life...with the diversity of Life...with the Unity of Life...you are united in a Love free from opinion...free from lesser and greater...all an integral part of the Whole...know your oneness with each person in this room as you find yourself back in your body with your eyes still closed...feel the Unity in this room...the Love that unites... everyone here rooted in that which is identical...now take a few deep breaths...and when you are ready, open your eyes.

1. Ernest Holmes, *Discover a Richer Life* (Misc. Writings, Vol. 1, Science of Mind Publishing), p. 28.

2. SOM 113:2.    3. *Webster's New Collegiate Dictionary*, G. & C. Merriam Co., 1977.

4. Alex Ayres, *The Wit & Wisdom of Mark Twain* (Harper & Row), p. 173.

5. *Around the Year with Emmet Fox* (Harper & Row), p. 187.    6. SOM 121:3.

# 13    The Power of Purpose

*The theme song from
the movie* Mahogany *asks
the question "Do you know
where you're going to?
Do you like the things
that life is showing you?"*

It is a wonderful question
for each of us to ask ourselves: "Do I have a plan and a conscious purpose for my life? Have I created or am I creating a
mental pattern for success–an inner template through which
the Infinite Creative Power can flow and create an incredible
life for me?"

When we have a purpose–an idea of how we want
to express ourselves in the world–we give direction to the
Divine Energy within us. We channel It like water through a
dam, and there is *Power* in our life! Our life becomes meaningful and effective because there is Purpose in what we do.
Just like the power generated by water through a dam, the
Power of Purpose can light up our whole life.

Each of us is an *individualization* of Spirit, a *point
of consciousness* in Universal Consciousness, a *microcosm* of
the Macrocosm, a *particularization* of the Impartial and
Unlimited. Unlimited Power is always available to us because
It is the Core and Substance of our being. But even though
Spirit is individualized wherever we are, we experience only
as much of Its Power as we choose to use. Unless we use It,
unless we require It in our life, It remains unexpressed
through us. When we have a purpose–motivation and inspiration for living our life–we open up the floodgates for Spirit

and all of Its richness to flow into our life. It springs forth as we require of It. It surges through us as we make use of It. We could say that a life without a purpose is like just so much water under the bridge!

Do you have a dream? You've got to have a dream in the first place if you're going to make your dream come true, right? Did a dream come to mind when you read the question just now? Are you conscious and aware of the kind of life you want to create? Is it alive and active in your mind? Would you recognize your dream if you were living it? Some of us may be certain that we're not living our dream, but we're not even clear *what* dream we're not living. We've forgotten to dream. We don't know what it is that we want to do that we're not doing. And some of us are not only not dreaming or living our dream—we're busy living a nightmare!

How do we dream our dream and how does that dream actualize into our earthly experience? We begin to discover the dream within us by first acknowledging that there *is* one to be found. The Creator must have a purpose for Its creation. Deep within every being is a Divine, Holy Purpose. We all have a dream within us because God's Dream is at the core of our life—God's Idea of Life—and that Divine Idea includes each of us living at our fullest potential. Even though it may seem like it, it isn't that some people have a specific purpose in life while the rest of us are simply aimless *extras*. We all play an integral part in the Divine Picture of Creation.

Everyone has the same potential for greatness in life, and by "greatness" I mean a self-expression that is spiritually magnificent and fulfilling whether the world knows that we exist or not. The important thing is that *God* knows we exist. Spirit knows *who* we are and *why* we are. "Man does not exist for the purpose of making an impression upon his environment. He does exist to express himself in and through his environment....All that means anything is that while we live, WE LIVE....we may assume that spiritual man is already a success, is already supplied with everything that he needs. The potential of all things exists in the Universal Wholeness."[1]

As children, we all had an idea that we were special; so distinctive, in fact, that we knew that we were going to be *famous* one day. We weren't going to be just a ballerina, but a world-famous *prima* ballerina, or a movie star, or President of the United States. We were aware of the Power of our potential, and we felt naturally unique and important. But then, as we began to grow up in the world, and only some people seemed important, we began to think that maybe life was made up of superstars, heroes, and extras. And most of us began feeling like extras! However, the Inner Truth that we were aware of as children hasn't changed. It is still at the heart of our being. We are still special and important, and there is still Power in our potential.

Everyone is important to God. Nothing in nature is an exact duplication. There is no one who expresses life quite the way you do, or quite the way I do. Each of us is unique. An infinite Creator must forever create; and even though it is the One Spirit expressing through each of us–as each of us–It expresses uniquely since It is *individualized* through us. Who we are will not be duplicated in all of eternity! Our purpose is to tap into the Dream that God is having and give that dream a unique outlet in our life. "Each state of thought taps the same Principle, each uses the same Law, is inspired by the same Spirit, but each draws forth a different result."[2]

## "MAN IS AN IDENTITY IN THE UNIVERSE"[3]

Our spiritual identity is intact in the Mind of God–in the Dream that God is dreaming. We find it as we look within ourselves, "in faith believing" that It is there. Your dream is waiting for *you* to come true. It is waiting for you to get real, and for you to acknowledge that there is a purpose to your being. All Life, including your life, has meaning. When we find ourselves within ourselves, we discover our spiritual identity, and we begin to more fully live the idea God has of us.

How do we discover our spiritual identity and what will best serve the Spirit in our life? How do we find our unique expression and draw forth our part in the Whole? We begin by asking ourselves what it is that we love to do: "What is it that I would do even if I didn't get paid to do it? What is it that I would do with *no strings attached* and for nothing material in return? What is it that, when I do it, I feel the most connected with Life and the most centered and fulfilled within myself? What is that thing that, when I'm doing it, everything else in my world could be falling by the wayside and I could still feel content doing it?" Close your eyes before you continue reading, and think about it for a moment: the thing that you would *do for free* is the very thing that will *set you free*. The impetus to your spiritual growth and the inspiration for your self-knowledge lie within that activity–because as you do that thing, you will naturally call upon the Divine qualities within yourself–require them and use them–and you will learn more about the Power within you.

If you already know what it is that you love to do, are you doing it at least part of the time every day? Often we divide our lives into what we *love* to do and what we *have* to do. We have an idea of the life we'd like to live "one day," but we often view it as a fantasy–an idea whose time may never come.

It is essential that we pursue our greatest joy, or, as Joseph Campbell put it: "follow our bliss." As we do what we love to do even part of the day, we activate the dream within us, and the Power behind our dream brings about the ways and means for us to live it. The Universal Creative Force moves through us, and It multiplies our vision until it is our life. We don't have to worry about how we can make a job out of our true love. That's the function of the Universe. "If we keep our thought fixed upon the idea that this Energy, which is also Intelligence, is now taking the form of some desire in our lives, then it will begin to take this form....Therefore, there must be a definite purpose in our imagination."[4]

## SHE TOLD THE TRUTH

We begin to activate the Power within us by being honest with ourselves–by acknowledging where we are in our life. Nancy, who lives in Southern California, discovered that real "truth-telling" can bring very precise results. Nancy's sister, Barbara, was a new student of the Science of Mind several years ago. One day Barbara called Nancy to tell her about an empowering seminar she had just attended where she had gotten in touch with her dream to be an artist, and that she had gone out and purchased new canvases and oils, and was looking forward to her first showing. Nancy tried to feel happy for her sister, but Nancy had lost her job at the library because of cuts in the county budget, and though she had been looking through the want ads, she was unenthusiastic about the availability of fulfilling employment. Barbara said excitedly, "You know, Sis, you can do anything you truly want to do!" Nancy replied that that sounded wonderful, but that she didn't know what she "truly" wanted to do, and that she certainly hadn't found it advertised in the classifieds. The only thing she could think of that she truly liked to do was to sit in the big, comfortable chair in her den and read. Barbara was silent for a moment, and then said confidently, "Okay, then I know that there is something wonderful for you that meets that description because I know in my mind, and in my heart, that there is Power in your potential! You can know it, too!" Nancy agreed to keep it in mind.

The following week Nancy sat down in her big den chair, with a hot cup of tea on the table beside her and her cat curled up next to her, and scanned the want ads. But she found nothing of interest. Then the telephone rang and a friend whom she had not talked with since leaving her job asked her if she was still looking for work. When Nancy replied Yes, the friend told her that her brother, who was a script reader for a studio in Hollywood, had a backlog of scripts and needed an assistant. The pay was good, and Nancy could do all the reading at home!

Needless to say, Nancy took the job. In fact, after reading a few scripts, she was so inspired that she wrote one of her own. Today, Nancy is a successful script *writer.*

There is no desire too small for Life to acknowledge, and no dream too big for the Power within us to bring it about. There can be no plan too grand, nor purpose out of reach, because the very inspiration for our dreams comes from the Spirit within us. Spirit can bring about whatever It inspires. All we need to do is trust that the Power of Purpose carries with It the ways and means for that purpose to reach fulfillment.

## GOALS AND PURPOSE

It is important to note that there is a distinction between *a goal* in life and *our purpose* in living. A goal is something that we can gauge *materially* even though our goals begin in our mind. Career goals, financial goals, relationship goals, family goals, and retirement goals can be calculated *in the world* even though they originate *within us*. Our goals have to do with what we want to create "out there" in manifested form—*measurable* achievements. Purpose, on the other hand, is *how* Spirit expresses through us and into our goals. Purpose has more to do with our spiritual utilization and activation of the Power within us. Purpose is immeasurable because it has no limits or boundaries. We achieve our purpose moment to moment as we live our life. It is the "point of fulfillment" and the "Presence of Spirit" in whatever we are doing.

We could say that we *bring* our purpose *to* our goals. Reaching a particular goal, in and of itself, can be empty if we haven't reached within ourselves in the process and brought forth more of our spiritual nature; if we haven't challenged ourselves to be more, and to express new and greater aspects of our Divine potential. "Our individualized Universe is forever complete, yet forever completing Itself, in order that every experience may teach us to transcend some previous one, in ever ascending cycles, upward bound."[5] It is through our expression of the qualities of our spiritual nature that our goals have meaning. Have you ever finished a task—or completed an entire day—and then asked yourself what the "point" was to it all? Have you ever reached a short-term, or even a long-term, goal and asked yourself the same question?

No matter how much the world may admire a goal we've achieved, if we are not experiencing meaning and purpose in our life, if we know that we have not reached into the Great Reservoir of our being to "transcend" our previous self-expression, there is little value in our having reached that goal. Purpose is our sense that Life, Itself, has significance–that *our* life within Life has significance. Purpose is something that we experience *on our way* to a goal. "We may be quite emphatic in saying that we think the Universe exists for the expression of Spirit, and man exists for self-expression, because he is the expression of Spirit."[6] What could be a greater purpose than to express the All-Loving, All-Powerful Nature of Spirit wherever we are and in whatever we do?

As we realize that we are a significant part of Life, we are empowered to express more of ourselves, to do more with ourselves, to participate more in life, to share more with others–in other words, *to give more from within*. Our goals become the outlet for our purpose rather than ends in themselves. It is out of our sense of purpose that we form meaningful goals. "Let us feel that our purposes are animated and inspired from on high and then let us go forth and make our dream come true in human experience. With an invisible Intelligence to guide, and an immutable Law to direct, let us take our place in any legitimate activity, and thus cause our dreams to come to full fruition."[7]

## "THE PENT-UP ENERGY OF LIFE, AND THE POSSIBILITY OF FURTHER HUMAN EVOLUTION, WORK THROUGH MAN'S IMAGINATION AND WILL"[8]

Can you imagine that there is a Power for Good in the Universe that is unlimited in every way, and that It desires expression through you? Can you imagine that there is an Intelligence that is All-Knowing and is willing to give you all of Its ideas–that "all that It has" is yours? Can you imagine such greatness taking shape as *your* life? Or do you imagine that all the good ideas are already claimed, or that good ideas can be taken advantage of only by people who have more money, more education, more contacts, fewer responsibilities, and more opportunities than you?

The only *more* of anything that you will ever need in order for you to take advantage of *any* idea is more courage–*the courage to go for it!* Episcopal clergyman Phillips Brooks wrote: "Set yourself earnestly to see what you were made to do, and then set yourself earnestly to do it; and the loftier your purpose is, the more sure you will be to make the world richer with every enrichment of yourself."[9]

How we will live our life is our choice. We can choose to cruise in a big luxury liner or in a little rowboat. The smaller our dreams (the less our idea is of who we are and what we can accomplish), the smaller our vessel. If our vessel is small, a lot of power isn't needed. A big steam engine would overpower a little rowboat. All that is necessary to move it is a paddle and a lot of personal energy. However, a long trip in a small vessel can be tiring. In the same way, when our idea of ourselves is small, we use up a lot of personal energy, and we often exhaust ourselves trying to get where we want to go.

A large ship, however, can take advantage of the power of a big engine; in fact, a lot of power is necessary to move it. Personal energy wouldn't budge it. When our dreams are large, and our purpose is to achieve spiritual greatness, we can take advantage of the Unlimited Power of Spirit. A large vessel is not only more comfortable, it can weather the storms much better than a small one. Small boats can be damaged or wrecked by the big swells and high waves that are a natural part of the life of an ocean. When our vision of life is spiritually large, the swells and unrest that are a natural part of earthly life won't affect us so much. Granted, there can be a certain thrill in overcoming the risks of being tossed about in a small vessel, but mostly it's just easier to get seasick!

The larger our dreams, the greater our purpose, the more Spiritual Power we'll require–and more will be given to us. As we commit to following our dream and living our purpose, we shall have all that is necessary to live it successfully. When we say Yes to the greatness of life, we activate a Power within us that cannot be exhausted and that will supply all of our needs and bring fulfillment to our life. THERE IS POWER IN PURPOSE!

*Process Sheet Thirteen*

# The Power of Purpose

## *INDIVIDUAL*

1. "The thing that you would do for free is the very thing that will 'set you free.'" What is it that you feel totally fulfilled doing?

_____

_____

_____

_____

2. What qualities of Spirit do you express in the above activity?

_____

_____

_____

_____

3. "Can you imagine that there is a Power for Good in the Universe that is unlimited in every way, and that It desires expression through you"–that the Intelligence of the All-Knowing, the Joy of the Free Spirit, the Creativity of the Universe experiences pleasure when It expresses *as you*–? Turn within, now, to that Power which finds joy in your self-expression–to that Presence that *is* the Joy you express as you do what you love to do, know that your purpose in life is to express the Spirit through the uniqueness of your being, and make an inner commitment of your time, focus, and energy to that Purpose.

## *GROUP*

Discussion of Lesson.

**Activity:** Sections 1 and 2 of *Individual*, above.

**Meditation:** There Is Power in *Your* Purpose

*(Facilitator: read slowly with restful music in background, if desired. Begin with one of the Relaxation Techniques on pages 299-300.)*
Imagine yourself doing what you love to do...feel the qualities of your spiritual nature as you express yourself in the activity...do you feel joy and happiness?...do you feel love and compassion?...do you feel excited and enthusiastic just to be alive?...the spiritual qualities that you are feeling right now *are* the very Presence of the Spirit within you...every time you do what you love to do, and you bring love to what you do, you activate the Power of Spirit within you...this Power can and will bring about successful ventures...enriching experiences... prosperous undertakings...your Purpose is to fully express the Spirit within you in a unique and special way...a purposeful way that not only enriches and fulfills your soul, but touches life...how does your highest self-expression touch the world?... take a moment to imagine yourself doing what you love to do and imagine that action touching others in some way...see how others benefit from your spiritual self-expression...*(Facilitator: allow one to two minutes)*...spiritual self-denial, suppression of individual joy and fulfillment lead to weakness and exhaustion, but spiritual self-expression and emancipation of individual joy and fulfillment lead to Power and Energy...the Power within you finds joy in your self-expression–the Presence within you *is* the Joy you express as you do what you love to do...your purpose in life is to express this Divine and Holy Presence through the uniqueness of your being...make an inner commitment of your time, focus, and energy to that Purpose...now, focus your

thought back to your body and the room, and take three deep breaths, with each one feeling more and more energized and joy-filled, and then open your eyes...one...two...three.

1. SOM 270:4, 6.    2. SOM 45:4.    3. SOM 132:10.    4. SOM 195:2.    5. SOM 336:2.
6. SOM 270:3.    7. SOM 477:4.    8. SOM 151:4.    9. Phillips Brooks, *Lectures on Preaching*,
(Yale University Press, 1877).

# 14    To Have, Not to Hold

*Mark Twain wrote:*
*"What, then, is the true*
*Gospel of consistency?*
*Change." Most of us*
*appear to accept the*
*premise that the only*
*true constant is change.*

Yet, in spite of the warning
that change is inevitable, we often try to live our life in "sus-
pended animation." We seem to have taken the traditional
marriage vow, "to have and to hold until death do us part,"
and then applied it to everyone and everything in our life.
We don't want anything to move, change, or end. We hold
on for dear life to the status quo (which includes our limitations), and the result is spiritual, mental, and emotional stagnation.

We cannot move forward in our life–expand, grow,
progress–if we are unwilling to move from where we are. Do
you remember the "rings" in the schoolyard we played on as
children? We could move forward and around the circle of
rings by swinging from one ring to another, grabbing onto
the one ahead of us by letting go of the one behind us–right
hand over left hand, then right again, all the way around the
circle. But if we didn't let go of one ring so that we could
grab onto the next, we didn't get anywhere. We were stuck.
Just hanging in one spot got to be pretty boring and so tiring
that eventually we let go with both hands, fell to the ground,
and the game was over. Staying in one spot in our life is a lot
like that. We get stuck, but we're unwilling to let go of where

we are so that we can progress. Even if we feel comfortable and safe hanging in the same place, holding on tightly to the same spot can get get tiring, if not boring; and sometimes, by the time we are exhausted enough to let go, the game of life is over.

As It is impressed with ideas (both human and Divine), Spirit, the One Creative Medium, is forever giving form to the world in which we live. Through our receptivity (or lack of it) to the Divine Wisdom within us, and through our use (or misuse) of the Creative Power of the Universe, our thoughts have created everything we experience in our world: All of our relationships, all of our activities, and all of our "stuff." When we forget that everything is made from the same thing, Spirit in form, and that everything begins in mind as a thought, it appears to us instead that everything we love or desire is "outside" of us, made from something different from ourselves, and that we have to *get* it if we want it. Then, when we get it, we believe that we must hold on to it for dear life, whether the "it" is money, prestige, a job, a house, or a person. Unless we remind ourselves *often*–in fact, unless we "pray without ceasing"[1]–it is hard for us to remember that everything that is "seen," everything in the material world, is made from that which is "not seen," the unseen substance of Creative Energy which is activated by thought.

## "EVERYTHING IS A THING OF THOUGHT"[2]

However, when we are conscious that the outer world is composed of inner thought, and that every material effect has a mental origin, we realize that it is unnecessary for us to hold on to things, or to hoard or hide them, because we cannot lose that which has its origin in mind. We cannot lose our thoughts. No one can take our thoughts away from us, and, of course, our thoughts are not in any danger of falling unnoticed out of our mind. Thoughts are unlimited. We can have as many or as few of them as we choose. We can think about the same things over and over again, or we can come up with something new.

What we think about and what we believe and accept actually makes up who we are and what we experience. Our outer life reflects the inner content of our mind. "What we outwardly are, and what we are to become, *depends upon what we are thinking*, for this is the way we are using Creative Power."[3] All that is manifest in our life at this moment is what we have allowed to come into expression. What we have, and what we experience, is as much as we've been willing to accept or believed that we were allowed to have and experience. It is what we have mentally acquired for ourselves from the Unlimited Creative Source of the Universe Who would withhold nothing from us. "Since we are dealing with an Infinite Power, which knows only Its own ability to do, and since It can objectify any idea impressed upon It, there can be no limit to what It can or would do for us, other than the limit of our inward embodiment."[4]

We often get confused and think that the *vehicle* through which Spirit gives to us is "the Thing itself," and that it exists separate from the thought or Creative Medium that created it. For instance, most of us believe that our job is the source of our prosperity or lack of it. However, our job is merely the vehicle through which Spirit gives to us, because that is an area in our life through which we have agreed to receive. The job is the "middle-man," so to speak, not *The Man*, the Spirit Almighty. When we believe that our job is our source, we become worried about losing it or afraid to leave it even though we may be unhappy and limited in what we are doing. We may put up with less than the best, worried about getting fired or afraid to quit because we believe that we will end up with even less if we do. It is important for us to remember that when we leave our job, voluntarily or otherwise, we leave only an outer form, a *vehicle* for our financial abundance. We don't leave our Source, because Spirit is our Source, and Spirit is everywhere present–closer than our next breath or our next thought.

We don't worry that our thoughts will disappear or that we won't have enough thoughts to think, do we? More often than not, we wish certain thoughts *would* disappear, and that we could think less! We aren't concerned that someone will come along and steal our thoughts from us, since most of the time we can't even give our thoughts away because no one wants them!

We may be willing to accept that just *some* things have a mental origin, but we may also believe that other things are the result of luck, fate, or faking it. We may trust that Spirit will manifest *some* of our desires but that we must get the rest on our own. So we must affirm, over and over again–until such thinking is *automatic*–that *everything* in our life is a thought form, and that *nothing* exists (because it cannot exist), separate from the thought that created it. Material results are the finite effect of eternal thought in action.

## "CHANGE IS ALWAYS TAKING PLACE..."[5]

When we're *not* happy, we *want* to believe that material life is finite and temporary. We're *hoping* that the lows in our life are not everlasting. But when our life starts to look just the way we want it to, we sometimes become rigid, inflexible, fearful, and possessive. We want our material world to suddenly take on infinite and eternal characteristics! Emerson tells us to "beware of holding too much good in our hands." It is "the good" that we don't want to let go of and that we grasp with white-knuckle intensity. When

our world is in order, and everything is in place–the perfect spot
to live, the wonderful job, the great relationship, the 2.5 children,
the rose-covered cottage, and the good retirement plan–or any
other version we may have of "worldly perfection"–we try to hold
it all together, protect it, control it, and keep it from changing.
We are afraid that all the good we have accumulated will become
*less* rather than *more* if it is allowed to move at all. In our joy, we
tell ourselves, "It doesn't get any better then this," and then we set
out to prove it by making sure that everything stays fixed and
static. We dig our heels in, and then dare Life to move us.

I know that sometimes I take the attitude, "Thank you
God, I'll take it from here!" as if I had the power to take "it" anywhere, *in and of myself*; as if I could make anything happen *by
myself*–including maintenance of the status quo–without the
movement of Spirit upon my life. Jesus asked, "Which of you by
taking thought can add one cubit unto his stature?"[6] If we are
afraid of losing what we have, it is usually because we feel personally responsible for getting it. We see God as somewhere "out
there" giving us love and peace, and ourselves here earning, buy-
ing, attracting, and accumulating everything else on our own! Of
course, we can't do *anything* without God, but that doesn't keep us
from trying!

Life appears to be an ever-flowing, ever-evolving process.
When we hold on too tightly to our life, no matter how good our
life may be, we limit our spiritual growth and self-discovery.
"When the law of circulation is retarded, stagnation results. It
is only as we allow the Divine current to flow through us on
and out, that we really express life."[7] Sometimes we hang onto
our job here, grasp our money there, keep a "tight rein" on our
relationship over here, and maybe our children over there. We
become mentally contorted and spiritually distorted. When our

hands are full (mentally as well as physically), we cannot receive any more. Then not only *can't* things get any better for us, materially and emotionally, but we are unable to expand and grow mentally and spiritually. Hands that are closed in the grasping position are not open to receiving anything new. Inspirational author and lecturer Anna Lindsay wrote: "Life is large. We cannot possibly grasp the whole of it in the few years that we have to live. What is vital? What is essential? What may be profitably let go? Let us ask ourselves these questions."

## "LET GO AND LET GOD"

Most of us are familiar with the admonition "Let go and let God." If we are to experience a greater sense of the Divine Life, we must "let go" of the *death-grip* we have on our worldly life, i.e. our limited ideas of just how good "good" can get and *how* that good should come about; our self-righteous concepts of the "perfect" outcome of a situation; and our desire to control others. Then we can "let God" show us more than we've seen and tell us more than we think we know. We can let God lead us and reveal to us what "He" has in Mind for us. Spirit knows our heart's desire, and Spirit desires good for us even more than *we* do, and even *greater* good than we can imagine on our own. Jesus said, "For worldly people seek after all these things. Your Father in heaven knows that all of these things are also necessary for you. But seek first the kingdom of God and his righteousness, and all these things shall be added to you."[8] When we *let God*, we are open to the Unlimited Kingdom of Creativity, and the Wisdom that creates for us all that we desire, and then some. But we must be willing to give up self-righteousness to receive "his righteousness."

Of course, it isn't easy to let go of how we think things

*ought* to be. Most of us have ideas and opinions about everyone and everything in our life and how it all should operate. We not only think that our ideas are *good*, we believe that our ideas are *right*–the gospel according to us! Why should we let go and let God handle things that are already good and working, especially when we've got it all under control?! But what is *under* control cannot be inspired or enriched from *Above*. "Do not will or try to compel things to happen. Things happen by an immutable law...L-E-T is a big word and an important one. By taking thought, you do not add one cubit to Reality, but you do *allow* (let) Reality to manifest in the things you are doing."[9]

I know that there have been times in my life when I was willing to surrender my control to God only when I thought that I had *nothing to lose*–either I'd messed things up and couldn't fig-ure out how to unravel them, or I hadn't been able to get what I wanted through control and manipulation. About twelve years ago I wanted to create a "significant" relationship in my life. I wasn't having much luck *on my own*, so I decided to ask for "God's help." I prayed for my *soul-mate*; I wrote my affirmations of self-worth every day and verbally affirmed them; I visualized togetherness with the "man of my dreams," then I "let" God handle the details. I figured the worst thing God could do was to set me up with a boring date. But since I'd already been doing that on my own, I knew that I had nothing to lose. And, of course, I got what I wanted: a wonderful relationship with a "significant other." I knew when we met that he was the direct result of my "letting go and letting God." However, it wasn't long before I forgot that my bliss was Divinely Orchestrated, and that the substance of my new rela-tionship was Spirit. I forgot how capable God was at managing my affairs. In fact, I took my gift of love and said, "Thank you, God, I'll take it from here."

My response to Life was similar to what a dog does when given a bone. He takes it in his teeth, puts it on the ground, wraps his paws around it, and then if anyone gets near it, including the giver of the bone, he growls. He no longer cares who the giver was. His friendly begging has gotten him what he wanted, and his appreciation has turned into possessiveness.

Without consciously knowing when the shift happens, our mind often moves from gratitude to God for the gifts of the Spirit to possessiveness and fear of loss. We become afraid of losing the good we have been given. We are fearful that our life will somehow go backwards if we don't hang onto it to keep it from rolling downhill. Our sense of what we have, whether it is money, a job, a relationship, a new home, a new baby, etc., moves from spiritual confidence and acceptance that what we have is a part of us–a resonating and reflecting form of our consciousness–to fear.

## "THE GIFT WITHOUT THE GIVER IS BARE"[10]

In our fear, our mind shifts from recognizing that whatever we have is an expression of our eternal, abundant, unlimited relationship with God–a way in which Spirit manifests love for us, a way in which Spirit gives to us–to believing that we could lose the goodness in our life. We see things as separate from us that we must hold onto or they'll be lost. We start living *for* the gift, and we forget the Giver, and we lose sight of the *reality* that all of our good comes from our living for God. We stop looking inside ourselves for the Truth of who we are, and Its expression in our life, and instead we begin looking to the outside for approval.

Sometimes it looks as though we won't have money, or someone to love, or a place to work, or nice surroundings, if we don't hold onto them. However, by stifling the movement of our life, we are going against the "Natural Law" that governs our success and happiness, and we end up with the very thing we are trying to prevent: lack and limitation. "There is no stagnation in Spirit....Spirit is alive, conscious, aware and active."[11] Movement and circulation are necessary to life. We limit our ability to *have* by our desire to *hold*.

Earthly life is temporary, and we take nothing material with us when we leave. Even if we try to hold on to it, "it" is not going anywhere when "we" go. We are not making mortgage payments on earthly things; we are renting them. However, reminding ourselves of the finite, temporary nature of the material world should not make us appreciate it less but rather allow us the freedom to appreciate it more. Every experience, every moment, becomes a gift in the moment it is given because we understand that we shall not "pass this way again."

I had heard that the practice of "detachment" was an important part of spiritual growth; but the idea of detachment seemed *cold*–a state of mind in which an individual did not care about anyone or anything. I assumed that real love demanded attachment and worry. If someone I loved was late, I "awfulized" about their having been in an accident or kidnapped. I was frantic that some terrible "twist of fate" could take that person away from me. However, I discovered that detachment didn't mean not caring, but rather loving deeply and completely–caring about everything, and *then* letting it all go, surrendering it all to God, knowing that everything has come from God. Detachment meant trusting that God forever holds for me what is highest and best, and therefore that I do not have to hold on to it all. Detachment also meant trusting that what *remained* in my experience would continue to enrich me and teach me to love even more, and that what had *left* had taught me all that it could.

Some people stay in one job until they retire. Some people stay in one relationship until death do them part. I believe that some experiences are meant for a lifetime, while others are not. But that doesn't mean that the experiences that are more temporal are less valuable. We can learn from a job that lasts a day. We can learn from a relationship that doesn't last much longer. Even a *miscarried* baby has a lesson to teach and comes briefly into one's experience with a gift in hand. It is as we look within ourselves and discover the Unchanging Presence that we receive our ever-changing gifts. When we know that God won't let go, we are able to let go and trust God to hold our good.

After eight years of living "for the gift," existing solely for another human being, I realized that I needed to live "for the Giver," for God. I wanted to feel Life's Power inside of myself rather than feeling that my power was dangling just out of my reach in the hands of another. I needed to cease making someone else not only responsible for my happiness but the *reason* for it. It was a struggle for me to loose the grip I had on my relationship and everything that revolved around it. But as I moved my trust to the Spirit within me, knowing that what I let go of would be in Good Hands, I could slowly release my hold, one finger at a time, until I finally gave it all to God. When I surrendered completely, I felt an inner *explosion* of my own individual spirituality and power. And, as I stopped holding on to the outer form of love so tightly, I discovered I loved even more. I experience a deeper relationship of peace with the God within me. I gave my gift back to God and said, "Thank you very much; *you* take it from here." And He did.

As I sat alone one afternoon after my relationship had ended, the torrential rain that had been pounding the island most of the day suddenly stopped. The intense light of the emerging sun created a spectacular rainbow. I had been looking for a little "reassurance" that day, and Nature provided it in living color. The rainbow was larger than I'd ever experienced and the colors seemed brighter than I had ever seen. It began far out in the ocean and arched across the sky until it ended just in front of the hillside in front of me, so that all of the trees at the base of the mountain were bathed in color. As I sat there in absolute awe, I heard a gentle whisper, "You had placed your trust in the rainbow," and I understood. I realized in that moment that in my letting go to that Power, that Creative Energy, that Loving Presence that causes the beauty and goodness of life to *be* in the first place, I had lost nothing, but rather I had gained the Kingdom. God was still holding all of my good for me, and God would continue to create even greater good in my life.

The rainbows in life fade away, but they come back again and again, often brighter than before. Just because rainbows are temporary doesn't take away from their beauty or our appreciation of them. Perhaps, it even adds to our reverence for their radiance. Our good is to *have*, in every moment—not to hold. Let us celebrate the temporary and worship the Eternal. We don't need to hold on to the rainbows when we trust the Rainbow Maker.

*Process Sheet Fourteen*

# To Have, Not to Hold

### INDIVIDUAL

Who or what in your life are you holding on to or attempting to control?

_____

_____

_____

_____

_____

What do you believe might happen if you "let go"?

_____

_____

_____

_____

Write affirmations to assist you in "letting go and letting God" relating to the people and/or situations above.

_____

_____

_____

_____

_____

### GROUP

Discussion of Lesson.

**Activity:** (*Materials: water-filled balloons or raw eggs.*)
In groups of two or three, all join hands and keep a solid

grip on one another's hands. The facilitator places a water-filled balloon or raw egg on the floor in the center of each group, and without letting go of the *solidly* held hands, the group must move the balloon or egg from one side of the room to the other. (Bottom line after process: It is much easier to get things moving in life when we let go.)

**Meditation:** Mentally Releasing People and Events

*(Facilitator: read slowly with restful music in background, if desired.)*
    Sitting comfortably, take in a few deep breaths...now imagine that there is a peaceful white light surrounding you, and with every inhalation, you are breathing in this peaceful white light into every area of your body...deep...all the way to your toes...imagine that as you exhale you are releasing any stress or tightness in the body...breathing in deeply...exhaling...completing...feeling relaxed...your body feeling lighter...and lighter...feel yourself moving deeper...and deeper within yourself...now imagine that you are standing in a white-walled room, without a ceiling, that is floating in a beautiful azure sky...sit down in the center of the room and feel comfortable...perhaps there are pillows to sit on...there is a box of colorful balloons next to the pillows, close and easy to reach...now allow the image of a person or event that you have been holding on to to appear in front of you...take a balloon and gently blow it up until the person or event is surrounded by the balloon...choose a beautiful color...the person or event is now in the balloon...the balloon is transparent, you can see them...and now, with the words "I release you to the Highest Good," let the balloon slowly drift up through the ceilingless room and on into the "blue heavens"...continue this process until you have released all people and events that come to mind...

*(Facilitator may wait five minutes, silently, as music plays)*...now look up and see all of the colorful balloons as they float farther and father away from you...notice how they have colored your sky for a moment...watch them disappear...now see the room dissolve and see the peaceful white light surround you again...breath it in...feel the peace and freedom of releasing and letting go...focus on your breathing...inhale...exhale...feeling relaxed, at peace...and on the count of three, you will open your eyes feeling refreshed...one...two...three.

1. 1 Thessalonians 5:17 (KJV).   2. SOM 224:3.   3. SOM 140:4.   4. SOM 118:2.
5. SOM 131:5.   6. Matthew 6:27 (KJV).   7. SOM 440:4.   8. Matthew 6:32-33 (Lamsa).
9. SOM 489:3.   10. James Russell Lowell.   11. SOM 67:2.

# 15   Life Is a Moving Experience

Shifting Our Attitudes from Mediocre to Magnificent

*We need only look at ourselves and the world around us to realize that life is a moving experience. Blood constantly flows through our veins and arteries.*

Rivers flow into current-filled oceans that ebb and flow at the shoreline. Winds circle the planet, gathering clouds and scattering leaves and seeds. The earth rotates on its axis as it travels around the sun at incredible speeds, while the sun itself speeds through space even faster. On a starry night we can see the ever-changing configuration of the heavens. From the smallest speck of life on our planet to the outermost galaxies, life is in motion!

Yet sometimes in our own individual life, we don't seem to be moving at all. We feel stuck in a rut, immobilized by indecision. We may have been thinking for some time about making a move, but we just haven't moved on that thought yet. Perhaps we've been thinking of moving to another city, state, or country, but our address is still the same. Maybe we've been thinking about moving into a relationship or moving out of one, but our status is still "status quo." Or perhaps we've been considering moving from one job to another, or changing our career entirely, but we're still getting up and going to the same place every day.

Often we become stuck when there is a decision to be made that involves change. We are afraid we may make the "wrong" choice and lose what we already have, even though what we have may feel limited and unfulfilling. Or else we are afraid to make any choice, "right" or "wrong," because someone else might not approve of the choice we make. So we stay stuck in our rut, living a life of mediocrity, or even misery, rather than trusting ourselves to make life-enriching choices that will move us to greater levels of life experiences.

## "LIFE IS TO BE LIVED, ALL OF IT"[1]

Are you excited about your life? Do you live on the edge? In the middle? Or have you found a safe little crack in the framework of life to hide in? Do you risk and actually make a choice for change now and then? Or are you so cautious about every decision that comes along that by the time you make a choice, the opportunity has passed you by? Do you try new avenues or are you stuck in a rut in the same old road? Does your life feel *comfortable* like an old shoe–or simply *worn out* like an old shoe? Composer John Cage has written: "We are involved in a life that passes understanding, and our highest business is our daily life." How high are you willing to fly in your daily business of living?

When guests are visiting us, we are concerned about them. We want to make sure that they eat well, that they are comfortable, and that they are having a good time. We ask them, "How are you feeling?" "How did you sleep?" "Did you have fun today?" "What are your plans for tomorrow?" But do we ever stop to consider if *we* are having a good time visiting the planet? "One should analyze himself, saying, 'Do I look at myself from a standpoint of restriction? Do I see life limited to the eternal round of getting up in the morning, eating, going to work, coming home, going to bed, sleeping, getting up again and so on?' Break the bonds of apparent necessity and see life as one continuous expression of the Infinite Self."[2]

We are each an integral part of the Infinite Self. We are spiritual beings created by an Unlimited Power. We have the potential to be, do, and have anything we desire. We have the ability to express ourselves fully in the image and likeness of our Creator, Who is Boundless and Ever-Creative. The expression of Life is Love, Joy, Peace, Energy, Creativity, Color, Beauty, and Abundant Good. Does your life reflect the qualities of Spirit? Is it filled with freshness, spontaneity, and vitality, or is the only thing "growing" in your life the moss under your feet? Are you living the life you fantasize about? Are you living a life *anyone* would fantasize about?!

Perhaps we don't feel particularly bad, but, then again, we don't feel extraordinarily good either. Our life may be "just fine," but it is definitely not *fantastic*. *Fine* sounds rather gray. *Fine* has about as much color as lint from the dryer. Lint is usually gray when we dry bright red, blue, yellow, and green clothes *together*. Why does lint turn gray? Where do all the colors go? In the drying process, the strands of bright color lose their individuality, just as some of us, in the living process, seem to have lost *our* individuality. We have ceased to express ourselves through choice and change, and our life has become dull and gray.

However, the Spiritual Realm in which we live, and which lives in us, is filled with unlimited, colorful ideas. We can choose (if we choose to choose) from a rainbow of opportunities and potentialities. But often, because of fear, we don't make the choices that will enhance our life. We make "safe" choices or no choices, and our life becomes boring, like lint. It would be fine to have merely a *fine* life, if we did not have the potential to have a *fantastic* one.

But we do.

## WE HAVE NO CHOICE BUT TO CHOOSE

If we're feeling fine about our life, instead of fantastic, it could be time for us to look at some of our choices. We might want to check our excitement barometer to see if we've been mistaking boredom for peace of mind! If we are to find our true potential, if we want to move beyond *fine*, and feel *fantastic*, we must push ourselves beyond our comfort zone. Do we always make the safe choice–the one that won't rock the boat or the one where we risk the least? Or do we try to avoid making choices altogether?

It is important for us to realize that although we may think we're not choosing, our "choosing to not choose" is actually a choice. "We cannot live a choiceless life. Every day, every moment, every second, there is choice. If it were not so we would not be individuals."[3] So even though we think that we are playing it safe by not making certain choices, because we are immersed in a Life that is continuously active and creative, our indecision is reflected in the wishy-washy condition of our life.

The inherent Wisdom within us will never fail to guide us into positive, life-enriching choices. Yet rather than seeking Inner Guidance, we often look for outer approval when making our choices. We ask, "How will I look to others? What will people think of me?" Then we usually assume the worst and make a safe choice to avoid criticism, embarrassment, or ridicule. Some people actually live miserable or mediocre lives because they are afraid that if they choose something different, someone will disapprove! Social philosopher and author Eric Hoffer wrote: "However much we guard ourselves against it, we tend to shape ourselves in the image others have of us. It is not so much the example of others we imitate, as the reflection of ourselves in their eyes and the echo of ourselves in their words."

It is easy for others to tell us what we ought to do, because they don't have to live with the choice–*we* do! Yet because of "public opinion," we choose to live where we don't want to live, in a relationship we don't want to have, in a job that we don't want to perform, all because of what others might say if we chose something else. We sell out on our soul and on the potential greatness of our life all because of what people might think. *But what about what God thinks?!* Spirit, Infinite Mind, is filled with grand and glorious ideas *of* us and *for* us; yet some of us are willing to shrink down our self-expression to fit into the minute idea that some other person may have of us!

We must be willing to lose the approval of others, we must be willing to risk judgment and criticism, if we are to discover God's plan for us. "For whoever wishes to save his life shall lose it; and whoever loses his life for my sake shall find it."[4] When we are willing to risk it all for the sake of the Spirit within us, we shall find meaning and purpose in our life, and we shall move from *fine* to *fantastic*.

## WE SHOULD BE CAUTIOUS WITH CAUTION

We all need to ask, "What would I be doing today if I weren't afraid of losing money, esteem, position, or the support of family, friends, or colleagues? How would my life be different if I felt that I could be as outgoing and uninhibited as I wished?" Life is about moving beyond what we already know and reaching inside ourselves to the Unknown. Life is about our taking risks for the Spirit within. Unfortunately, some people live their life as if there were a PROCEED WITH CAUTION  sign in the birth canal when they were born!

A friend of mine who is a risk-taker and very successful at

whatever she chooses to do said, "Caution will get you a nine-to-five job pushing paper–doing time–not living life." The need for security has made many of us prisoners of life rather than masters of fate. We might as well risk that "nest egg" we've been protecting because our fears and insecurity will probably keep it from hatching anyway. We can never get to where we want to go unless we're willing to move from where we are.

The Divine Life inside us desires to move more fully into our life and to create the life of our dream. "Free yourself forever from the thought that God may be pleased by a life of sacrifice, that the world is any better because of your misery, or that righteousness is more perfectly expressed through poverty than abundance. Know that the greater the abundance of every good thing which you are bringing out in your life, the more perfectly you are satisfying the Divine Urge within you." [5]

When we seek security in the material world, we limit the good that could be ours. People who succeed in this world are risk-takers who are not afraid to lose. Many millionaires will tell you that they've gained and lost millions of dollars over the years. Some have lost everything, been totally bankrupt, and have gained it all back–and more. In the material world, sometimes we risk and win, sometimes we risk and lose. But we never lose spiritually when we take a chance on life. We gain in spiritual self-knowledge every time we are willing to let go of our security blanket and embrace more of our potential. What we discover about ourselves by *asking more of ourselves* is beyond measure.

Courage is not the absence of fear. When we're not afraid, courage isn't necessary. Courage is our willingness to feel the fear and test our limits anyway. When we do, what we will find is that we have no limits except the ones we have placed upon ourselves. We are never too young or too old to do anything. People on both sides of the age scale have proved that–from the six-year-old chess master to the man in his eighties on the "Armor-All" commercial who water-skies (barefoot!). If no one your age has done what you want to do–be the first! We don't have to wait around for someone else to live the life we want to live before we give ourselves permission to go for it!

The Spirit of God has given us freedom to "go for it." We have free choice, and we are free to choose to live fully and completely every day of our life–to keep moving *forward* and *upward* until our life on earth is completed. There is no higher authority than the Spirit within us. No one can stop the spiritual surge if we choose to allow it to move into our life and move us forward in our life. The choice is up to each of us. Life is a moving experience, and if we'll let It, It will take us all the way to the top!

*Process Sheet Fifteen*

# Life Is a Moving Experience

*INDIVIDUAL*

If you are feeling *fine* about your life, instead of *fantastic*, it could be time for you to look at some of your choices. Ask yourself, "What would I be doing today if I weren't afraid of losing money, esteem, position, or the support of family, friends, or colleagues? How would my life be different if I felt that I could be as outgoing and uninhibited as I wished?"

_____

_____

_____

_____

_____

What we discover about ourselves, by asking more of ourselves, is beyond measure. Write down what "risk" you are willing to take *right now* toward the life you have just written about above.

_____

_____

_____

_____

_____

Compose an affirmative statement that you can write fifty times morning and evening, place on your mirror, and repeat throughout the day that will empower you to take the above risk and move forward in the direction you want to go.

_____

_____

*GROUP*
Discussion of Lesson.

**Activity:** This is a game of "verbal baseball." Designate four places in the room (one each) for first, second, third, and home bases. Divide the group into two teams. The first person "at bat" must take a "risk" to get to first base. The risk could be telling a secret about himself or herself to the group, singing a song, reciting a spontaneous poem, telling someone in the group something he or she feels about that person, etc. If the person at bat is not willing to take a risk, they are "out." Depending on the size of each team, the number of outs may vary from one to three before the other team is up to bat. The object of the game is for everyone to reach Home Base. The first team to do so wins.

**Meditation:** Onward and Upward

(*Facilitator: read slowly with restful music in background, if desired. Begin with one of the Relaxation Techniques on pages* 299-300.)
        Imagine that you are at the bottom of a large "rut" in a road…in fact, you *live* in the rut in the road…all around you are all of the comforts of home…everything you are familiar with…you cannot see anything else because the walls of the rut are too high…you could stay right where you are, but lately the same old scenery has gotten a little boring…you once thought that the rut was safe…even peaceful…but now something inside of you is urging you to get out of the rut and move farther along the road…you can vaguely hear laughter coming from somewhere down the road…the clinking of glasses, the gaiety of conversation…there is something wonderful going on down the road… you are invited, but you can't attend if you stay in the rut…as you

look up at the opening above you and the high ledges all around you, you notice that there are metal rings...handholds and footholds that you can use to climb out...but what will those who are also in the rut say if you leave?...what if life is better in the small rut in which you live than farther along down the path?... written on each of the handholds and footholds is something that you must be willing to do...some action or change in thought that must come from you in order for you to use the rings to pull yourself out of the rut...you sit and wonder if you really want to exert all that effort...if you want to risk the negative opinions of others...after all, life in the rut is not so bad...but then again, you are invited to a wonderful party down that road that might be fantastic...as you consider making a move, you hear a gentle voice whisper: "Know that with the greater abundance of every good thing which you are bringing out in your life, the more perfectly you are satisfying the Divine Urge within you"...there is so much more to Life...so much more to your life than you have discovered so far...Life is about moving beyond what you already know and reaching inside yourself to the Unknown...there are treasures for you in the Unknown...there are gifts waiting with your name... untapped abilities...unexpressed creativity...the Divine Life inside you desires to move more fully into your life...to create the life of your dreams...look at the risks you must take...and choose if you are willing to move onward and upward...grab the handholds and footholds and commit to taking the risks necessary...as you attempt to pull yourself up to the top you see a hand reaching down to help you and beyond that hand, the face of a loving, compassionate being...reach up and take the hand and feel your-self being uplifted like a weightless child...up...up...and out of the rut...you are free...and the party awaits you...feel your free-dom as you walk now down the road dressed in your party best,

invitation in hand...and feel that same freedom as you find yourself back in the room with your eyes still closed...know that the
party is right here...right now...as you open your eyes you open
them free of the rut...free of the fears and inertia that have held
you back...take a few deep breaths and feel the anticipation and
excitement of going to a party where you are loved and where you
love all those present...and on the count of three, open your eyes.

1. Ernest Holmes, in Reginald C. Armor, *Ernest Holmes: The Man* (Science of Mind Publishing), p. 29.
2. SOM 288:2.   3. SOM 143:3.   4. Matthew 16:25 (Lamsa).   5. SOM 288:2.

# 16  What's Wrong with This Picture?

## Realigning Our Mind with the Divine Design

*The other day, a friend offered to proofread something I'd written. She qualified her skills by explaining to me that spelling was not one of her strong points* but that she could always tell when a word was spelled wrong. She indicated that even though she would not be able to correct the misspelled words, she would have no problem recognizing the errors.

How often do we approach other areas of our life that way? We know what's wrong with something or someone. We have no problem in pointing out the error, misstep, or transgression. We judge and criticize. And even though we don't know how to correct the problem, we are convinced that it is important for us to target what's wrong with the picture.

Let's face it: Pointing out what is wrong in a given situation is a lot less challenging than taking the time to find a solution.

Some people, however, actually get a sense of being *right* simply because they have pointed out that something or someone is *wrong*. For instance, someone may ask you a question for which he or she has no answer. But when you answer the question to the best of your knowledge, then he or she responds, "No! That's not right!" with great satisfaction. Somehow, their being right that you were wrong was more satisfying to them than their getting closer to the "right" answer. However, the games of "greatness by comparison" and "one-upmanship" are spiritually dangerous ones.

## "THOSE WHO CAN'T, CRITICIZE"

I've never thought the facetious saying "Those who can, do; and those who can't, *teach*" was particularly amusing. A more astute observation might be that "those who can, *do*; and those who can't, criticize those who do." We as a society have become the indefatigable judge and jury. Even though we may know that the Higher Ground is not to "judge according to appearance," we may still entertain a self-satisfied opinion about the one whose trial in court makes the headlines, or is talked about in the media, even though there are hundreds of pages of recorded testimony that we have not heard or read. We may have reached conclusions about scandals in Washington when all we know is what we have heard from political "spin-doctors," pundits, and analysts. We may know exactly what is wrong with the government (it's corrupt), with our country (the welfare system), with our colleagues (they're inept), with our neighbors (they're too noisy), and with our mate or our date (they are just too insensitive!). But simply knowing what is wrong with the picture doesn't improve the view.

We've all heard it said that "If you are not part of the solution, you are part of the problem." Our knowing what is wrong with the picture is still *being a part of the problem* unless we have an idea of what the right picture looks like. It does little good for us to know that something is spelled wrong unless we know how to spell it right (or are willing to find out how to spell it right or to hand the misspelling over to someone who can spell it right). Fault-finding simply to find fault is fruitless and useless.

Criticism and judgment is an exercise in human ego. It

does nothing to expand our spiritual awareness or to heal any situation. In fact, criticism and judgment not only hinder a solution but inhibit the spiritual growth of the one focusing on what is wrong. "And it is the law that *the man who sees what he wants to see, regardless of what appears, will someday experience in the outer what he has so faithfully seen in the within.* From selfish reasons alone, if from no loftier reason, we cannot afford to find fault, to hate, or even to hold in mind *anything* against any living soul!"[1]

When our focus is on what's wrong with the picture, we overlook what is right with it. We fail to experience the perfection of Universal Goodness that is present within the picture. We lose sight of the Divine possibilities inherent in the moment and actually block what is "right with the picture" from manifesting. Henry Ford once said that "Obstacles are those frightful things you see when you take your eyes off your goal." When we practice the Science of Mind, our goal is to see the perfection of Spirit emerging in the midst of a problem–to see the Good that is present every time and everywhere. When we look for fault in ourselves and others or we need to be right by making others wrong, we take our eyes off that goal.

## "YOU CAN'T GET THERE FROM HERE"

People who tend to focus on what's wrong always know why things *can't* be done. They also don't seem interested in discovering how things *can* be done. It has been said, "People who say it cannot be done should not interrupt those who are doing it." We should not let ourselves be discouraged by the doomsayers around us who would place our dreams on the "Why it can't be done" side of life– those who would condemn us to failure because they are convinced that they know what's wrong with the picture we envision for our life.

The doomsayers are usually the ones who have given up on their own life and have defeated their own desires with "I can't do it" and "It can't be done." It is the one who has given up on his or her dreams, or who is afraid to dream at all, who continually finds fault with everything around them and who judges and criticizes the world so that he or she does not have to take responsibility for not pursuing his or her potential. We are not spiritually empowered by the false position of superiority we hold when we have declared someone else wrong. Spiritual expansion does not come through our recognizing and pointing out everyone else's mistakes. It occurs through our quietly seeking to correct our own. We are not spiritual by comparison. We are spiritual through individual action.

If we want to succeed in life, our decisions and motivation must be influenced by what is *right* with the picture we hold of our life and why we can live it that way. Anything can be accomplished when we believe that it can, and when we accept no opposition and no other picture. "There must be a recognition that the power of the Word, operating as the Truth and Reality of Being, can do all things."[2] Highly successful people see the possibilities in themselves and do not give up even when others have given up on them. We've all heard stories of famous writers, composers, sculptors, and painters who were told that they had no talent. For example, did you know that Walt Disney was fired by a newspaper editor for "lack of ideas"?! It is the one who is not deterred by what others say is wrong with the picture, but keeps focusing on his or her dreams, whose vision reaches fruition.

We cannot move forward by avoiding the "wrong picture," unless we replace it with the one we desire. A dear friend, whose childhood was scarred by a tyrannical alcoholic father and a sexually abusive neighbor, has made tremendous progress as an adult in working through the residue of a past that left him filled with self-loathing and self-sabotaging behaviors. Through the years he has slowly removed from his experience many of those things he believed were wrong with the picture of his life. He stopped using alcohol and drugs. He quit smoking cigarettes and drinking caffeine. He even gave up sugar.

However, although his mental and physical health improved, his sense of self-worth became attached to what he was *not doing*. His mind was continuously fixed upon what needed to be *eliminated* from the picture he was seeing of himself. What he was doing "right" was simply the absence of the "wrong" he was no longer doing. Eventually he began to feel the emptiness of the void he'd created in his life. He realized that it was not enough for him to see only what was wrong with him and eliminate that. He needed to perceive a "right" picture of himself, so that he could begin living from "right" action rather than merely not doing "wrong" actions.

## "WHEN WE DO RIGHT, WE ARE RIGHT"[3]

When we continue to look only at what's wrong with life, we are not inspired with the ideas that will bring about a better picture for us. An artist looks at the image he or she wants to reproduce on canvas. We too must look at what we want to emulate and recreate in our life. There is a whole, complete, and perfect picture of Life held forever in the Mind of the Creator. "Wilt thou not cease to pervert the right ways of the Lord?"[4] Although we do not have the power to change Changeless Perfection, we do have the seeming power to pervert our view of it. When we look only at what is wrong with ourselves and others, when we focus solely on the negative in daily events, when we dwell upon the error of our ways, we pervert our view of Reality, and the True Beauty of Life is lost to us.

We must close our eyes and let go of "what is wrong" and meditate upon the Perfection that is clearly there within us and that awaits only our acknowledgment. As we affirm that the "right ways of the Lord" are active in us, the outer picture of our life automatically changes. As we see "what is right" within us, we also begin to see what is right in the world around us, because the inner picture is reflected in the outer dreamscape. "As we look at the many millions of forms, all of different shape and color, and yet know that they all come from One Stuff, are we not compelled to accept the fact that there is a specific cause, or concrete mental image back of every idea or thing, a Divine Mental Picture?"[5]

There is nothing wrong with the Divine Mental Picture, which includes all life. Our mental reception is simply experiencing "interference." As we realign our mind with the Divine, as we look at the world around us and know that everyone and everything "comes from One Stuff," and that that "Stuff" is perfect, then...we shall surely "get the Right Picture."

*Process Sheet Sixteen*

# What's Wrong with This Picture?

### INDIVIDUAL

As we affirm that the "right ways of the Lord" are active in us, the outer picture of our life automatically changes. As we see "what is right" within us, we also begin to see "what is right" in the world around us because the inner picture is reflected in the outer dreamscape. Make a list of "what is right" with the picture you hold of yourself:

_____

_____

_____

Focus on these qualities all week.

### GROUP

Discussion of Lesson.

**Activity:** After completing the above Individual exercise, have the group sit in a circle. Each person takes turn "being the picture," as every other person in the circle completes the following statement about him or her: "The beauty I see in you is

_____

_____ "

The person "being the picture" may choose another in the group to record the statements of the others for him or her so that the statements can be added to the "picture" if desired. (Be certain that eye contact is made by the one being spoken to and the one speaking.)

**Meditation:** The Beauty God Sees *Is* Me

Have pencils or pens and paper ready to use following the
meditation.

*(Facilitator: read slowly with restful music in background, if desired.
Begin with one of the Relaxation Techniques on pages 299-300.)*
As we look at the many millions of forms in life...all of
different shape and color...and yet know that they all come from
One Stuff...we are compelled to accept the fact that there is a
specific cause...a concrete mental image back of every idea or
thing...a Divine Mental Picture...imagine now that you are holding a giant eraser...use it now to erase every thought or mental
image within your mind...move it back and forth until all
thoughts and mental images are erased...until there is just the cool
depths of clarity within you...a clean slate which is open to the
Imagination of the Divine...there is a Divine Mental picture back
of what you know as you...unseen to the outer eye...held in the
Mind of the Divine...a Holy and Perfect Idea that God holds of
you...in the inner place of imagination your mind is linked forever with the Divine Mind...with the Universal Mind of Unlimited
Potential...open your mind now to that Holy One who holds a
Divine Mental Picture of you...the Beauty God sees *is* you...allow
that picture to appear in your mind...in your imagination...do
not judge what you see, just allow It to appear across the clean
slate you have prepared in your mind...*(Facilitator: allow two or
three minutes)*...there is nothing wrong with the Divine Idea of
you...there is nothing wrong with the Picture Wisdom holds of
you...you can choose to focus your mind on what is "right" with
you...you can choose to allow the Divine Mental Picture of you
held in the Invisible Realm of Spirit to move into form in your

life...take a few deep breaths, open your eyes, and write about what you saw. (*If time permits, share with a partner.*)

1. SOM 299:1.   2. SOM 170:2.   3. SOM 503:5.   4. Acts 13:10 (KJV).   5. SOM 105:3.

# 17           **Fear Not**

## Facing and Overcoming Our Fears

*If all the problems
of humankind could be
summed up in just one
word, it would be fear.
Fear causes stagnation
when we are too afraid
to move and chaos*
when it is the reason for our
movement and actions. Fear is the parent of anger, jealousy,
hatred, greed, and all of the other problematic emotions and
actions of our world. It is the creator of the illusion of a
"separate" self, and its motivation is self-preservation. When
we are afraid that there isn't enough, we become greedy.
When we fear another can take our good, we become jealous.
Hate and anger are offspring of the fear that others control
our life and our destiny. All of the despair on earth, all of the
wars and devastation perpetrated by humankind, are caused
by fear, because when we are living from fear, we cannot live
from Love.

## FEAR'S INSUBSTANTIAL NATURE

Love, on the other hand, is the parent of unity, confidence,
compassion, generosity, honesty, joy, and peace. Its motivation is self-expression. It is the Father-Mother of all that is
good, beautiful, real, and eternal. The "foundation" upon
which fear stands is unreal, illusory, temporal, limited, and
changeable. Fear is fed and nourished by the belief that there
is a power other than, and opposed to, God. All true

Substance–all that is Everlasting, Infinite, and Unchangeable–is of Love. Love knows no other existence but Itself: "Fear not, neither be alarmed....You are my witnesses, that there is no God besides me, and no mighty one whom I do not know."[1]

The Divine creation–that which is real and eternal–is formed out of Life's Self-Contemplation and Self-Realization. What God knows is Truth, and God knows only Good. *What God doesn't know isn't so.* "If God could know evil, then evil would be an eternal reality. But God is sinless and perfect and *nothing can reflect itself in the Divine, save a perfect image.* If God could know sin, He would be a sinner. It is enough to know that this cannot be."[2] There is no other Power, no mighty one, no enemy that exists in Truth to hurt, to harm, or to hate. In Reality there is only God and what God knows. There is only the Perfect Creator and the perfection of creation.

So what are we afraid of? Well, to begin with, it certainly doesn't *look* like there is only God's perfect creation on earth. The world is filled with frightening images that seem real and threatening–personally and universally. The material world is not a fearless place, though some are far more frightened than others. Each of us, however, has fears that we must face and overcome if we are ever to experience the world of God's creation. That is why it is important for us to recognize, uncover, and face our fears. If we don't, our fears will run our life, ruin our happiness, and keep us feeling separate from God and each other. Fear will keep us from loving, risking, reaching out, and connecting with one another. Until we face our fears and resolve them, they will create havoc in our life. "To overcome fear is the greatest adventure of the mind of man."[3]

Some of our fears are easy to spot. They're obvious. They make our heart race and our skin turn cold. They make us scream

out loud. But we also have less conspicuous fears–hidden fears–
that can quietly paralyze us from within. Fear is a fact in our
human experience. It has been said that we are born with two
fears: a fear of loud noises and a fear of falling. It appears that we
take on others from that point–and we've apparently taken on
quite a few. There are so many human fears that they have been
analyzed and categorized into neuroses and phobias. In fact, hundreds of phobias have been classified in minute detail.

Did you know that there are people who have a morbid
fear of blushing or a morbid aversion to red? They have *erythro-
phobia*. Phobias run very narrow and very wide. There is the fear
of open spaces, *agoraphobia*, and of small places, *claustrophobia*.
Phobias cover the alphabet from *acrophobia*, the fear of heights to
*xenophobia*, the fear of strangers and foreigners. You've heard it
said that "The only thing we have to fear is fear itself"? That's
called *phobaphobia*, the fear of being afraid! You may be thinking
that you don't have any abnormal fears. But the question is: is any
fear "normal"? Can you relate to "riskaphobia," "commitmenta-
phobia," or "changeaphobia"?

## "FEAR MUST GO"[4]

The Bible is filled with many "fear not" advisories. Fear is not
Spiritually Normal or Divinely Natural. When we are filled with
fear, we cannot perceive the Ever-Presence of Love that would
guide us to safety. Not only are we not to fear, but in Truth, fear
is *not*. Fear is not a part of the Living Presence. "God is love....
There is no fear in love."[5] Fear is a shadowy illusion created by the
lie that we are separate from the Power of Good. It cannot exist in
the Presence of God, and the Presence of God is everywhere, all
the time. Fear can no more exist in the Presence of Pure Love than

darkness can exist in the Presence of Pure Light. "There is no fear in the Spirit, and there will be none in us when we realize who and what we are."[6] However, on our path to the full realization of "who and what we are," our limited awareness of what is Real and what is not causes us to fear. We can choose to deny it, avoid it, act upon it, or overcome it.

Sometimes we will do anything to keep from feeling afraid. We will avoid people, places, and things that seem threatening to us. In the process, we miss out on loving relationships, job promotions, travel opportunities, and positive changes in our life. *Phobaphobia*–our fear of fear–keeps us from moving forward and upward, and from growing in spirit, mind, and emotion. Most of us want change, but we don't want to feel the fear or anxiety that often accompanies changing. People often say, "I'll change later, when it doesn't scare me or make me uncomfortable." Our fear of fear keeps us doing the same thing the same way even though we may not like the results. Vice President Al Gore said: "If we keep doing what we've always done, we'll keep getting what we've always got!"

WHY FEAR FEAR?

Fear is nothing to be afraid of. In fact, it can be useful if we allow it to be. Fear can be our taskmaster or our teacher. It can overpower us or empower us. Lao-tsu said: "How do I know about the world? By what is within me." The world, individually and collectively, reflects our highest level of trust and our highest level of fear. We can learn a lot about ourselves–what we need to change or challenge in order to improve our lives–by looking at our fears. Where our fears lie is where we believe God is *not* in our life. *Our fears are our belief in the absence of God.* "The fear of lack is nothing more than the belief that God does not, and will not, supply us with whatever we need. The fear of death is the belief that the promises of eternal life may not be true. The fear of loss of health, loss of friends, loss of property–all arise from the belief that God is not all that we claim: Omniscience, Omnipotence, and Omnipresence."[7]

Look at your life to see where you are motivated (or frozen) by fear. This may take some time and true dedication, however, because most of our fearful responses have become habitual. They often feel so natural that either we've ceased to question them or we don't even notice they are there. Many of our reactions have become so automatic that the feeling of fear and our resulting reaction occur so quickly and simultaneously that we don't actually feel the fear anymore *before* we react. For example, we might react negatively or hostilely to something that someone says to us but not realize that our response is based on unconscious fear. We may even wonder later why we reacted the way we did. Yet somewhere within our subconscious mind there is a conditioned fear that corresponds exactly to our reaction. Even though we don't feel our fears, they are there and they are active (and causing our reaction) in our life.

Fear is a powerful pseudo-creator because we experience it with so much feeling and emotion that it deeply impresses our subjective mind. And it is out of the sum total of our subjective feelings and beliefs that our life is molded. The biblical Job said, "The thing which I greatly feared is come upon me, and that which I was afraid of has befallen me."[8] The reason Job experienced "the thing which he greatly feared" is because that is where he placed the most emotion *and* the greatest amount of creative energy. He focused on what he didn't want and created it with his fear. He embodied fear, and the fear took form in his life.

"What is fear? *Nothing more nor less than the negative use of faith*...faith misplaced; a belief in two powers instead of One; a belief that there can be a Power–opposed to God–whose influence and ability *may* bring us evil."[9] That is why we are told to "fear not." Fear is not *inert*. It is creative even though what it creates is not *real* or *everlasting*. It has no power to create, in and of itself. It creates because *we* give it power: The disease we fear *may* come upon us, the person we fear *may* come upon us, the poverty we fear *may* come upon us, the loss of esteem and position we fear *may* come upon us–all because we have used our creative energy *resisting* the thing which we greatly feared. When we *intensely oppose* what we do not want, we feed it with creative energy. We must learn to *focus on* and embrace what we *do* want.

Unresolved fears from the past can turn into anxieties about the future. When our mind is fixed on the past and in fear of the future, we miss the Power and Potential of the present moment altogether. "Because we fail to realize that Principle is not bound by precedent, we limit our faith to that which has already been accomplished, and few 'miracles' result."[10] The Spontaneous Goodness of Spirit is not dependent on historical events–ours or the world's. However, it seems that sometimes we would rather predict a bad result and be right and feel righteous ("I *knew* he wouldn't listen to me!" I *told you* it would end like this!") when it happens than take the time to look at the fears that are creating negative results over and over again in our life.

## LET'S SELF-EXAMINE HERE

When we live in fear and act from fear, we limit our true self-expression which is, owing to our spiritual origin, naturally fearless and confident. Our fears limit how much of Spirit and how much

Good can express through us. It is important for us to ask ourselves: "Where do I hold back in my life: in giving, in sharing, and
in expressing myself? Do I withhold love, forgiveness, understanding, compassion, or honesty from others? Where in my life am I
limited and lacking?" Wherever the answer to these questions
leads, you will find the dark places of your soul where you have
not opened up and allowed the Light of Truth and Love to shine.

Self-examination takes courage. Some of us may have to
dig deep within ourselves to find it and consciously work to activate it, but no one is bereft of courage. Courage by definition, is
"mental or moral strength to venture, persevere, and withstand
danger, fear, or difficulty. Firmness of mind and will in the face of
danger or extreme difficulty."[11] Courage is the bridge between the
spiritual and the material world. Courage is unnecessary in the
Spiritual world because there is nothing to fear and therefore no
fear to overcome. God is Good and the Kingdom of Heaven is
safe. But the journey home to that Kingdom takes courage
because it requires that we open the doors to our mind; and often
what we find behind those doors is darkened rooms that look
very frightening.

"Fear," Ernest Holmes tells us, "is the antithesis of
Faith."[12] Courage, however, is faith in action. In order for us to
face our fears and overcome them, we must have faith in a Truth
beyond the obvious and a Presence beyond the physical. We must
have an abiding trust in the intrinsic Goodness of a Power greater
than we are (and greater than the situation at hand) that is Present
right where we are. "Fear not," we are told, for "lo, I am with you
alway, even unto the end of the world."[13] We can trust that no
matter what illusions we have created through fear, no matter how
frightening the forms of the world may be, there are infinite
possibilities for good that lie beyond the world we have created.

A courageous person is not a fearless person, but rather someone who has not allowed fear to motivate his or her actions. A courageous person is one who has felt fear, been challenged by it, and done whatever was required anyway. Joe Garagiola said: "Bravery is the capacity to perform properly even when scared half to death." We love to hear about acts of courage. We celebrate courage because we all know what it feels like to be afraid. Courageous people don't lie down "for the count"; they don't let fear win over human spirit; and they don't settle for the world's opinion of what they can do and can't do. Courageous people look to a Greater Authority for their self-expression and a Higher Power for their perseverance.

A mind infected with and dominated by fear has no peace. It is filled with an *almost* impenetrable darkness, an obscurity that grows deeper as its fears are ignored or inflamed. But there is always a "light at the end of the tunnel." The Light of Truth that indwells each of us can never be extinguished. As we are courageous enough to walk through the "valley of the shadow" within us, we shall find that the fear we feared soon pales and disappears in the Presence of the Everlasting Love guiding our way. For "there is no fear in the Spirit, and there will be none in us when we realize who and what we are."

*Process Sheet Seventeen*

# Fear Not

### *INDIVIDUAL*

Where do you hold back in your life: in giving, in sharing, and in expressing yourself? Where do you withhold love, forgiveness, understanding, compassion, or honesty with others? Where do you feel limited and lacking? Give careful consideration to the answer, because "wherever the answer to these questions leads, you will find the dark places of your soul where you have not opened up and allowed the Light of Truth and Love to shine."

_____

_____

_____

_____

Write affirmations of Spiritual Truth that will help you to let the Light of Truth and Love shine into those dark places of fear and dissolve them:

_____

_____

_____

### *GROUP*

Discussion of Lesson.

**Activity:** We are empowered by every fear we overcome. This week face one of your fears. Stare it down with the Power of Truth and the Light of Love within you. Our overcoming even a "small" fear will empower us and move us towards facing "larger" ones. Next week share your experience with the group.

**Meditation:** "Fear Not, Neither Be Alarmed"

(*Facilitator: read slowly with restful music in background, if desired. Begin with one of the Relaxation Techniques on pages 299-300.*)
      Imagine, now, that you are walking along a dark path lined with tall trees on both sides...you can barely make out the shape of the trunks of the trees because of the darkness, and the upper branches and leaves disappear into blackness...although you know that there are more trees beyond those lining your path, all that you can see is unilluminated, pitch-black darkness...there is a chill in the air and sounds of movement among the trees... you begin to feel afraid, but as you do, you hear these peaceful words floating on a gentle breeze: "Fear not, neither be alarmed... for I am with you always...there is no God besides me, and no mighty one whom I do not know"...all at once you feel peaceful...and loved...certain that no matter how dark the path may be, you are safe...there is nothing to fear, nothing that can harm you, because there is a Great Power with you...and no other power around you at all...you have faith in that unseen Power... and that which is seen no longer frightens you...just up ahead, however, as the path becomes narrower, lies your greatest fear...it is time for you to face your fear knowing that there is a Great Power with you and that what is seen has no power at all...walk forward...and face your fear knowing that even though you may walk in the Valley of the *Shadow* of death, Spirit is with you, and the Presence of Spirit empowers you...and also know that on the other side of your fear is your freedom....(*Facilitator: allow three or four minutes*)...now, take in a few deep breaths...become more and more relaxed...feeling the Presence of Peace with every breath...come back into your body...back into the room...

open your eyes, and silently write about your experience.
(*If time permits, share with partners.*)

1. Isaiah 44:8 (Lamsa).    2. SOM  467:2.    3. SOM 404:4.    4. SOM 272:2.
5. 1 John 4:16, 18 (Lamsa).    6. SOM  485:1.    7. SOM 156:3.    8. Job 3:25 (Lamsa).
9. SOM 156:4.    10. SOM 162:3.    11. *Webster's New Collegiate Dictionary*, G. & C. Merriam , 1977.
12. SOM 593:5.    13. Matthew 28:20  (KJV).

# 18　So, Who's Stopping You?

## Getting Rid of the Excuses That Block Our Success

*There are those who
believe that there is a
waiting-line somewhere
on the astral plane for beings
"desiring" or "requiring"
earthly incarnations.*
They loiter there, according to
theory, because there are only a limited number of human
incarnations allowed on the planet at one time. The "disem-
bodied" have to wait in line for "available space." No one
can say for sure whether this conjecture is accurate; but if it
is, you may have been waiting centuries (of earthly time) for
your turn on the planet. However, whether you waited a
long time for planetary life or God just popped you into
existence, what is certain is that it's *your turn* now! You are
here! And, if you are not living a life worth waiting for; if
you have a lot of plans for one, but you haven't gotten
beyond the planning stage, the question is: "So, who's stopping you?"

"Today is the first day of the rest of your life" is a
wonderful concept. It allows us to see that each day is a fresh
start, a brand new opportunity for success. The past has been
rolled up behind us like a long carpet, and we are on the
threshold of creating our life anew. It is inspiring and ener-
gizing! But...it can also give us a reason to put things off. If
we look at today as the first day of the rest of our life, we can
also look at today as the beginning of a long time ahead in
which we can *think* about what we're *going* to do without
actually doing it. We have time to procrastinate: "I'll get

around to my spiritual quest when I'm not so busy with worldly interests, obligations, and responsibilities." A young woman I know has spiritual procrastination down to a fine art. She believes so thoroughly in *reincarnation* that she has relegated her focus on her spiritual growth issues to a future lifetime!

It is true that we have "all the time in the world" to get around to what we need to get around to, but it is important for us to remember that the time in *this* world is limited. The Greek Philosopher Epictetus wrote: "Do you know that death must needs overtake us, no matter what we are doing? What do you wish to be doing when it overtakes you? If you have anything better to be doing when you are so overtaken, get to work on that."

## WHY WE'RE HERE–NOW

Did you really wait for earthly life just so that you could collect earthly things? Did you come through the discomfort of the birth canal merely to get comfortable here? Or did you come to the planet to discover the magnificence of yourself and your potential, to learn to love what you discover within, and to share that love with others? "The aim of evolution is to produce a man who, at the objective point of his own self-determination, may completely manifest the inner life of the Spirit"[1] If we have come together to learn our inseparable oneness with each other and with Life Itself, we had better get busy, because the process of taking down the walls we've built up over the years to separate ourselves from God and humankind could take some time. If we don't get started now, we shall open our eyes one day, sooner or later, and see that our time here on the planet is up. We may find that we have barely begun getting "it" together before it's time to leave!

David wrote in a psalm, "This is the day which the Lord has made; we will rejoice and be glad in it."[2] Does your day look like something the *Lord made* or more like something the *dog did* ? Are your days filled with enthusiasm and joy–or burden and necessity? If you lived each day as if it were your last on earth, would your life look differently than it does right now?

We all know people who incessantly talk about what they are *going* to do "one of these days," while they are in the midst of complaining about the situation they are currently in: they are going to tell their boss exactly what they think, ask for that raise, or quit that job. As they complain about their relationship, they talk about how they are *going* to leave that "jerk," or stand up for themselves and ask for what they want. While you listen to all their complaining and their apparent knowledge of the solutions to their problems–conclusions they are doing nothing about– haven't you either thought to yourself or actually said out loud, "*So, who's stopping you?*"

Sometimes we live our life like Scarlett O'Hara in the movie *Gone With the Wind*: "Oh fiddle-dee-dee. After all, tomorrow is another day." But whether or not we accomplish what we came to the planet to accomplish, the attitude of the physical world is more like Rhett Butler: "Frankly, my dear, I don't give a damn." What we do here is up to us. Nobody is going to do our life for us. *We must WAKE UP if we want to live the life of our dreams.* "Live" is a verb. It isn't enough for us to merely dream of worthy accomplishments; we must wake up and *do* them. If every- one has the spiritual potential to do whatever they choose to do, who's stopping you?

Can you imagine yourself doing what you truly want to do without hesitation or excuses? "The Truth is God, and God is free, happy, peaceful and ever poised in His own Being....I *must be like God, if I wish to realize His Spirit in my life!"* [3] When God said, "Let there be light," do you think that He looked around to see if anyone would mind? We all have reasons and excuses for not doing whatever it is we want to do. But no matter how the reasons and excuses are phrased, the answer to "Who's stopping you?" of course, is YOU.

We can blame others and circumstances–past and present–for our not doing what we desire to do and for our *not* creating and *not* living the life of our dreams. However, nothing and no one can hold us back or keep us down, but we, ourselves. *We* are the ones who draw the boundaries around our infinite potential. We create what we perceive as a safety zone, a space of comfort, and we are afraid to go beyond the boundaries we've drawn. We start believing that the limitations we have set for ourselves, and the boundary lines we have drawn, have something to do with the Divine Picture of who we are. But they haven't.

## "THERE IS NOTHING BUT SPIRIT IN THE UNIVERSE" [4]

God is all there is. To be like God and to realize His Spirit in our Life is to know that there is no opposition to our good. God has no one to blame, for there is nothing outside of the Infinite. "It is Undivided, Complete and Perfect within Itself, having no opposites and no opposition. It knows only Its own ability and since It is ALL, It cannot be hindered in any way, shape or manner." [5] In order for us to be Godlike, we must cease blaming anyone or anything in the "outer" world for our inner fears. Once we take ownership of our fears–no matter who encouraged our fears in the first place–once they belong to us, once we take responsibility for them, we are free to do whatever we want with them–including healing them.

If something seems to be stopping us from moving forward from where we are to where we want to be, it is important for us to ask ourselves what we are afraid of: "What fear is keeping me from doing what I want to do?" It is vital for us to identify the underlying fear that is the origin of our excuses. Many of our excuses can be traced back to our fear of not being good enough to have what we want, of losing what we already have, or of not being accepted by others.

Sometimes, no matter how limiting, unsatisfying, or downright miserable our circumstances may be, we are afraid to risk what we have for what we want. We may want to leave our boring, uncreative, or miserable job–but the insurance benefits are so good. Perhaps we would be willing to leave that unhappy, unloving relationship–if we hadn't just taken out that second mortgage or we weren't afraid that we'd be lonely. Maybe we would pursue a relationship with that one who "looks interesting"–if we weren't afraid of being rejected or failing. We invest in our own misery, and we profit in pain.

We are the ones who are stopping ourselves from being happy and living a life that we truly enjoy. "Our belief sets the limit to our demonstration of a Principle which, of Itself, is without limit."[6] Even if it looks like someone else is holding us back or causing our suffering, we are the one who is giving that person power over our life. No one can stop us unless we put on our brakes when they put up the sign. Are we willing to allow mediocrity or misery to stop us from experiencing "the Great Unknown" just because we are more familiar with downhill skids than upward spirals?!

Excuses keep us hanging onto limitation. If we never stretch, we won't know how far we can truly reach. Robert

Browning wrote: "Man's reach should exceed his grasp." Our potential is unlimited, but if we never cross our own barriers, we may simply go around in circles. When we reach out into the Unknown, we have to reach inside ourselves for courage and strength to trust in that which we cannot see and have never experienced. When we are willing to move beyond our safety zone and beyond our self-made boundaries, we are affirming that there is something to the Unknown and that there is simply not a Great Abyss waiting to swallow us up just beyond our realm of experience. "Declare your freedom. Know that no matter what others may say, think or do, *you are a success now*, and nothing can hinder you from accomplishing your good."[7]

A young woman told me that she'd rather be treated badly in a relationship than be lonely (as if those were her only two choices). We must declare our freedom to be happy and trust that if we are willing to fling ourselves into Unknown territory, we shall find our true home.

## "THE SPIRIT KNOWS NO PAST"[8]

Fear keeps our mind stuck in the past because we're afraid of repeating past mistakes, or it keeps our mind in the future because we are worried about future consequences. Fear keeps us from experiencing the Presence and from knowing our true nature within God. The Power and potential of the Spirit within us exist in the Present. "Principle is not bound by precedent." No matter what has happened to us in the past, it has nothing to do with the potential of the moment we're in or the possibilities of the future. It's been said that the only advantage to living in the past is that it was cheaper! We can begin anew every moment because what we are capable of being and doing as the expression of Divine Spirit has nothing to do with what we have ever been or done before.

The past cannot stop us. Yet, often our excuse for not doing what we want to do is that we tried to do it before and it didn't work. Most of us know by now that Thomas Edison tried to invent the light bulb 10,000 times and when asked after the 5000th try how it felt to have failed so many times, he replied that he hadn't failed at all. He'd discovered 5000 ways how *not* to make a light bulb. So maybe we've discovered almost that many ways how *not* to have a happy relationship. Maybe we know a lot of ways *not* to lose weight, or *not* to have a fulfilling job, or *not* to be prosperous. But, *there is a way* to what we *do* want, and that way is within each of us. We must trust that there is a Divine Plan with our joy and happiness in Mind.

When we're not afraid to fail big, we open up our life to succeeding greatly. The biggest failures may come when we put ourselves out there, but the greatest rewards do too. There are people who seem to have very little talent in the direction they are headed, but they still put themselves out there in life. They aren't letting anything stop them. *The Book of Heroic Failures* tells of an explorer with no sense of direction whatsoever who was perpetually lost. His colleagues had to light fires at night so he could find his way back to the camp.

We really cannot fail in life, anyway. It isn't a pass/fail proposition. When we win in what we attempt, we win. And when we lose, we learn. There can never be a true "downhill skid," because we can never "go back" to anything as the same person we were. "The spiral of life is upward. Evolution carries us forward, not backward."[9]

## FEAR OF FLYING

It takes courage to take our turn in life, especially when those around us think that we should be going in another direction. We can seek insight from the experience of others, we can get pointers from those who are moving forward; but it is God's Expectation that we must live up to. We must be willing to lose the respect of others, their friendship, even their love. But we might find that if we could look through the eyes of those who would attempt to control and manipulate what we do, many of those we've been trying to please are a lot more near-sighted than we are! We must be willing to give up the lesser for the greater. We must be willing to let go of our foothold on earth if we want to soar in the heavens.

## THE BOOK OF ME

Often what stops us from making a change and from taking a step forward is that we want to know how everything is going to turn out before we BEGIN—before we even take the first step. Do we want to know how a novel ends before we begin to read it? Probably not. We read a book for the joy of the adventure as we go. Good fiction, especially a good mystery, keeps us on the edge of our seats, totally focused on the scene at hand, eager to turn the page, but unwilling to rush through it for fear of missing key passages that may be a clue to solving the mystery.

Our life is a mystery, too. It is only by our living it fully moment to moment, focused on the scene at hand, that we discover the clues, the keys to the mystery. We don't want to put a good mystery down. I have often read into the wee hours of the morning unable to put down a good book. I'll say to myself, "Okay, one more hour, and then I'll go to sleep"; and after that hour goes by, I'll usually bargain with myself for another. We may want to ask of our life, "Is the story I'm writing about *me* exciting and interesting enough to keep me up all night, or is it so boring that I keep nodding off?" Life is an adventure, and many of us don't even have our suitcases packed!

There may be people who don't want you to write your true life story–the one that you know is inside you. They may want you to write a biography and be someone else. Are you willing to compromise your spiritual self-discovery in order to write about someone else's dreams and successes? As you live each day, you are in the process of writing "the novel of a lifetime"– your lifetime. You have been given "Creative Freedom" to write whatever you choose. You can create fascinating characters, luxurious scenery, and action-packed adventure. You can write a classic that enriches the world as well as your own life. You can create a wonderful chapter, today. And...no one can stop you!

## *Process Sheet Eighteen*

# So, Who's Stopping You?

*INDIVIDUAL*

"We can blame others and circumstances–past and present–for our *not* doing what we desire to do, and for our *not* creating and not living the life of our dreams." Who or what circumstances have you been allowing to stop you from creating and living the life of your dreams?

_____

_____

_____

_____

Once we take ownership of our fears–no matter who encouraged our fears in the first place–once they belong to us, and we take responsibility for them, we are free to do whatever we want with them, including healing them. God is all there is. To be like God, and to realize His Spirit in our Life, is to know that there is no opposition to our good. Write affirmations that assist you to knowing that there is no opposition, nothing to stop you from doing whatever you desire or from creating and living the life of your dreams. (Example: "*Because I am the unlimited and free child of God, there is no opposition to my good, and I am creating and living the life of my dreams*" or "*No one and nothing can stop me from being all that I am created by Spirit to be!*")

_____

_____

_____

_____

## *GROUP*
Discussion of Lesson.

**Activity:** (*Materials: red and green construction paper. If none is available white paper will do. Black crayons or marking pens. If using white paper, use red and green crayons.*)

Each member of the group cuts hexagonal shapes out of red construction paper (or white paper for use with red crayon). On one side of the hexagon write the word *Stop* and whatever it is that you desire to do or create in your life that you believe that you cannot do. On the other side write the name of the person, or a description of the circumstance, that you believe is stopping you. Make one for each area of your life where you believe you are being prevented from moving forward. Then do the following guided meditation:

**Meditation:** You've Got to Go Where You Want to Go and Do What You Want to Do

(*Facilitator: read slowly with restful music in background, if desired. Begin with one of the Relaxation Techniques on pages 299-300.*)

Imagine now that you are driving on a paved road...you are sitting in the driver's seat of a luxury vehicle...perhaps it is a car...but perhaps it is something more futuristic than an automobile...whatever it is, *you* are in the driver's seat...your destination is up to you...up ahead of you is an intersection with roads leading out in all directions from it...as you reach the intersection you notice that at the beginning of every road there is a stop sign... it appears that you cannot go forward in any direction...but you know the Truth...you know that you are a child of Spirit...free to travel the roads of Life without opposition...remind yourself now of your spiritual freedom...say within yourself, "I am a beautiful, creative spiritual being...my life is unlimited and boundless... there are no conditions placed upon me to limit my self-expression...the Power within me which is the Spirit of the Universe expressing as me moves me unimpeded in the direction I choose to go...there is no opposition to my good...no one and no thing to stop me, for my full self-expression enriches the world around me...it is good for me to move forward into fuller self-expression...I am ready...I am willing...I can create and live the life of my dreams"...and suddenly a municipal vehicle pulls along side of you...it is a truck painted iridescent gold, and written on its doors are the words "Universal City"...the truck pulls ahead of you, and where every Stop sign is the workers, dressed in white robes, replace them with green lights...so that everywhere you look...at the beginning of every road...there is a green light...the roads ahead of you are clear and you are free to move forward...there is nothing stopping you...as you begin to move ahead, drive yourself back into the room...when you open your eyes, take a piece of green construction paper and cut out a circle for each area of your life in which you now feel free to "go for it"...write the word *Go* on the green circle creating a green light, and also write on it what you plan to create now that you know nothing can stop you... open your eyes.

(*When they leave, the group members should be advised to drop their Stop signs in the wastebasket, and take their Go lights home to paste on their mirrors, refrigerators, etc.*)

1. SOM 338:2   2. Psalms 118:24 (Lamsa).   3. SOM 446:4.   4. SOM 209:5.   5. SOM 82:1.
6. SOM 37:4.   7. SOM 302:2.   8. SOM 245:4.   9. SOM 387:1.

# Mental Floss

Removing the Negative Beliefs That Undermine Our Good

*Dentists tell us that it is not only important but imperative that we floss our teeth every day if we are to have a healthy mouth.* Along that same line, if we are to have a healthy mind, it is imperative that we clear away any unnecessary and harmful thoughts we may have accumulated during the course of the day. We could say that we need to "mental floss" daily for *comprehensive* hygiene! To mental floss is to use affirmative, spiritual threads of thought to remove embedded beliefs that can lead to decaying attitudes and loss of self-worth in our lives.

Mental flossing, like dental flossing, has long-term, preventative effects. Most of us brush our teeth, but how many of us take the time to floss as well, even though we have been told by tooth experts that it is vital? Even though we know that we really *ought* to floss, when it comes right down to it, we are often in too much of a hurry to take the time for it, especially when it *seems* that we can get away with just brushing. Flossing, both mental and dental, takes time.

Today, we live in a "hurry-up" world. It used to be that we were content with getting things ASAP, but now we want them yesterday. We can get our glasses and photos done in an hour, and our printing and oatmeal instantly. Most things can be done "while you wait"; but then, who has time to wait?! We rush through our fast-food and speed on our expressways.

We are in such a hurry to *do* that we forget to *be*. English poet and essayist Austin Dobson wrote: "Time goes, you say? Ah no! Alas, Time stays, we go." We all have a lot to do and a lot to learn before we go. If we don't use our time on the planet wisely, we shall be gone before we know it; and, if we don't mental floss daily, we shall rot and decay along the way.

It isn't just that we're too busy to mental floss. Sometimes we're too lazy as well. Mental flossing, like dental flossing, takes effort on our part. Why floss our teeth since we can't see plaque, anyway? As long as our mouth tastes nice and minty, why concern ourselves with the unseen enemy that may be busy undermining our efforts and attacking our gums, and which will, over time, create some very devastating problems?

The same lackadaisical attitude is often applied to our mental hygiene. Most of our destructive beliefs are hidden beneath the observation of our conscious mind in the subjective or subconscious aspect of our thinking process. It is much easier for us to pretend that they don't exist until some devastating problem comes up and we have to look at our thinking. Let's face it: sometimes we'd rather vegetate than meditate! We need to ask: "Am I a spiritual couch potato?" "Am I sitting around waiting for Enlightenment to somehow dawn upon me without my active participation?" "Do I choose to remain ignorant of who I truly am until who I believe I am becomes a problem?"

When I was a little girl, once a year a dentist from the community would bring to our school a huge, plastic replica of human teeth and gums. He would use a giant toothbrush to show us the proper way to brush our teeth. The artificial teeth and gums were so shiny, I couldn't wait to get home to brush my own teeth so they'd look like the big plastic ones. In those days, the dentist never mentioned flossing. He told us that if we just brushed our teeth "properly," we would be able to rush home after a dental checkup and shout, "Look, mom: no cavities!" for the rest of our life. Today, however, almost all dentists will tell us that "brushing alone isn't enough." Merely brushing our teeth doesn't get rid of the hidden plaque that can cause tooth decay and gum disease (dreaded gingivitis!) which in turn can result in the loss of our teeth–the loss of the very things we've been polishing all our life.

## WE MUST PENETRATE THE SURFACE

When we were growing up, perhaps no one told us the importance of mental flossing, either. We weren't told how to think properly and that positive thoughts running through our consciousness have the power to prevent future problems. We weren't told how important it is for us to examine our life, to take the time and make the effort to floss our mind to remove the tacky, limited, and negative beliefs that can create devastating problems for us over time. In fact, most of us probably got the impression that if things looked good on the surface, we wouldn't have any problems. We weren't told about the unseen enemy, our unhealthy beliefs and the limited thinking that often go unnoticed in our subconscious. Perhaps, we were not informed that such thoughts could undermine the good we desire and keep our natural spiritual beauty from expressing in a healthy way in our life.

"So we learn to go deeply within ourselves, and speak as though there were a Presence there that knows; and we should take the time to unearth this hidden cause, to penetrate this inner chamber of consciousness."[1] We live in a sea of Perfect Life, and we should take time to understand and sense this within our consciousness. We must rid ourselves of rotten beliefs, the negative "contemplative plaque" that builds upon our erroneous concepts. It is those unchecked thoughts that undermine our efforts for true self-expression and spiritual growth and create decay and loss in our life–the loss of the very things we care about.

Often we treat our mind the same way we treat our mouth. We do some surface work like brushing up our positive attitude with a few affirmative thoughts. We don't take the time to notice the deeper crevices of our mind or to examine the habitual beliefs that may be creating havoc by breaking down the inherently perfect foundation of our life. Just as there is a possibility of our losing our teeth if we don't use dental floss, when we don't use mental floss there is a possibility that we may lose our dreams, because they cannot stay rooted in the unhealthy terrain of our belief system.

Our thoughts are active whether we are busy or lazy, just as plaque germs are active no matter what we're doing. We must take the time to allow the threads of Love to move across our mind and clean out every unloving and conflicting thought, because if we don't take the time or exert the effort, eventually we may experience some pretty devastating results in our world. "The one who wishes scientifically to work out his problems must daily take the time to meditate and mentally treat the condition, no matter what the apparent contradictions may be."[2]

## "BUT ONE THING IS MORE IMPORTANT"[3]

There was a song in the Sixties that began: "Slow down, you're movin' too fast." It's a good suggestion for all of us. We fool ourselves if we think that we are *really* doing something just because we are *doing* something. If we are not about our Father's business;

if we are not about expressing love, peace, joy, compassion, and abundant good; if we are not about spiritual self-expression, and discovering our true potential; then whatever we are doing is about nothing at all. We are just going through the motions of life without a true connection with Life.

We can put together a million-dollar deal, make our quota in sales, bring home twenty extra hours of overtime, but if we have not taken the time to experience the Presence of the life within us, if we have not taken a moment to consciously quiet our mind and listen to the Inner Voice of Spirit, if we have not allowed Wisdom and Love to motivate our activities, we haven't enriched our life by all of our doing. The true Spirit of Life cannot shine through a mind that is coated with layers of fear and material dependency.

We will never simply "find" the time for anything we want to do. *If we want time, we must make it,* the way we make everything else–through our thinking. If we think there is "never enough time" to meditate or quietly ponder the "meaning" of life, then there never will be enough time. We'll fill up our day with other, "more important," activities. We'll get side-tracked by the tug of worldly obligations. We'll let ourselves be pulled in so many directions that the very meaning and purpose of our existence will get lost in the shuffle. How can we hope to *seize the day* if it already has a death grip on us? Spirit whispers every moment for us to *slow down because we're movin' too fast* to catch a glimpse of who we truly are. God beckons us to "come to the garden, alone" and walk and talk with Him. And what is our response? "Love to, when I have the time."

There is a saying: "If you don't have time to do it right, when will you have time to do it over?" If we don't have the time to examine our life and our thinking *now,* when shall we have time to deal with the results of the build-up of beliefs, values, and attitudes within us that are undermining our good? "*The time is now; the place is where we are, and it is done unto us as we believe.*"[4] None of us wants to lose our teeth, yet are we doing everything possible *right now* to prevent it? None of us wants to create negative experiences in our life, but are we doing anything about our thinking *right now* to prevent it? Just as plaque germs continue their activity in our teeth and gums until they are removed, our beliefs continue their activity in our life until they are removed.

Does your list of daily activities include affirmative prayer and meditation? Sitting down and cleaning out the little, limited particles of thought that have stuck in your mind? Are you so busy with all the things that you think *must* get done that you can't seem to get "Turn to God" checked off your list? Did you come to the planet to get a job and build an empire, or did you come to *catch the Spirit* and build your consciousness?

## WHAT ARE YOU CHEWING ON?

Poet Grenville Kleiser wrote: "Give your mind positive thoughts to chew on. To think constructively, examine your daily thought habits. It is in your power to choose the thoughts that are to govern your life. Right thinking will lead you to true knowledge." Dentists tell us that *every time* we eat, we are supposed to brush and floss. The same is true in the mental realm. Every time we take in an idea or concept, it is important for us to "chew on the positive," absorb what is good for us, and consciously remove what is not. We can't get away with "just brushing." It is not enough for us merely to brush aside those negative or limited thoughts that we don't want to think about, because the harmful particles are still there. We need to dig in with the silken floss of

Spirit every day–and many times throughout the day–running the thread of Truth across our mind, removing through treatment, affirmation, and meditation all that is not serving our spirituality. "We should come daily to the Spirit of Goodness for a complete washing away of all mistakes, fears and troubles."[5]

Shall we require a mandatory stoppage in our life so that we shall finally take the time for God? Do we want to live by default and let our experiences *force* us to look within by bringing our life to a screeching halt through some catastrophic illness or devastating experience? We can wait for our negative thoughts to build up and create pain and disease, or we can take the time daily to clean up our act. We can choose to come daily to the Spirit of Goodness for a complete washing.

If we think about it, all we need to do for our teeth is keep them clean and let them be, because they are innately healthy and beautiful. The same is true of our mind. We don't have to do anything to our consciousness except to keep it clean–free from cumulative harmful beliefs–because it is naturally healthy and beautiful. We are the offspring of a Perfect Creator, the expression of a Magnificent, Awesome Spirit. We could say that each of us is like *a radiant smile of God.* If we could see ourselves that way for just one moment, we'd never again forget to use mental floss!

## *Process Sheet Nineteen*

# Mental Floss

### *INDIVIDUAL*

Often, if we write down positive statements about ourselves and life, hidden beliefs may surface, just as particles of food are loosened by brushing. Then, when the belief appears, the mental floss to use is another affirmation to rid ourselves of the negative beliefs.

Write a positive, personal statement for each of the following: money, health, relationships, self-worth.

_____

_____

_____

_____

_____

Did a hidden belief come up as you wrote the above statements? If so, use a little mental floss and another affirmation to remove it:

_____

_____

_____

_____

_____

### *GROUP*
Discussion of Lesson.

**Activity:** (*Materials: chalk board or dry erase board or large sheet of paper; chalk or marking pens; paper and pens/pencils.*)

Each member of the group is given a piece of paper and a pen or pencil. The facilitator writes on the board or large sheet of paper a list of words, such as *Mother, Father, Child, Church, Spirit, Jesus, Christ, Family, Prosperity, Body, Mind, Home, Heaven, Earth.* Everyone in the group writes down their first response to those words. Share responses in group or with a partner. Purpose: Hidden beliefs may be revealed, discussed, and an affirmation can be written for each belief to assist in eliminating it.

**Meditation:** Flossing Our Mind with Threads of Truth

*(Facilitator: read slowly with restful music in background, if desired. Begin with one of the Relaxation Techniques on pages 299-300.)*
    You live in a sea of Perfect Life...you exist in an atmosphere of Health and Wholeness...there is nothing you need to do to make this happen...It simply is...you simply are...complete and perfect...all that is required of you is to remove false concepts from your consciousness...beliefs about yourself and others that do not support or affirm the Perfection of Life in which you exist...imagine now that you are holding a long golden thread with both of your hands...the thread is so iridescent that it looks as if you were holding a thread of light...now take the thread and mentally move it back and forth in your mind...see it removing false ideas...eliminating negative concepts...ridding your mind of beliefs about lack and limitation...be very thorough in this cleansing process...for when the lies are removed, all that is left is the Truth...the Truth of your Perfection...the Truth of the Perfection of all Life within you...*(Facilitator: allow two to three minutes)*... now feel your health and wholeness...it is as if the whole Universe were smiling at you from within...and as if you were smiling back...now feel yourself back in the room...still feeling the joy of pure health and

wholeness...perfect life within and around you...now open your eyes, look around the room, and give the group a big, beautiful smile.

1. SOM 153:3.   2. SOM 57:4.   3. Luke 10:42 (Lamsa).   4. SOM 151:4.   5. SOM 502:1.

# 20 **Can You Relate?**

*When someone tells
us how they feel about
a particular situation,
and they want to know
if we understand how
they feel or what they
have gone through,*
they might say to us after telling
their story: "Can you relate?" And if we wanted to convey
to that person that we too have felt what they are feeling or
that we also might have acted in the same way they did
under the same circumstances, we might answer, "Yes, I can
relate." When we relate to something, it's because whatever
it is strikes a "familiar chord" within us. It is something that
we can *imagine,* an *inner concept* that is not first dependent
on outer confirmation, a sense that *preexists* in our awareness
before it occurs in the world, an inner chord of recognition
that *resonates* to the outer event.

The reverse situation can also happen to us: someone may tell us about something and we may think to
ourselves, or say out loud, "I just can't relate to that." That
is, we can't get a feeling for, or an understanding of, what
that person is saying to us. When we don't "relate" to something, it's because we haven't an inner sense of its meaning.
We can't *imagine* it, or we don't *resonate* to it.

The choices we make in our life (when we are being
honest about how we feel) are choices based upon that to
which we relate. Our likes and dislikes in food, clothing,
people, and every other area of our life have to do with what

we resonate to–what *feels* right and what *doesn't feel* right for us. There is, however, a distinction between what "feels right to us" and what "is good for us." Sometimes we don't resonate to experiences that are good for us. We relate to outer experiences that symbolize and reflect the ideas we hold as true about ourselves, positive and negative. So what we resonate to may not bring us the joy and fulfillment we desire if we are not loving ourselves or if we are feeling unworthy. Our feelings are drawn from, and dwell in, our subconscious state, and we are not always conscious of what our feelings mean. For instance, a woman who is in an unloving or abusive relationship may have resonated to that relationship because of unconscious beliefs about her unworthiness to be loved. She may believe that she honestly loves the one who abuses her because she has an emotional response to that person. But what she may actually be feeling is her own inner chord of recognition and familiarity that she doesn't deserve any better. Her unconscious embodiment of the idea of her unworthiness is merely resonating to the outer experience of someone who does not love her. It may *not* feel "good" to her, but it *does* feel "right."

EMBODIMENT

The concept of embodiment is an important one for us to understand. When we embody an idea, we *internalize* it. We give it meaning in our mind by shaping the idea into a mental form or image. We create a mental equivalent within us. For example, more than likely all of us have embodied the idea of an apple–which means that when we hear the word *apple*, read about an apple, or think of an apple, we have a mental image of what an apple is. We have a picture in mind. We can relate to it. On the other hand, someone unfamiliar with the vegetation in Hawaii would probably not have a mental equivalent for a *kukui nut* or *breadfruit*. If that person heard those words or read them, they could not relate to them because they would have no mental concept or picture of what they were.

## THE MENTAL EQUIVALENT

We cannot experience anything for which we have no mental equivalent. "The Law is Infinite and Perfect but in order to make a demonstration WE MUST HAVE A MENTAL EQUIVALENT OF THE THING WE DESIRE."[1] In order for us to make a personal demonstration of the thing we desire, we must not only maintain a mental equivalent within us of what we desire, but we must be able to *relate* to that mental image as *belonging* to us. For instance, if we don't have a mental equivalent for success and prosperity that we take "personally," we cannot experience success and prosperity for ourselves no matter how much we desire to do so.

We may be able to see the forms of success and prosperity that others are experiencing, but unless we can imagine ourselves as *capable and worthy* of such an experience, our mental equivalent for success and prosperity will contain a "Belongs to Others" clause. We need to equate ourselves with abundant livingness, see it as a natural part of who we are, and visualize and imagine ourselves as financially free. We must not only be able to conceptualize *what* success and prosperity mean, but also give them *personal definition*. Unless we can see it for ourselves, the Creative Process within us cannot create the outer life we desire for ourselves.

## "WHAT WE DRAW FROM IT WE MUST DRAW THROUGH THE CHANNEL OF OUR OWN MINDS"[2]

Each of us has a mental equivalent for everything that we perceive as "reality" even though most of our mental images remain "unconscious" to us until we "consciously" call upon them. But it is important to understand that even though we may not consciously remember every one of our personal mental equivalents, we still "draw" from the Creative Medium the mental images we have about life.

We cannot actually recognize anything in the outer world unless we *first* identify it within our mind. That is why some things in the world–such as loving relationships, job opportunities, social solutions, labor-saving inventions, etc.–are more "obvious" to some than to others. Have you ever said to someone, "Why didn't you do (whatever) when the solution was so apparent!?" What is evident to one person may be a total mystery to another. Just because we presume that we have an answer for someone else's situation based on the mental equivalents of our world view, we cannot assume that a person is lazy, indolent, or indifferent because they have not resolved their problem.

In order for an individual to reach beyond a ghetto, to move out of an abusive relationship, to strive for more than a mediocre or mundane existence, he or she must have a mental equivalent–a personal concept–of something greater than his or her current experience. "We cannot demonstrate beyond our ability to provide a mental equivalent of our desire."[3]

## WE ARE OUR MENTAL EQUIVALENTS

Our mental equivalents are our inner level of understanding and perception of what life is and how our life can be. At this very moment you have within you–contained and maintained within your subconscious mind–thousands, even hundreds of thousands of thoughts, which are your individual mental equivalents of life: close your eyes and visualize a beautiful house; see yourself dressed the way you feel the best; imagine a "perfect" day in which you are doing what you enjoy doing; and visualize that "special" someone with you. (Before reading on, take a moment to do this visualization.) Each individual will have a different mental equivalent for each of the things listed above. The house you imagined may have been a rose-covered cottage in the country, a condo in the city, or a mansion on the beach. The "perfect" day and activity, and the manner of dress you chose, would differ from someone else's choices according to your mental equivalent of perfection. And the one you visualized being with may have been a lover, a friend, a child, or a parent. (Unless you are into self-abuse and you visualized being with someone you don't like!)

We cannot experience a life beyond our mental ability to relate to the life we desire. Unless we can make our dreams mentally palpable, and until we experience our thoughts as "tangibly" real, we shall go on talking about a life that we shall never give birth to within us or experience in the world. Our mental equivalents become the forms which are acted upon by Universal Creative Energy. The flow of Life through us must take the form we give to it. If we want a particular something in our life, we must have an equivalent of it *first* within our mind. We must *know* before we *see*.

## ANATOMY OF A MENTAL EQUIVALENT

A mental equivalent is more than just a mind picture. Its shape is held together by our feelings and emotions. A mental equivalent is visualization *plus* our acceptance in mind and emotion. That is why some of our visualizations don't "actualize" or take form in our life. We might be *thinking* about a wonderful relationship, but our *emotions* hold our mental equivalent—the "shape" of relationship within us—in the form of a broken heart. Then, rather than drawing to us the loving relationship we desire, we continue to experience loneliness or unloving alliances.

Perhaps we desire expanded prosperity but we are forcing the grandeur of the Creative Medium to squeeze through our mental form of unworthiness. We may want more Life, but more Life can't get through our limited mental equivalents. We repel what we desire because it can't fit into the smallness of our self-image and our restricted ideas about life.

"A demonstration...is born out of a mental concept. The mind is the fashioning factor, and according to its range, vision and positiveness, will be the circumstance or experience."[4] The Creative Medium which brings subjective thought into objective life is Limitless. The possibilities of our experience rest solely in our resonance to, and embodiment of, the ideas we desire experienced.

It makes no difference how other people see us. We can experience only the mental equivalent we hold of ourselves. Has someone bought you a gift and said: "I saw this and I knew it was you!" Maybe it was; but then again, perhaps you thought to yourself, "That's not me." Often, our self-image is hidden from others under layers of self-denial and a desire to please others. Self-denial multiplies upon itself so that without our noticing it, we can bury the self we truly desire to express and present a total stranger to the world.

A friend of mine was recently given a lovely necklace of amber stones with a matching set of earrings that another friend had brought back from Russia. The ensemble was striking, and since my friend had worn large, beaded necklaces for the six years I had known her, I commented that the gift was certainly, "her." She replied, "I cannot stand big necklaces, beads, stones, or pearls!" I was surprised and asked her why she wore them all the time. She told me that years ago a close friend had given her a large, beaded necklace. Because she felt great affection for her friend, and would have felt guilty not wearing the gift, she wore the necklace even though she felt uncomfortable wearing such a large piece of jewelry on her rather small-framed body. Because the necklace was so noticeable on her petit form, those around her began to have a mental image of her as a person who wears big jewelry. Year after year on her birthday, at Christmas, and on other special occasions, her friends bestowed upon her gifts of large necklaces. She told me that guilt became her "accessorizer," and that she hadn't dressed like "herself" in years!

## WHEN IT'S TIME FOR A CHANGE OF MIND

Our mental images of others, ourselves, and life are not always accurate and are almost always limited. When our limited mental equivalents restrict our experience of the Greater Good, it is time for us to change our mind. "The Eternal Gift is always made.... *it must be measured out to us according to our own measuring.*"[5] If we believe a little, we receive only a little. This is the Law of Mental Equivalents.

If we don't like what we are experiencing, we need to

change our mental equivalent, expand our mind, and reshape its forms. We must begin right where we are in consciousness. We may not be able to imagine—in mind *and* emotion—a million dollars, but we can begin to free ourselves, day by day, of the mental image of financial burden and limitation. It is through our mental equivalent of freedom that the richness of Life flows into our experience. To the degree that we release the Spirit within us by expanding our mental images and acceptance of abundant good, we will experience a richer life. Marcel Proust wrote: "The real voyage of discovery consists not in seeking new landscapes, but in having new eyes."

We must look upon life with new inner eyes—through greater spiritual perceptions and more magnificent mental equivalents of being. We must learn to "relate" to the Unconditioned, Unrestricted Self within us before we can experience a greater objectified self in the world. Remember, we can only relate to that in the outer world which touches something already existing within us—an existing chord of resonance—that which is awake in us as a possibility—something we can imagine.

"How much life can any man experience? As much as he can embody....We are so constituted that we can continuously increase our embodiment."[6] We must increase our idea of Life in order to increase our experience of Life. Within each of us is the Greatness of the Almighty desiring a fuller expression through us. Within each of us is the Unlimited Power and Potential to bring every desire to fruition. Within all is the Perfect Child of God— fully whole, capable, and complete. This is the Truth of being.

Can you relate?

*Process Sheet Twenty*

# Can You Relate?

*INDIVIDUAL*

What do you desire in your life that you are not currently experiencing?

_____

_____

_____

"If we want to do a thing that is really worth doing, we must mentally grow until we are that thing....We must see it, think it, realize it, before the creative power of Mind can work it out for us."[7] Realization is visualization *plus* acceptance in mind and emotion. Close your eyes and visualize that very thing you desire as already existing for you. Meditate upon the vision until it is "tangible" in your mind–until you can feel it as the very reality of who you are. Use your *inner* five senses to touch, taste, see, feel, and smell the internal existence of your desire. Impress the mental equivalent of your desire upon the Creative Medium of Mind. When you are convinced that what you desire is present right where you are–that the One Whose pleasure it is to give you your heart's desire is acting upon your mental image–silently speak words of thanksgiving for the inner Divine Action that is bringing about your greater outer experience.

Write an affirmation that will assist you in daily maintaining your mental equivalent:

_____

_____

_____

## *GROUP*
Discussion of Lesson.

**Activity:** (*Materials: pencil/pen and paper.*)
The difference between fiction and nonfiction writing is that fiction is a description of the activity of the mind, while non-fiction is a description of what has already occurred in the world. Ernest Holmes wrote, "A demonstration, like anything else in the objective life, is born out of a mental concept."[8] We could say, then, that because all that has transpired in the world occurred in mind first, that all nonfiction stories start out as fiction–an activity of the mind. Write a "fiction" story about your heart's desire as if it were nonfiction. For example: If I am not currently in a loving, satisfying relationship but I would like to be, my story will be about the loving, satisfying relationship I am *already* experiencing. (Allow fifteen to thirty minutes for this activity.)

If the group is small enough, each member may want to read his or her story to the group. Otherwise, each may share with a partner.

Instruct the group to read their stories every day, out loud, as if reading a newspaper article.

**Meditation:** I Must Be It to See It

(*Facilitator: read slowly with restful music in background, if desired. Begin with one of the Relaxation Techniques on pages 299-300.*)
Visualize the story that you have just written...using your inner five senses, touch, taste, see, feel, and smell the inner actuality of your heart's desire...(*Facilitator: allow three to five minutes*)...visualization *plus* acceptance brings about realization... accept this inner vision as a living, tangible part of who you are...

as an actual component of your being...inseparable from your life experience..."A demonstration, like anything else in the objective life, is born out of a mental concept"...all objective life begins in mind...your objective life begins in mind...this place within you...this Holy place of Imagination...is your inner oneness with Divine Creativity...It is the genesis of all life...the very origin of your life and all that you have ever experienced or will ever experience...accept this inner life as the source of your outer life... silently speak words of thanksgiving for the Divine Givingness of your heart's desire...for the Inner Presence of that which is projecting Itself into your world of experience...and with a deep breath of gratitude and expectancy, open your eyes.

1. SOM 281:4.   2. SOM 40:3.   3. SOM 118:2.   4. SOM 281:4.   5. SOM 280:3.
6. SOM 280:2.   7. Ernest Holmes, *Creative Mind and Success* (New York: G. P. Putnam's Sons), p. 74.
8. SOM 281:4.

Freeing Our Unlimited Imagination

*When we think of a
newborn baby, we imagine
a pure consciousness–
an untainted being filled
with a sense of intrinsic
goodness and inherent
freedom to express itself.*
Some children, it seems,
entertain that unadulterated inner awareness for only a split
second of earthly life before the harmful effects of the world
take hold. Others appear to perceive it throughout their
entire childhood, experiencing the joy and confidence that
come from the knowledge that the world is on their side and
is filled with unlimited potential and wonderful possibilities.

Author and environmentalist Rachel Carson wrote
of children: "A child's world is fresh and new and beautiful,
full of wonder and excitement. It is our misfortune that for
most of us that clear-eyed vision, that true instinct for what
is beautiful and awe-inspiring, is dimmed and even lost
before we reach adulthood." Most of us can think back (perhaps way, "waaay" back) to a time when we felt excited about
life and believed that the world was our "oyster." We felt certain that we could be anything we could imagine ourselves
being, and we were also sure that just being ourselves was
joy enough.

For many of us, as time marched on, the adult that
we became–even the adolescent that we became–forgot what
we knew and felt as a child. Our earthly "education" taught
us lessons of limitation and self-doubt. Our child's mind was

willing to believe that we were good, creative, and valuable. Children do not naturally embody guilt, self-doubt, and self-condemnation; these are instilled in them by the world and validated by experience. French author Alexandre Dumas wrote: "How is it that little children are so intelligent and men so stupid? It must be education that does it." As adults, most of us are trying to unlearn our limitations. The path of *un*learning includes our search for–and our finding–that childlike awareness of freedom and possibilities that we once knew.

## THE CHILDLIKE MIND

"Truly I say to you, Unless you change and become like little children, you shall not enter into the kingdom of heaven."[1] One of the things we knew as children was that we didn't know much of anything at all. Therefore, we didn't block new and valuable information with hardened opinions and opposition. We were mentally and emotionally pliable. We were open to new ideas. We didn't overanalyze, critically judge, or look for loopholes. "Jesus tells us that the childlike mind is more receptive to Truth than the over-intellectual who demand too rational an explanation of those truths which must be accepted on faith alone."[2] When we were children we believed that anything was possible because we didn't have mental boundaries to limit our vision. Our mind was open–our thoughts soared as if on the wings of fairies and angels–and we were free to spire as far as we wanted to go.

Unfortunately, it seems that as our body grew larger, our imagination grew smaller. We learned the words *can't, shouldn't,* and *shame on you,* and we experienced the limited self-expression that came with their meanings. Our embarrassments, disappointments, failures, and learned fears created walls of limitation within our potentially unlimited mind, and many of us have not been able to scale those inner walls to see the many options and possibilities that are still there for us."The Universal Mind contains all knowledge. It is the potential ultimate of all things. To It, all things are possible. To us, as much is possible as we can conceive...."[3]

The Kingdom of Heaven–the Realm of Unlimited Imagination–is within us. However, unless we become as children–open and receptive–and unless we can believe in the possibilities that exist within us, we cannot enter the Kingdom. We must be willing to take down or break through our walls of limited thinking–our *can'ts, shouldn'ts,* and *won'ts*–and all of the conditions that we have placed upon our success, health, and happiness. Then our true magnificence–born of Unconditioned Life–can and will unfold unimpeded. "Impossibility" doesn't exist in the realm of "Unlimited Possibility." We are the offspring of the One Who knows no limitations. We cannot enter into our Father's Kingdom of Boundless Life while we are shackled to limitations of the world.

## BELIEF

"Whoever...believes that what he says will be done, it will be done to him."[4] Children are true believers. They believe that stories always have a happy ending. They believe that no matter how bad or scary things look or seem, things can get better instantaneously. If there is a monster lurking in their closet or under their bed, they are willing to believe that a tiny nightlight will keep it away. Wouldn't it be wonderful if we adults believed that the monsters in our life could be kept away so easily? Instead, we are often unconvinced that the fullness of the Light of Spirit and the Power of the entire Universe is enough to chase our mental demons away or heal our bodies, enrich our finances, or bring love into our life.

## IMAGINATION

When we were children, our imagination was the substance of our life. We filled our mind with vivid images, and those images were just as real to us as anything in three-dimensional material form. In fact, our imagination could bring two-dimensional images to life as well. As children, my sister and I spent hours sitting together with a thick *Sears Catalog* opened between us. The items pictured on each page of that wonderful publication (depending on which side of the catalog each of us was sitting on) became ours for the choosing: toys, jewelry, clothes–even tools, car parts, and gardening equipment–were ours (in our minds) simply by pointing a finger. According to our rules, each of us was allowed one item per page. Within no time our imaginations carried away a bounty of goodies.

Because our child-mind was so rich, most of us never doubted that our life would follow along the same abundant line of our childhood dreams. It was only as we were taught the "cold, hard facts of life" that the space for our existence narrowed: "Life isn't always fair," "You can't always have what you want (therefore you should settle for what you get)," "Practicality outweighs imagination," and, "Dreamers are simply idle people with their heads in the clouds."

Eventually, many of us stopped believing in our dreams, while some of us stopped dreaming at all–like "Kim," who was about to turn forty years old. A week before her birthday we sat together in a coffee house and she shared with me how empty her life had become. She said that she feared that her imagination and creativity had "atrophied" or even disappeared altogether from lack of use.

Although she had loved art throughout her childhood and

had majored in Fine Arts in college, she had not touched her oils, or so much as picked up a sketch pad, since leaving school. She had married during her senior year of college, and by the time she graduated, she was pregnant. After a sixteen-year marriage to an abusive, violent man, she moved with her two children to start over. She took a job at a minimal salary, and although she was able to make ends meet, and found joy in her children's activities, she felt personally empty and unfulfilled. Her eyes filled with tears as she whispered to me that she still believed that dreams could come true, but that she had forgotten *how* to dream.

As we sat through several cappuccinos and talked about the True Nature of her childhood Imagination and its relationship to the One Mind, she realized that her Imagination could never really "go" anywhere. It couldn't shrivel up or disappear, because It was an Unlimited, Boundless, Ever-Present Place within her. "We are one with unmanifest Substance whose business it is to forever take form and we are one with the Law which gives form....Man has the ability to choose what he will do with his life, and is unified with a Law which automatically produces his choice."[5]

Kim understood that she had stopped using her Imagination to enrich and enhance her life because she had been focusing on the acute, limited circumstances of her situation. She decided that in order to find her dreams, she needed to stimulate her Imagination again. She knew from her study of the Science of Mind that "our mental acceptances should be filled with conviction, warmth, color and imagination" and that "the creative power responds to feeling more quickly than to any other mental attitude."[6] So she set out to "prime" her inner creativity and to make an "impression" on the Creative Medium that would give form to her dreams. She knew that it was her Father's good pleasure to give her the Kingdom, and she wanted to fill the Kingdom of her

Imagination with all that she desired to experience.

## SHE "CATALOGUED" HER DREAMS

She had heard me talk about my sister and me and the *Sears Catalog*, and she resolved to spend her fortieth birthday making a picture book that she called "Kim's Catalog." But instead of allowing herself only one item per page (as my sister and I had), she filled the pages with every desire that she could imagine for her life: a picture of herself painting a picture, a picture of a gallery filled with people looking at her paintings, a picture of a silver Jaguar, a large house surrounded by rolling hills and fruit trees, and two college degrees with her children's names on them.

The more pictures she placed in her catalog, the more she imagined. When she was finally finished, she looked at her catalog often throughout each day, and she shared the pictures with her children. Their enthusiasm added to the excitement. She quietly closed her eyes every morning and evening and gave thanks for the images in mind that were taking form in her life.

When Kim "lost" her job, she didn't panic. With faithful trust in the Power of her Imagination that was now stimulated and overflowing, rather than looking for another full-time position, she found a part-time job and began painting in her spare time each day. In the meantime, her former husband (who had been delinquent in his child-support payments in the past) suddenly began sending checks regularly. When Kim had enough paintings completed, she found a gallery that agreed to show her work. At one of the showings, a distinguished-looking man bought two of her pieces. Kim was so appreciative that she helped him carry them out to his new silver Jaguar.

The last time I heard from Kim, she was painting

full-time and successfully selling her work. She had married the wealthy businessman with the Jaguar. They moved to the rolling hills of Kentucky where they have a lovely home with plenty of fruit trees (and a stable full of horses). One of Kim's children was already attending college, and the other was on the honor roll in high school! "To imagine, without the power to manifest such imagination, would be to remain in a dream world which would never come to self-realization."[7]

It may sound overly simple, and perhaps even trite, to state that if we merely catalog our desires, or make a picture book of our dreams, they will come true. Life is more complex than that, isn't it? At least we seem to *make* it more complicated. Besides we're all grownup and busy with our life. Who has time to paint pictures in a book, or cut them out and paste them in one, and then look through the pictures day after day? We have to earn a living; we have responsibilities and obligations! In fact, some of us are so busy living the life we *didn't* imagine we would be living, that we don't have time to picture the life we *want* to live! When we were children, no matter what else we *had* to do, we always found time to play—to draw pictures, to look at books, to make a playmate out of thin air. We used our Imagination to make magic out of simple moments that might have seemed mundane and boring to an adult too busy to imagine anything beyond the obvious.

## IT'S NEVER TOO LATE

We still have that same Imagination available to us. It hasn't gone anywhere. It has just seemed to shrivel up because we have limited its joyous possibilities by using it to imagine the worst—to foresee a restricted future based upon a limited past. "Worry is the misuse of imagination," so the saying goes. Isn't it time that we began to use our Imagination to bring fulfillment rather than anxiety into our life? The Universe is *still* on our side. The world is *still* our oyster. Our potential for happiness, love, creativity, and joyous, unfettered self-expression is still within us. We are *still* the unlimited child of an Unlimited Father. "Our outlook on life must be transformed by the renewing of the mind. We must relight the torch of our Imagination by 'fire caught from heaven.'"[8]

The "fire caught from heaven" is aflame with passion and enthusiasm. We must renew our minds by seeing ourselves and the world around us the way we once did: filled with potential and possibility. We must call forth that childlike mind that sees the wonder and magic of life and believes in the Power and Substance of Imagination. We must turn to the Creative Force within us that desires to express Itself through our Imagination and is waiting to give to us the desires of our heart. And...we must return to simplicity. Our spiritual path need not be a tangled maze that we must try to figure out every moment. Life will be to us only as complex and confusing as we make it within our mind. We can use our imagination to fill us with excitement, enthusiasm, and energy–or we can use it to wear us out. A student of the Science of Mind who had apparently taken "one class too many" without a recess told me wearily, "I know that 'the unexamined life is not worth living,' but the over-examined life is no picnic either!" Playtime–time to let the thinking mind rest and the imagination soar–is vital to our spiritual growth and self-fulfillment.

Children do not give up on their dreams until the adult world convinces them of the impossibility of their dreams coming true. But the Bible tells us that "With God all things are possible,"[9] and God expresses through our dreams and creates within the Realm of Imagination. Kim had a childlike faith in her oneness with a Power that would give her the desires of her heart. She accepted the Good within her Imagination as Real and Substantial, and the images of her mind became the forms of her life.

## IT'S NEVER TOO SOON

Perhaps you have been telling yourself that your dreams are impossible. This could be the time for you to change your mind and become like a child–accepting and believing in your unlimited potential. The Creative Power of the Universe honors our faith in It. We must learn to trust the Spirit and return to the joy and richness of our Imagination. "We must return the way we came, as little children, who know that life is good."[10] How wonderful can your life be as the unlimited offspring of an Unlimited Creator? Use your Imagination!

*Process Sheet Twenty-One*

# Like a Child

### INDIVIDUAL

"A child's world is fresh and new and beautiful, full of wonder and excitement. It is our misfortune that for most of us that clear-eyed vision, that true instinct for what is beautiful and awe-inspiring, is dimmed and even lost before we reach adulthood." We can never truly lose the beautiful and awe-inspiring, but we can forget how to see it. Close your eyes and open your Imagination. Know that your mind is still filled with beautiful and awe-inspiring images even though it may have been quite a while since you've called them to your conscious mind. Take time, now, to quietly meditate upon your inner world of endless wonder. Begin by breathing deeply and slowly, allowing your body to relax with each breath. Let the "busy thoughts" of your mind slowly drift away and open your awareness to that Holy Place of Imagination. Quietly let your Imagination speak to you. (When you feel complete with this exercise, write down your experience and keep it in a notebook.)

### GROUP
Discussion of Lesson.

**Activity 1:** (*Materials: pencils/pens, paper; perhaps some fabric for simple costumes and cardboard to cut out to use for props.*)

　　Children use their imaginations to make magic out of the seemingly mundane. They find within themselves and their friends a "cast of characters" and they create a wonderland out of whatever environment they find themselves in. This process is to assist the participants in rediscovering and reactivating their imaginations. If the group is small, the whole group may participate as one.

Otherwise, a large group can be divided into smaller groups of four or five people. Each group is to write a short play–a fun, happy, "earthly" event, a mythical story, a story with a moral, etc. Each member of each group becomes a character in the play. When the plays have been written, each group performs its play for the others. (Allow a half hour to an hour for the groups to write their plays and make costumes and props.)

**Activity 2:** During the week make a "catalog" with your name on it, drawing or pasting pictures of those things that represent your dreams. Share with supportive family members or friends. Or, bring to the next group meeting to share with the group.

**Meditation:** Like a Child

(*Facilitator: read slowly with restful music in background, if desired. Begin with one of the Relaxation Techniques on pages 299-300.*)
    A child's world is fresh and new and beautiful...full of wonder and excitement...this world dwells within you...you have never truly lost the beautiful and awe-inspiring within you, but you may have forgotten how to see it...move your focus deeper and deeper within...to that inner place where *all* things are possible because *anything* can be imagined...this Realm of Possibilities belongs to you...It has been yours from the "beginning"...yours since Creation began...It is your special place to play in...your special place to create from...meditate upon your inner world of endless wonder...open your awareness to that Holy Place of Imagination...and quietly let your Imagination speak to you in colors, images and forms...let It tell you about you...let It tell you about life...relax and allow...(*Facilitator: allow five minutes*)...it is time now to slowly move your awareness to your body and the

room...when you open your eyes, take a few minutes to write about your experience. Then find a partner and share your experience with him or her.

1. Matthew 18:3 (Lamsa).   2. SOM 443:1.   3. SOM  44:5.   4. Mark 11:23 (Lamsa).
5. SOM 195:3.   6. SOM 398:4.   7. SOM 108:3.   8. SOM 218:3.   9. Mark 10:27 (KJV).
10. SOM 456:4.

Eliminating Our Belief in Duality
through Trust in Divine Unity

*Eighteen-year-old Sara
lived with a roommate in
one of the newly renovated
condominium complexes
that border the Arena in
the heart of Miami Beach.*
Although the planned
civic refurbishing was well under way, the poverty of the
inner city was still evidenced by gang-related graffiti covering
overpasses and building walls, the homeless sleeping in parks
and storefront doorways, and small clusters of young boys
whose daily interests did not include attending school.

Since Sara worked nights as a waitress and often
drove home at two in the morning, her parents were happy
when she found a place to live that was only a five-minute
drive from her job. She moved into a protected condo in a
building that was fortified by high security walls and guarded
twenty-four hours a day by an attendant.

One sunny day at two in the afternoon Sara was driving home from a shopping mall. She stopped for a red light
at an intersection several blocks from home. There were two
cars ahead of hers as she waited for the light to change. She
casually glanced around her and noticed a group of teenage
boys walking towards her car. Feeling anxious, she reached
around her small compact, locked the doors and tucked her
purse under her seat. The boys had gotten within a few feet
of her car when the light turned green. As the other two cars
pulled away, Sara tried to shift her car into first gear but in
her panic stalled it instead. The young boys surrounded her

car and began pounding on the windows. The sound of shattering glass was terrifying, and Sara's shaking hand turned the ignition switch only with difficulty. Just as she heard the engine start again, several arms reached into the back seat through the broken glass of a rear window and grabbed a shopping bag containing a pair of nylons and Chapstick. Sara shifted hard into first gear and sped away, tears burning her cheeks.

She hysterically recounted the story to her roommates, the police, and her worried parents whom she had telephoned in Orlando. Sara was ready to quit her job and move out of Miami Beach to a less threatening environment. As she considered other places to live, discounting the larger cities because she was afraid of crime and smaller towns because she was afraid of feeling isolated, she wondered aloud if she would ever be able to find a "safe place."

Like Sara, we may ask, "Is there a safe place?" The answer is: "Yes and no," depending on where we are placing our sense of security—in spirituality or in geography. The spiritual realm is one of wholeness and unity. The material realm is one of duality and opposing forces. "We experience good and evil because we perceive a presence of duality rather than unity."[1]

In the physical world, the best chances of survival seem to go to the fittest, the most prepared, the one with the best protection, the most weapons, or the most elaborate security system. Even then, one can be "in the wrong place at the wrong time" and get into trouble, and being "in the right place" is difficult to determine. In an unpredictable, chaotic society, being in "the right place" seems to occur more by chance than by intention, as if our safety were linked to some cosmic flip-of-the-coin. In the material world, "luck" is often seen as the saving grace.

## DUAL-ING FORCES

The world with its dueling (and dual-ing) forces cannot be trusted to protect us. There are planned acts of kindness *and* random acts of violence; there are people bound together by love *and* warring factions torn apart by hate, racism, and prejudice; there are loving sexual unions *and* acts of rape and humiliation; and there are joyous births of children met with welcoming arms *and* children who have died or are dying of starvation or from violence or neglect. Psychologists tell us that we cannot focus on two opposites at the same time. But in the material world good and evil seem to walk hand in hand and occur so close together as to appear simultaneous. For every right, there's a wrong; for every justice, an injustice; for every joy, a sorrow. Even when things seem to be going well, some people are waiting for the other shoe to drop.

In history books it appears that every generation has thought that their generation was the worst. Today isn't any different. Terrorism, drugs, racism, greed, poverty, social and political violence certainly seem to be increasing. But, rather than increasing, perhaps they are really just reappearing from the collective unconscious–emerging from a human race that has never resolved, dissolved or transcended the issues when they first appeared in our world. "When the whole world sees the right and does it; then, and not until then, will the problem of evil be solved for the entire race."[2]

The atrocities that are reported in the news every day are difficult for most of us to comprehend. We are angry because we want to do something about what we hear, and we're afraid because the violence seems to be moving closer to home. There is no concrete evidence *on earth* that God is the *only* One in charge, that God is Good, or that God is all there is. It doesn't *appear* that peace, love, joy, harmony, and abundance are the natural state of our being or could ever reign supreme.

## "BELIEF IN DUALITY HAS MADE MAN SICK"[3]

But what is spiritually true can become materially evident only as we hold to the consciousness of God as good despite appearances. As long as we allow duality to govern our thinking, we can never truly be safe no matter where we place ourselves on the map of the physical world. "The whole confusion of the world arises from fundamental errors of thought. Chief among these errors–and the father to a greater part of the others–is a belief in duality."[4] When we fight evil as though it were a separate power or hide from it as though it could harm us without our permission, we add to its validation in the world and give it power over our life.

The only security we shall ever have is our steadfast belief in, and focus on, the unity and harmony of the Divine Presence– the One who is everywhere, all of the time, despite what appears to be. We must be convinced in our own mind that wherever we are, *God is*, and that Spirit does not reside only in upper-middle-class neighborhoods, where the streets are well lit and regularly patrolled, but that God and All His Glory is present in the slums and ghettos, and on dark, lonely roads as well. "Yea, though I walk through the valley of the shadow of death, I will fear no evil: for thou art with me."[5]

## "HEAVEN IS ALREADY WITHIN"[6]

In these troubled times it is essential for us to turn to that safe place within ourselves, to that Invisible Sanctuary of Indestructible Wholeness, and seek the Wisdom of Spirit to guide our every step and guard us on our journey. "If one will have faith in himself, faith in his fellowmen, in the Universe, and in God, that faith will light the place in which he finds himself, and by the light of this faith, he will be able to see that ALL IS GOOD."[7] With the All-knowing Presence uppermost in our mind, we are *always* in a safe place, because from this higher vantagepoint in consciousness there is no opposition to Good, no dark corner in which evil can lurk, and no neighborhood in which it can dwell.

## "NONRESISTANCE IS THE ONLY THING THAT CANNOT BE RESISTED"[8]

The one who neither fights nor fears evil in mind will not find it in manifestation. The path of nonresistance to some appears passive, and perhaps, viewed from a purely materialistic standpoint, it is. But from a spiritual viewpoint–from the knowledge that our thoughts are creative–nonresistance is a powerful position. When we know that our thoughts are creative, we understand that the more we *fight* evil in the world, the more we *create* evil in the world.

"We are thinking, willing, knowing, conscious centers of Life. We are surrounded by, immersed in, and there is flowing through us, a creative Something...call It what you will...our thought, will, purpose, and belief, create a tendency in this Law that causes It to react to us according to the sum total of that belief. Ignorance of the law excuses no one from its effects."[9] If the sum total of our thinking adds up to a belief in the power of evil, which we must fight or from which we must hide or protect ourselves, then the Law that reacts to us will create evils for us to fight or from which we must flee, because that is where we are directing our creative energy.

If we take a stand that is merely *against* something in the world—no matter how great the evil may appear to be or how noble the cause against it may be—we tend to perpetuate its existence. Why? Because as we focus our creative energy on something, even if we are against it, we feed it with living substance. Our creative energy is like the air that causes the fire's flame to leap and grow as it is stoked. That is why the Bible tells us to "resist not evil[10]...but overcome evil with good."[11] *Our resistance creates evil's persistence.*

We seem to be fascinated by the morbid details of evil. Murder trials are televised with all of the grizzly detail. The cameras zoom in and catch in "dying" color the atrocities of humanity against itself. We sit spellbound as the mind of the terrorist or serial killer is scrutinized and dissected in public forum. We may ask, "What makes anyone commit an atrocity?" Although the question and the circumstances may be complex, the answer is simple: *the belief in a power other than good.* And, "What makes us so fascinated by evil, angry with it, and fearful of it?" The same thing: *our belief in a power other than good.* Our *fear* of evil and our *fascination* with it become the living fuel that allows evil to continue its mass destruction.

The Scriptures tell us of our ability to bring evil into our life through our focus on it: "The light of the body is the eye: if therefore thine eye be single, thy whole body shall be full of light. But if thine eye be evil, thy whole body shall be full of darkness. If therefore the light that is in thee be darkness, how great is that darkness."[12] Rather than resist evil, we must be willing to overcome its bogus power through our tenacious mental focus on the One that is Good and Ever-Present no matter what appears to be. Our thoughts are powerful. When our *singleness of purpose* is to *eliminate* evil, we only serve to bring more of it to life, personally and as a global race. The Light—the Creative Energy within us—becomes to us what we believe, and with it we can create a whole world of darkness.

"The emphasis on true mental healing is insistently on God, the One Mind, the One Soul, the One Being, ever-present and ever-available; and on man's ability and right to make himself receptive to this healing Presence–a realization of the essential divinity of our own nature, and the truth that no evil can live in this Presence."[13] It is our singleness of focus–our holding to the consciousness of Good, no matter what the situation before us appears to be–that has the power to heal by resolving, dissolving, and transcending the appearance of evil.

## HE LOOKED BEYOND APPEARANCES

The new chaplain of a state penitentiary was determined to perceive the good inherent in the prisoners he served. He was committed to seeing before him–in place of the criminal–the innocent child that had somehow gone astray. But he was having a difficult time overcoming appearances with one inmate in particular, an angry and abusive convict who had been put into solitary confinement, where he threw his food on the floor and smeared excrement on the walls. When the young chaplain attempted to talk with him, the prisoner spit in his face.

Still determined to see the good that seemed to be evading detection, the chaplain waited one evening until just after midnight and asked a reluctant guard to allow him to enter the solitary cell. The prisoner lay sound asleep on a narrow cot, a thin blanket pulled tightly around him. As the chaplain looked down at the silent man, he prayed for the eyes of the Father–the Mind of the Creator who eternally knows the goodness of all creation. With a sudden rush of love, the chaplain reached out and touched the man's hand. The prisoner opened his eyes and tears began to stream down his face.

As they talked together the man explained to the chaplain that, up until that moment, he had never felt ashamed of his behavior. In fact, bad behavior had felt justified. But, when the chaplain touched his hand, he felt suddenly worth loving for the first time. He told the chaplain that he knew that he had seen something worthwhile in him, and he wanted to see it, too. He vowed to the chaplain that he *would* do better because he knew that he *could* do better.

The Science of Mind instructs us to "turn entirely from the condition" if we want to heal it. If we focus on the lie, we can't see the Truth. We cannot see opposites simultaneously. Like the black and white picture used in the psychological study of perception, where either a beautiful young woman or an ugly old hag with a wart on her nose can be perceived emerging from the same picture, but not at the same time, the picture of our life changes, depending on where we focus. "Whatever one thinks tends to take form and become a part of his experience."[14] "Cause and effect are but two sides of the same thing, one being an image in mind and the other its objective condition."[15]

## WE CAN'T "TURN OFF" OUR WORLD

This is not to say that we should ignore world events any more than we should ignore our personal circumstances. We don't want to simply look at the world through "rose-colored glasses," denying the existence of facts and pretending that everything is perfect and in Divine Order when people are dying needlessly and our environment is in crisis. Evil doesn't disappear because we stick our head in the sand like an ostrich–because just like the ostrich, we are still exposed.

There are people who are quite "righteous" about the fact that they don't read a newspaper or watch the news on TV. But it is not enough for us to cancel our subscription to the newspaper or to turn off the television set. We cannot cancel our subscription to life, and we cannot merely "turn off" bad news. Ignoring bad news is not creating *good news*. We create good news by constantly filling our mind with good news *whether or not* we're reading *The Times* or watching CNN.

The violence of the world is alive and rampant in race consciousness, whether we are conscious of what is going on or not. Race consciousness, which psychologist Carl Jung called the "collective unconscious," includes every thought, belief and activity on the planet–every mental concept including yours, mine, Mother Teresa's and Saddam Hussein's. Even though we may not listen to the news or read a newspaper, our subconscious is a world-wide receiver, and we are susceptible to every activity of humankind through our connected consciousness. "Mental suggestion operates through the subjective mind, and a silent influence is always going on through this avenue in the form of race-suggestion."[16]

The good news is that we can take part in the healing of the planet through the very same connection. As we heal ourselves of the belief in the power of evil, our thoughts–focused on the one and only Power of Good–affect not only ourselves but others as well, because we are also a subconscious world-wide *transmitter*. "Our theory is that the medium is a Universal, simultaneous Presence and in this Presence all live; and *that whatever is known at one point in It is known at all points, instantly!*"[17] Because we are one with all Life, and Universal on the subjective side or inner side of Life, what we think can and does subconsciously influence others.

## WHAT ARE WE AGREEING WITH?

If someone behaves like an imbecile (because he thinks he is) and we agree that he is just that, we are joining together with that person in creating a more solid fact. When we are in agreement with others about a situation–when we take a collective position–that stand becomes even more powerful than a single thought. "Whatsoever ye shall bind on earth shall be bound in heaven: and whatsoever ye shall loose on earth shall be loosed in heaven....If two of you shall agree on earth as touching any thing that they shall ask, it shall be done for them of my Father which is in heaven."[18] When we are in agreement about a thing, whether that thing is holy or unholy, it manifests more fully in our life.

It is important for us to remind ourselves daily that a human position is not a Divine proclamation. There is a difference between our looking for the Truth in a situation so that the perfection of Spirit can be revealed, and our looking for personal validation of our position. The Truth can be revealed only when we are willing to lay our earthly position aside. It is a difficult thing when we believe that *our* position is right and in everyone's best interest. It is tough for us to get out of the way when we believe that our truth is *truest*. But opinions tugging on either side of an issue cannot heal the issue. Whether we are liberal or conservative in our views, it is important for us to remember that there is no human formula and no law of government that can answer every need or that will be appropriate in every situation. *Only Spirit is right every time.*

## OUR MENTAL ATMOSPHERE
If we're wondering just how our thoughts are affecting the world, we only need to look at how our thoughts are affecting our own

life. Ask yourself: "What kind of people do I attract into my life on a consistent basis? What kind of experiences do I have and what kind of results do I get?" "Each person has a mental atmosphere which is the result of all that he has thought, said and done, and consciously or unconsciously perceived. The mental atmosphere is very real, and is that subtle influence which constitutes the power of personal attraction."[19]

People are drawn to us and remain with us because they respond to our beliefs and values. They resonate to what we think about ourselves and our beliefs about the world. If we are constantly feeling guilty, angry, and resentful; if we blame and accuse; we shall attract people who feel the same as we do, because they will feel comfortable around us. Occasionally, people who are miserable will hang around a positive person for a while hoping that the positive energy will buoy them up. But they generally move on because they can't feel comfortable for too long in a space unlike themselves. When we love and respect ourselves and others, problem people drop away automatically and we draw to us people who love and respect themselves, and us too.

If we want to change the world, if we want to change our friends, we need to change our mind. When we believe that we have a personal enemy, we validate the wars in the world because all enemies are a multiple of one. We are subconsciously connected through the One Subjective Mind to all of life, and our unloving or angry thoughts add to the lovelessness and violence in the world. We must consciously choose a spiritual attitude that affirms the Allness of God, the perpetuation of Peace, the validation of Love, and the activity of Harmony. In this way we shall not inadvertently affect the planet adversely. Of course, we shall also improve our personal life.

In a world where evil is screaming for attention, where the

Garden of Eden seems to be filled with thieves and thugs and the branches of the "tree of life" appear to be dying, it is vital for us to turn our mind to God. We must so fill our mind with the Spirit that nothing unlike It can take form.

Life manifests the contents of our thinking. Goodness, Peace and Harmony are ever-present–willing to guide and pro-tect–ready to take form for us even in the darkest places. When we think about the things of Spirit, our security does not rest upon a geographical location. We recognize that wherever we are, we are standing on Holy Ground, and we know without a shadow of a doubt that we have found a *safe place.*

*Process Sheet Twenty-Two*

# Is There a Safe Place?

*INDIVIDUAL*

Ernest Holmes reminds us to turn away from a condition if we want to heal it. If we focus on the lie, we can't see the Truth. Write down a "world" issue, e.g. social, political, economic, environmental, etc., in which you have been focusing on "the lie":

_____

_____

_____

_____

Write the Spiritual Truth regarding the above issue:

_____

_____

_____

Condense what you have just written into a one-line "Statement of Truth" that you can write at least ten times a day, morning and evening, and mentally affirm every time you hear or read anything about the issue:

_____

_____

_____

*GROUP*

Discussion of Lesson.

**Activity:** Same as for Individual.

**Meditation:** This is a good time for the familiar "Faith Walk," in which one of two partners is blindfolded and *silently* led around a darkened environment by the other. The blindfolded partner should be reminded that every step he or she takes is on Holy Ground and that geographical safety is first established spiritually. Allow twenty minutes, then the one who has not been blindfolded takes the blindfold and finds *another* partner to walk with as he or she wears the blindfold. This meditation is most effective when performed outdoors in the evening.

1. SOM 39:4.    2. SOM 111:3.    3. SOM 597:4.    4. SOM 453:6.    5. Psalms 23:4 (KJV).
6. SOM 472:4.    7. SOM 217:2.    8. Ernest Holmes, *The Anatomy of Healing Prayer* (DeVorss), p. 52.
9. SOM 38:3.    10. Matthew 5:39 (KJV).    11. Romans 12:21 (KJV).    12. Matthew 6:22 (KJV).
13. SOM 142:3.    14. SOM 320:4.    15. SOM 321:2.    16. SOM 421:4.    17. SOM 94:1.
18. Matthew 18:18, 19 (KJV).    19. SOM 350:3.

# 23  It's the Law!

The Impersonal and Universal Aspects
of the Divine Process

*Many verses from the
Bible frightened me as a
child. But two that sent
goose bumps up my spine
were: "Vengeance belongeth
unto me, I will recompense,
saith the Lord"*
and the verse that followed it: "It is a
fearful thing to fall into the hands of the living God."[1] I had
been taught that God was a little like Santa Claus: He knew
if you'd been bad or good no matter how secret your misdeeds were. Whew! My parents were strict, but at least they
could punish me only for the things that they found out
about. God, on the other hand, knew what you were up to
all of the time!

Not only was I afraid of the Holy Vengeance that
might be directed my way; I was concerned that well-
deserved retribution toward my adversaries might be overlooked by a busy God. The Lord's "ownership" of vengeance
seemed to imply that if someone did something bad to me,
I was not supposed to retaliate; *He* was in charge of "getting
even." It was difficult for me to stand by and wait for the
Lord to take revenge, because it seemed to me that the Lord
was not always paying attention to the misdeeds of my enemies.

Many years later, through the study of the Science
of Mind, I discovered a less literal, more metaphysical interpretation of the Bible; one far more comforting and uplifting
than my fundamentalist conditioning had afforded me. I

255

began to view Scripture in terms of *Love and Law.* "We live in a Universe of Love as well as a Universe of Law. One is the complement of the other–the Universe of Love pulsating with feeling, with emotion, and the Universe of Law, the Executor of all feeling and all emotion."[2] And Ernest Holmes says of these two, "We must understand both."[3]

## "LORD" = LAW

Sometimes those who are looking for a less orthodox interpretation of the Bible will substitute the word *Law* for the word *Lord* in certain verses because *Lord* seems to imply a person, whereas *Law* denotes an impartial principle. This is helpful when a biblical passage is referring to a "basic truth, law, or assumption," and not a "physical personage." For example, the word *Law*, substituted for the word *Lord* in the verse "The Lord will destroy the house of the proud," would remove the mental concept of a *personal* and seemingly *partial* "Someone in the heavens" visiting punishment on vanity and conceit. Instead, it would suggest that pride by its nature (i.e. the *law* of its nature) leads to destruction.

Law is the "Impersonal and Universal" aspect of the Creative Process. It is a "blind force" which the Mind of God *and* the human mind activate. As It is animated by our thinking, It turns the contents of our mind into the experiences of our life. The Law re-creates for us in worldly form the thought forms of our belief system: It does unto us as we believe.

When I substituted the word *Law* for the word *Lord* in my "menacing" verse and added a dictionary definition of the word *vengeance*, I had a better understanding of the *reciprocal* Nature of Life. According to the dictionary, *vengeance* means "retribution" or "to pay back by dispensing of reward or punishment."

"Vengeance belongeth to me, I will recompense, saith the Lord," could be translated as "Payback by reward or punishment is a function of the Law." In other words: what we put out we get back; what we sow, we reap; and what goes around comes around. IT'S THE LAW! This is actually good news and not something to cause goose bumps, because the reciprocal action of the Law also "rewards" when we put positive, life-enhancing thoughts into the Law.

## "GOD IS LAW"[4]

The Law is *the way* Spirit functions and operates. It is not separate from Spirit but Co-Existent with Spirit. "God did not make Law; Law is Co-Eternal with God. God did not make Substance, this is also Co-Existent and Co-Eternal with God. BUT GOD DID MAKE, AND DOES MAKE, and IS MAKING AND WILL CONTINUE TO MAKE, FROM ETERNITY TO ETERNITY, *FORMS*. We live in a universe of Infinite Substance and numberless forms, wherein nothing is moved unless Intelligence moves it, in accord with law."[5]

The Law is consistent and unerring, a "blind force" that unfailingly responds without prejudice to *all* of our thoughts. It cannot "edit" our thoughts in order to create only positive conditions for us, but It would never prevent good from coming our way. IT'S THE LAW! Its action depends on our input. If our mind contains beliefs, concepts, and ideas that are negative and life-depleting, the Law must act upon those thoughts.

*We cannot get away with the luxury of a negative thought,* because "there is nothing that is covered that will not be uncovered; and hidden that will not be known."[6] The Law responds to inner thoughts, hidden beliefs, and covert concepts. It is as useless for us to try to "cover our tracks" as it is for us to worry about someone else getting away with something, because *everyone* gets what they deserve and *no one* gets away with anything at all. IT'S THE LAW!

There is only One God Who is both Love and Law. "God is natural Goodness, Eternal Freedom, and pure Loving-kindness. But the Law is a cold, hard fact, returning to each the result of his own acts, be they false or true."[7] The negative or limited appearances in our life are not the result of a Love that has abandoned us or a Universal Law that has failed us. God isn't out to get us. The Law is merely re-creating in perfect form our imperfect thoughts! What appears to be "vengeance" is simply "Law and Order."

## WE'RE "PAID IN MENTAL AND SPIRITUAL COIN"[8]

Everyone is repaid in like manner according to his or her own individual thought and activity. If someone lives in the "realm" or "consciousness" of lies and dishonesty, he or she receives from that realm. We never have to hold on to resentment or wish ill-will toward anyone no matter what they have done to us because the Law has a repayment plan that is much more comprehensive than we could ever imagine.

In fact, it is not only unnecessary for us to concern ourselves with others "getting theirs"; it is in our best interest to let go of thoughts of revenge as quickly as they enter our mind. The Law acts upon our thoughts every moment, and what we desire for another cannot help but come back to us. The activity of mind precedes the movement of matter, and the two are actually one and the same. The condition of our life is as much the result of our *unspoken desires* as our *direct actions*. "I say unto you that whoever looks at a woman with lust, has already committed adultery with her in his heart."[9] We can present a pleasant or pious exterior to the world, but if we are entertaining unpleasant or unholy thoughts, those thoughts will come back to us in form. IT'S THE LAW!

## "WE ARE SURROUNDED BY A UNIVERSAL LAW"[10]

Unlike human laws that are often changeable (depending upon who's in charge), vague (and arguable), and biased (in favor of a particular group), the Law of Spirit is changeless, clear, and always just. There is no way to get around the Law of our Being, because It is around us. It is Boundless and moves in, through, above, and beneath us. There is no way to circumvent it. It cannot be changed or overruled. It cannot be manipulated, fooled, or defrauded. It remains in Integrity eternally, creating specifically and perfectly the ideas, concepts, and notions given to It.

The Law acts only upon belief and conviction, not whimsy and wishes. We can wish all day for prosperity, but if our mind is filled with images of lack and limitation, we are not going to be prosperous. The law will respond to our belief in scarcity and will create more and more lack by creating less and less in our world. "For whosoever hath, to him shall be given, and he shall have more abundance: but whosoever hath not, from him shall be taken away even that he hath."[11]

The Law gives to us our *convictions*, not our hopes and wishes. It is clear, concise, and exact. Jesus asked, "If a son shall ask bread of any of you that is a father, will he give him a stone? or if he ask a fish, will he for a fish give him a serpent?"[12] We may ask for bread when, in fact, we *believe* that we deserve only a stone.

Then, when the stone appears, we blame God for punishing us by not giving to us that for which we asked.

The Law creates for us out of the seeds of our thought. Just as we can depend upon the laws of nature to bring forth from the soil whatever we plant–e.g. a carrot, not a cucumber, from a carrot seed, and an oak tree, not a palm tree, from an acorn–so we can depend upon the Law of Spirit–the Law of our Being–to bring forth into our experience exactly what we think into it. It creates forms from the thought seeds that we plant into Its Receptive, Powerful, and Active Substance. IT'S THE LAW! If we are not getting what we want from life, we need to look at what we're putting into It through our thoughts and beliefs.

Seeds planted in fertile soil will always sprout. Our thoughts are always creative, because the Substance into which they go is Infinitely Fertile. When our life is not blooming with roses, we need to check the seeds, not the Soil. The Creative Medium of Spirit "receives all ideas given It, and tends to create a form around them. If It could choose, It could *reject*, and this is as impossible as for the soil to say, 'You must not plant spinach this year, you must plant cauliflower.'...It does not argue but at once begins to create a likeness of the pattern given it."[13]

There is no trick to the way the Law works–no cosmic pranks. We are all created with "green thumbs" and the ability to bring into our experience all that we desire. We can depend upon the Law to be consistent in every way, every time. Just as the fertile soil will not give us what we have not planted, and just as it will grow a weed as well as a fruit tree, our thoughts operate through a Creative Medium that will give us only what we have planted through solid belief, even when we believe in pain, suffering, and limitation.

## "WHY DID THIS HAPPEN TO ME?"

Most of the time we are not conscious of what we've planted. We
have thousands of thoughts every day. Most of them have become
so habitual that we don't even notice what we are thinking most of
the time. It isn't until our thoughts begin taking form (sometimes
really ugly forms) that they get our attention. Then we ask,
"Where in the world did this experience come from?!" We don't
remember that we planted the seed for it years ago, perhaps even
in childhood. We don't realize that we not only didn't dig the seed
up, but that we've actually been giving it nourishment through the
years with more and more thoughts just like it. Most of the time
we don't notice the sprouts in our life (those little manifestations
of things we don't want to grow). It isn't until they grow large and
cover our path that we finally see them.

Just as a sprout needs nourishment to continue until it is
fully grown, once we plant an idea in Mind–one that is positive
and life-enriching–we must nourish it if we want it to come to
fruition. We need to be careful that we are not nourishing weeds
instead of roses. If we consciously plant a seed of prosperity, it is
important for us to nourish and feed it all day long with spiritually rich thinking. We may speak our treatment for prosperity,
we may make a few affirmations during the day,  but abundant
good can't take form in our life if the majority of our words and
thoughts throughout the day affirm lack and limitation. If we look
at the economy or our material resources and believe that they
determine our abundance or lack of it; if we are not certain that
we are worthy; if we are selfish with what we have and judgmental
in what we see; it all adds up to lack and limitation. We have,
unintentionally, nourished the weeds of poverty and allowed the
blossoms of Abundant Good to wither.

## THE LAW THAT BINDS CAN ALSO FREE

God can give to us only what we are truly willing to accept through our belief system. IT'S THE LAW! We are bound, shackled, and imprisoned by our beliefs through a Law *that can also set us free*. "Nature seems to await our comprehension of her and, since she is governed by immutable laws–the ignorance of which excuses no man from their effects–the bondage of humanity must be a result of our ignorance of the true nature of Reality."[14] We cannot live an unlimited, fulfilling life and experience the freedom of our spirituality while we are thinking of ourselves as limited, material beings.

Through the Law we have the potential to bring into our life every beautiful experience we desire: love in all of our relationships, success in all of our endeavors, health and vitality in our body all of the days of our earthly life, and guidance and direction in all of our activities. If we want to return to the Garden of Eden, we must plant the seeds of acceptance of our true spiritual nature into the Fertile Soil of Spirit, where our faith and belief is acted upon by the Powerful Creative Medium of the Universe.

Then every day and every moment of every day, we must feed and nourish those thoughts so that our Tree of Life will grow large and beautiful, and bear abundant fruit. Then our life will be a place for the songbirds to sing and build their nests. All of this can happen–does happen and will happen–as we live the Truth of our Being. The Truth automatically sets us free. IT'S THE LAW!

## *Process Sheet Twenty-Three*

# It's the Law!

*INDIVIDUAL*

We hurt ourselves and no one else by our fantasies of revenge even though we may never take outward action on our flights of fancy. Knowing that you reap what you sow, even though you may never consider taking action on such thoughts, examine your consciousness to see if you have been sowing thoughts of revenge or ill-will. Write them down on a separate piece of paper.

We are all here for the same purpose: to learn more of our innate spiritual nature and to express it. Close your eyes and imagine any individual about whom you have entertained revengeful thoughts. "Release" that person with loving thoughts of support as you watch them walk away along their path of spiritual learning. Remember, this person belongs to "the Lord." We are all subject to the same Law, and we all reap what we sow. (This process could take five to ten minutes or longer.)

Now you have cleared some space in the "garden" of your mind. The Law is working for you at this very moment. The Soil of the Creative Medium is Fertile. What seeds of thought do you want to plant?

_____

_____

_____

What weeds will you need to pull up?

_____

_____

_____

What will you do to nourish these seeds (what "supporting" thoughts will you pour upon them?)

_____

_____

(*This week, consciously write, speak, and act upon all thoughts that will nourish the seeds you desire to grow in your life.*)

### GROUP
Discussion of Lesson.

**Activity:** Same as for Individual.

**Additional Activity:** (*Materials: pencil/pen, paper.*)
Write a personal poem about the garden you have planted up until now. (Pattern your poem after "Mary, Mary, quite contrary, how does your garden grow?" Begin your poem with "(*Your Name*)_____ , quite (*a spiritual quality*)_____, how does your garden grow? With ..." (*Example: "Denise, Denise, quite at peace, how does your garden grow,? With health and clarity, wealth and charity, and good friends all in a row."*) Your poem does not have to rhyme. (*Example: "Bill, Bill, quite loving and kind..."*)
Share with partner or group. Be sure to tend your garden all week and make any changes in your garden poem as new forms "sprout."

**Meditation:** The Godseed

(*Facilitator: read slowly with restful music in background, if desired. Begin with one of the Relaxation Techniques on pages 299-300.*)
You are a beautiful idea in the Mind of God...a perfect seed Spirit has planted within Itself...within you is everything that

you will ever require to grow into the idea God has of you...imagine that you are planted deep within the warm, nurturing Soil of Spirit...the Creative Medium of Life...what kind of seed are you? ...feel who you are...what will you grow into?...what are your special qualities; what makes you unique in the Great Garden of Life?...(*Facilitator allow one to two minutes*)...every good thought that you think nourishes you–the Godseed that is you–with the Sunlight of Love...every act of forgiveness allows the Waters of Peace to pour into your experience...take a few moments now to continue the act of releasing that you began earlier this evening... let go of any desire for another's pain or punishment and, as you do, feel the Waters of Peace pour into your soul...(*Facilitator: allow one minute*)...now think of that person or those people whom you have just released and place into that space of forgiveness thoughts of good toward them...thoughts of Love and, as you do, feel the Sunlight of Love warm you...nourish you...feel the Godseed that is you growing healthier, stronger, more radiant, and more beautiful...(*Facilitator: allow one minute*)...now bring your awareness back to the room, and with your eyes still closed, imagine that you are a beautiful part of the smaller garden in this room...your spiritual expression blending with and enhancing the group...feel your connectedness with everyone in the room...each and every person here adding to this special garden...and on the count of three open your eyes...one...two...three.

1. Hebrews 10:30, 31 (KJV).   2. SOM 196:2.   3. SOM 26:2.   4. SOM 186:4.   5. SOM 70:1.
6. Luke 12:2 (Lamsa).   7. SOM 500:2.   8. SOM 268:2.   9. Matthew 5:28 (Lamsa).   10. SOM 458:4.   11. Matthew 13:12 (KJV).   12. Luke 11:11 (KJV).   13. SOM 92:2.   14. SOM 33:2.

# 24     Beyond Suspicion

Conviction in the Power of Mind to Bring About Change

*Before we attempt to improve the conditions of our life through "mental healing," it is necessary for us to be certain in our mind*
that we believe that thought is creative. We cannot effectively change "the outer" through *Mind Power* if we believe that there is actual *physical power* to oppose our endeavors. We cannot hope to change the "effects" in our life by changing their mental "cause" if we believe that *some* conditions are completely physical in origin and have no mental basis. What good would it do for us to attempt to "change our thinking," if we did not believe that through that change we could "change our life"?

The Science of Mind is a philosophy of living as well as a faith in an Ever-Present Power greater than ourselves. In order for us to move our faith from "crisis management" to day-to-day spiritual awareness, we must be convinced not only that thoughts are creative, but that thought itself is *all* there is to creation—in ourselves and in the world. We must live from the clear, conscious knowledge that every time we think, we are molding our life *within and out of* the Universal Creative Substance of Spirit. "Thoughts are more than things, they are the cause of things."

How much of the time are you certain beyond a shadow of a doubt that there is nothing in the outer world—no person, job, germ, or circumstance—that can harm, diminish, deplete, or affect your health, wealth, or happiness?

How often, instead, do you find yourself thinking, speaking, and acting as though the physical world were concrete, rather than fluid thought-form; as though it had a separate life of its own apart from you and the influence of your thought, and as though it were separate from the Mind of God?

## HAVE YOU HAD THIS CHECK-UP LATELY?

It is important for us to take an "attitude check" every now and then–in fact, as often as possible. We need to observe and see whether we are living out of clear, confident spiritual intention–consciously knowing our spiritual nature–or whether we are living under a cloud of suspicion with doubts about the creativity of our thoughts and the effectiveness of our words.

We may *suspect* that there is more to life than what we are experiencing. We may *presume* that some people can create what they want through their thinking. We may even *understand* that if we took the time to really "get in touch" with our spiritual nature and clarified what we desire in life, we *might* be able to create it with our thinking. But too often we are so busy dealing with, and surviving in, a world we believe is not influenced by our thought that we just haven't gotten around to attempting to make a change in mind.

A friend told me the other day that she was finally cutting her "ambivalence cord"! To be ambivalent is to fluctuate between one thing and its opposite. Sometimes it seems as if we were attached to an ambivalence cord that keeps us vacillating between spirit and matter, between using the power and creativity of our thinking and believing that we are a victim of circumstances. If we don't consciously cut that cord, it will continue to "feed" thoughts that are wishy-washy, inconsistent, doubtful, and cloudy. It will keep us stuck in Never-Never Land because we will never-never do what we dream of doing or accomplish what we are capable of accomplishing.

Ambivalence makes us spiritual couch-potatoes in the Universal creation of our life. We need to make a choice as to what we are going to trust and believe in. We can't have it both ways. "The conviction that heals is that God is all in all and that there is no material cause or effect."[2] We can't believe that "thoughts are things" while also believing that some things are simply *things*. We can't believe that we can "make" things happen through faith and focus while also believing that things just happen. "Ye cannot serve God and mammon[3]...choose you this day whom ye will serve."[4]

We need to examine our thoughts. We can fool ourselves into believing that we are spiritually focused when, in fact, our thinking has not risen above the mountaintops. Traveler and writer E. Stanley Jones tells the story about visiting a Hindu ascetic who sought to escape the temptations of the world by going to live in a cave in an isolated forest and spending all his time in spiritual meditation. He said that the first thing the Hindu said to him when they met was, "I haven't thought about a woman for forty years." Stanley Jones said he thought to himself how interesting it was that that was the first thing he said to him! We need to be clear, moment to moment, about where our thoughts are *really* focused: on what the world is doing *to* us, or on what Spirit is doing *through* us. When we fluctuate between the two types of thinking, spiritual and material, we are ineffective in both.

## "KNOW–WITHOUT A SHADOW OF A DOUBT"[5]

We must have faith beyond a shadow of a doubt that what we desire in this lifetime is ours to experience if we want to live our dreams and assist others. We must be convinced that Spirit can and does move through our thoughts and that Divine Substance gives form to our thinking. "It is done unto us as we believe," not as we *suspect*.

Through our own experience of our "faith becoming flesh," by the *manifestation* or *materialization* of that for which we have treated and which we have accepted as undeniable, we build certainty that there is an Intelligence in the Universe that responds to us, guides and inspires us, and loves us Unconditionally. God is real only to the one who believes in Spiritual Reality and to the one who stands unmoved by material circumstances, stoic in his or her unity with the Whole. "Faith is mental assertion elevated to the plane of realization. It is beyond the mere quibbling or mumbling of words for it identifies itself with Reality in such a manner that Reality becomes real to the believer."[6]

Ask yourself, "How real is God to me in my day-to-day thinking? How often do I consider the spiritual nature of what I am doing? How often do I pause to look for the Truth and Meaning in my thoughts and activities? How often, instead, does the world, and my thinking about the world, get me sidetracked into meaningless and mundane routine?"

We are living, breathing points of Unlimited Potential and Eternal Possibility. We can achieve anything we want to achieve. We are not so much defeated by facing a challenge as we are defeated by *not trying* anything at all. How many dreams have you had in your life that you have given up on and will never strive to achieve? How many dreams do you have that you don't support with your day-to-day thinking?

"Could we see the mentality of a successful man, we should find the imprint of success written in bold letters across the doorway of his consciousness. The successful man is sure of himself, sure of what he is doing, and certain of the outcome of his undertakings."[7] We cannot create a successful life out of *ambivalent* thinking. Creating out of uncertainty, fluctuating between faith and fear, is like filling a balloon with water instead of air. Our dreams wiggle here and bulge over there, changing shape with the movement of each passing thought, until at last we cannot hold onto them and they fall from our grasp and burst. An affirmative statement begins with "I am," "I know," "I accept," or "I believe"– not "I suspect."

We must learn to think and act with spiritual confidence and not waver even if others disapprove or reject our ideas. We must *move* on our ideas rather than letting them sit unattended in the back of our mind. When we are focused on expressing our spiritual potential in everything we do, our mind doesn't drift to unpleasant events of the past or previous fears or failures. When our thoughts are based upon the conviction that there is a Power fully *for* us, we won't view challenges as a sign that life is against us, and we won't waste time with negative, unproductive, or fearful thoughts.

In the material world, we call those who have accomplished much with their lives "superachievers." But "average" is merely an agreed-upon middle ground on which the majority of humankind has agreed to stand. "Average" has nothing to do with the potential of who we truly are. We are *unlimited* spiritual beings. The ones who are called "superachievers" have barely even scratched the surface of human potentiality much less peaked the possibilities of spiritual beingness. Yet they far surpass the majority. Why would we choose to be "average" if we were *certain* of our spiritual potential?

If we want to change our life through "mind power" and have true confidence in our ability to succeed, we must have

unshakable faith that God "has made us, and not we ourselves."[8]
We must be convinced that we live, move, and have our being in
a Universe that is Spiritual and that we are given that spiritual
kingdom for our use. We must be certain that our thoughts are
creative and that by thinking into the Universal Creative Medium
of Life, our thoughts become the "things" of our life. And we must
never let anything cause us to doubt our ability to demonstrate the
Truth.

## "ALL DOUBT AND FEAR MUST GO"[9]

The flow of Life through us cannot bring about our desires if our
faith is not whole. "We must not only believe, we must know that
our belief measures the extent and degree of our blessing. If our
belief is limited only a little can come to us, because that is *as we
believe*."[10] If we *suspect* that it takes more than what is available to
us to create what we want, and if we *fear* that we can't live the life
we want to live, then our faith is fragmented between Spirit and
matter. We must be *certain* that when we speak our word, IT IS
SO! Mediocre faith causes our thoughts to be wishy-washy, uncertain, and ambivalent. True creation is beyond suspicion. It comes
out of certainty–an absolute belief in Spirit and in ourselves as
spiritual offspring.

They say that the only "certainty" is death and taxes. We
can be certain that this earthly life is finite and will end. If we are
not living the life we want to live now, when will we start to live it?
If we don't believe in our dreams, how can Life give them to us,
since it is done unto us as we believe? If we suspect that there is
more to this life than we are experiencing, why aren't we experi-
menting? We won't know what we are capable of creating in our

life solely through our thinking until we rely solely upon our
thinking and upon the Spirit that creates through our thoughts.

"There's no time like the present." In fact, it is the only
time we have. Our thoughts are as spiritual and creative now as
they will ever be. If we don't get busy and test the Power within us,
we shall miss out on the life that Power could, and would, have
created for us. There was an avocado rancher in Santa Paula,
California, who was given two apricot trees as a gift. He planted
them near his house and fertilized and cared for them faithfully.
But for seven years they produced no apricots. As his orchards
were filled with fruit-laden trees each season and he fancied himself to have quite a "green thumb," he considered the two barren
apricot trees a personal failure.

One day in late December, he got out a large ax with the
intention of cutting down both trees which, by then, had grown
quite large. He was about to make the first chop, when relatives
pulled up unexpectedly in the driveway. He laid the ax beside one
of the trees and never got around to cutting them down the rest
of the winter. The following spring they bloomed and produced
bushels of apricots. One day, as he stood admiring his now
fruitful trees, he noticed the ax, still leaning where he'd left it the
previous winter. He told friends later that he didn't know if the ax
had anything to do with it, but something had surely motivated
those trees!

Metaphorically, we all have an "ax" leaning against our
earthly trunks. We are only promised so much time on earth to
grow, to bloom, and to bear fruit. If we want to live our dream,
Universal Creative Substance can make it happen. But *we* have to
participate through our total, unwavering commitment to our
dreams, and our unshakable conviction that all that we desire

originates in the realm of Spirit.

You can begin creating your dreams right now if you move your faith beyond suspicion and choose this day whom you will serve.

*Process Sheet Twenty-Four*

# Beyond Suspicion

*INDIVIDUAL*

Do you believe that some conditions are completely physical in origin? If so, what are those conditions?

_____

_____

_____

_____

In order for you to move your faith from "crisis management" to day-to-day spiritual awareness, you must be convinced that thoughts are not only creative, but that thought itself is *all* there is to creation–in yourself and in the world. Consider the above conditions as originating in thought first, and write down a possible mental concept or "cause" for each. (If you are certain that all is thought, choose issues in your life that you want to change or improve, and write the mental concept or "cause" you believe is behind each one.)

_____

_____

_____

_____

Write affirmations to assist you in creating a *new* mental cause based upon Spiritual conviction for the above conditions:

_____

_____

_____

_____

## *GROUP*
Discussion of Lesson.

**Activity:** Same as for Individual.

**Meditation:** Mind, the Creator

(*Facilitator: read slowly with restful music in background, if desired. Begin with one of the Relaxation Techniques on pages 299-300.*)
   Thought itself is *all* there is to creation–in yourself and in the world...all originates in the Mind of God...the Only Mind... your mind...all is Divine Creative Energy...and It is right where you are right now...Infinite Imagination is right where you are... in the Unlimited Space of the One Mind...your mind...you can imagine anything you choose...all your desires fit within Infinity...imagine now your ideal home...see it in full detail... now imagine the perfect car parked in the driveway...see it, too, in full detail...a house, a car, so "big" in the world, fit in the Infinity of your mind...imagine a perfect relationship, if you choose...see yourself in the ideal career, if you like...see yourself on a perfect vacation...all originates in the One Mind...your mind...what in your life would you like to change?...see the change in mind...see the perfect outcome...all begins in the One Mind...your mind...if you can see it here, you can experience it in your life...take time now to set a new mental cause in motion for each change, for each desire...(*Facilitator: allow three to five minutes*)...accept, with conviction, that all you have seen in mind is now taking place in your world of affairs...there is no physical cause nor separate physical solution...all originates in mind...the One Mind...your mind...here and now...find yourself back in the room with your eyes still closed...feel the expectation and

conviction that you have set a new cause or causes in motion that cannot be prevented from manifesting in your physical world... and on the count of three...feeling elated and elevated with gratitude and anticipation...open your eyes, one...two...three.

1. SOM 414:2.   2. SOM 413:5.   3. Matthew 6:24 (KJV).   4. Joshua 24:15 (KJV).
5. SOM 188:3.   6. SOM 283:6.   7. SOM 450:3.   8. Psalms 100:3 (Lamsa).
9. SOM 272:2.   10. SOM 280:2.

# Scared Stiff

Transcending Fear through Trust
in the Ever-Presence of Spirit

*Phrases such as
"I'm scared to death" or
"It scares the living daylights
out of me" indicate that
we understand the
detrimental effect that fear
can have on us.*

When we say that we are "petrified"
or "scared stiff," it is evident that we know that fear can keep
us immobilized and unable to move forward in our life. Fear
keeps us from stepping out and exploring the greatness and
magnitude of our self-expression because we would rather
feel the security of knowing what to expect (even though
what we expect is not what we want) than to feel the fear
that accompanies our journeying into the unknown and
experiencing something new.

An earthly life that is lived *totally without fear* is usually lived by one who is either completely enlightened or
totally unconscious–for in the material world there seems to
be a need for caution and security. Most of us would probably think of ourselves as somewhere in between "enlightened" and "unconscious"–*semiconscious* so to speak–aware of
the potential dangers of the material world and trying to
protect ourselves from them, while glimpsing a spiritual state
of being that is untouched by worldly conditions.

We may experience fearless *moments* in our life
when we feel peaceful, harmonious, and safe–occasions when
we are convinced that there is nothing in the world (or in
ourselves) to harm us. But often when we are faced with

something outside of our accepted comfort zone, the unresolved fear that has been looming all along just beneath the surface of our awareness quickly invades our consciousness. When fear appears, if we are willing to face it rather than run from it–and move through it rather than become immobilized by it–we have the opportunity to grow in faith, increase in spiritual understanding, and to express ourselves more fully. "To overcome fear is the greatest adventure of the mind of man."[1]

Feeling fear does not have to prevent us from doing what we want to do in our life. After all, we've all moved through certain levels of fear to get us where we are today. Some of us have moved through the fear of tests in order to get through school, or overcome the fear of looking awkward in order to learn a new sport, or overcome shyness to interact with co-workers or the opposite sex.

## WE CAN CHOOSE TO MOVE

Fear is not a reason for us to do (or not do) anything. Fear "hovers" in human consciousness like a huge cloud casting a shadow over many of our activities–but it does not need to be the main event. When we feel afraid, we have two choices: Either (1) we can acknowledge our fear and do what we want to do anyway by increasing our faith in the One Mind in us. This is overcoming or transcending fear. Or (2) we can retreat by increasing our "faith in fear" and letting fear immobilize us until we are literally scared stiff, unable to make effective decisions, take positive actions, or relate harmoniously in the world. This is allowing fear to control us.

You have probably known people who have a knack for taking the simple worries and common fears of everyday life and transforming them into true misery-making, immobilizing anxieties that keep them petrified. These are the truly negative thinkers who can picture a rose-covered cottage and think only of mortgage payments, thorns, and allergies.

In their "training manual" *How to Make Yourself Miserable,* authors Dan Greenburg and Marcia Jacobs describe the elements necessary to "turn an ordinary fear into a full-blown, major anxiety," one in which we shall find ourselves scared stiff. There are three elements: (1) there must be hell to pay if our fear proves to be true, (2) there must be some evidence that our fear will prove to be true, and most importantly (3) there must be a substantial period of time to wait before we can find out if our fear is true.[2]

## THE DECEPTIVE ELEMENT OF TIME

Debilitating fear or chronic anxiety requires time for anticipation in order for it to be effective. Fear is "nothing more nor less than the negative use of faith"[3] and the misuse of our imagination. Fear has more to do with our imagination and expectation than with an actual event. We are afraid because we anticipate something unpleasant is *going to* happen. The Greek philosopher Epictetus wrote, "For it is not death or hardship that is a fearful thing, but the fear of death and hardship." Fear is *anticipated* rather than *actual* failure, pain, or loss. Fear occurs when we're *not doing* the actual thing we're afraid of, but *waiting* for it to happen. For example: *waiting* to confront someone, *waiting* for test results, or *waiting* in the dentist's office. "The Divine intends freedom for us but the very fact that we have creative thought, and that we are real individuals, presupposes the use of our creativeness in more than one way."[4] And that way isn't always by our imagining peaceful, pain-free events.

Then there is the event that has already occurred—that when we think of it in retrospect frightens us. While the event was actually occurring, however, we were too involved in the emergency to be afraid. A friend of mine who is a physical therapist experienced just such an the event. The ordeal was so unexpected, happened so suddenly, was over so quickly, and he was so busy handling the situation, that he didn't have time to be afraid. He was driving in his Jeep Cherokee to the post office late one afternoon when he crossed an intersection and was hit broadside by a car running a red light.

He remembers seeing the car just as it hit the rear passenger door. He felt his car rolling over and over as the sounds of glass shattering and metal bending filled his ears. He was wearing his seatbelt and, as a therapist, he knew that the best thing he could do at that moment was to relax his body–which he focused on doing. He said that everything seemed to be happening quickly and in slow motion at the same time. As his car finally came to rest right side up, he was able to get out on the driver's side. He was not seriously injured, but the driver of the other car was and had to be taken to the hospital. He said that he realized in retrospect that he had been so busy taking action in the situation that he hadn't been afraid–but he shook all the way home!

Often when an emergency situation is actually occurring, we're so busy with our involvement in the predicament that we don't feel afraid. If we lived totally involved in each moment of our day-to-day lives focused on being present–crisis or not–we would most likely never feel fear no matter what was going on because we would not be anticipating the worst that could happen or fearing that the past would repeat itself. There is no future to be afraid of and no past to bring discord into the present. "Let us forget the past and live in the eternal present of God's happy smile. Today is good; tomorrow will be even better...for the nature of Reality cannot change."[5]

# FUTURE FEAR

It seems to be human nature for us to anticipate the future and fear its potential for disaster. We feel sudden fear when a future event is just moments away–like just before we stand up to speak in public. Or, we experience chronic fear when we think something will *inevitably* happen to us at some point in our life. Today there are women who are having their healthy breasts removed and hysterectomies performed because they have a family history of breast and cervical cancer. These women would rather remove part of their healthy body than live with the fear of developing the disease.

Prolonged worry and fear can actually make us sick; and, like Job in the Bible, the thing we most fear often comes upon us, not because it existed as an inevitability or certainty, but because that is where we put most of our focus and energy. "Fear arises from that mental attitude which limits the possibility and the willingness of Spirit to give us the good we so greatly desire,"[6] and it actually helps to prepare the way for whatever we fear to come about in our life.

Fear robs us of our awareness and utilization of the Healing Presence within us. If we were to live each moment *within* that moment only, if we were to be "present in the present," all anxiety and worry would dissolve in the Allness of the Presence of Good. There would be no basis for fear if there were no concern about the future. If we could leave the negativity of the past (ours and our ancestors') behind us, where it belongs, and focus our attention on creating a new pattern in our life, we would not dread a future that resembled our past. We would be free to experience the fullness of the Present in which the Spirit of Spontaneous Goodness dwells and prevails. "Never limit your view of life by any past experience. *The possibility of life is inherent within the capacity to imagine what life is.*[7] "The Kingdom of God is now present, and NEEDS BUT TO BE REALIZED."[8]

## NOW IS THE APPOINTED TIME

The Kingdom of Heaven can only be realized NOW. *Spirit doesn't dwell in memories or work through anticipation.* We cannot experience the Unlimited Potential available to us or utilize the Power that is Present in us–in each moment–when the past and the future are colliding in our mind. In the mental and emotional chaos created by fear, the Magic of the Moment is lost to us. "Fear brings limitation and lack in its wake and destroys the happiness and possibility of a greater degree of livingness."[9] Our focus on fear blocks the Wisdom that is available to guide us into positive decision-making. It inhibits Love and hinders compassion for ourselves and those around us. And it prevents the Peace that would keep us centered and free us from panic.

Swami Chetanananda has written: "Your resources are infinite events, which you organize and mobilize to the depth of your capability at the moment." It is not possible for us to organize or mobilize our resources when we are scared stiff or in a state of panic. The Resource of knowledge that Spirit provides is unavailable to us when we are focused on fear, because we cannot be attuned to the One Power while believing in another power. It is only as we center ourselves in God–by turning within to the All-Embracing Presence and by opening to the Peace at the core of our being that is unmoved by circumstances–that we are able to organize and mobilize that Power through us.

Fear dissolves in the realization that God is available to us under all circumstances, and that we cannot create a situation that could eliminate Divine authority no matter how frightening the surroundings might be. It is both empowering and *sedative* at the same time for us to know that, no matter where we are, all of the Resources of the Universe are there, too. We don't need to worry about tomorrow (or an hour from now) when we trust that when we get there, God will be there, too. "Lo, I am with you always."[10] If Spirit were to leave us for a microsecond, we would have nothing to fear because we would be nothing at all. Our life depends upon the Presence of God because our life *is* the Presence of God. The movement of our body is the Movement of Spirit. The words that we speak float upon the Breath of Spirit. The thoughts that we think occur within the Mind of Spirit. We are never alone, because *to be alive is to live in God.*

Fear not only keeps us from recognizing the Spiritual Truth of our own being, but it keeps us from recognizing the Spiritual Truth of the world around us. Fear separates us from each other. It emphasizes our differences and hides our unity. We become afraid of the people we've already met: what they will think of us; how harshly they may judge us; and how thoroughly they may reject us. We fear those we haven't met and what they might do to us when we do meet them.

The material world seems to be filled with escalating crime and senseless violence. If we were to judge only by appearances, we would have much to fear. A friend commented to me as we watched a news report of yet another shooting: "It's beginning to look like the wild West all over again!" It would certainly appear that we have not progressed much as a race when our most obvious evolution is from a Colt 45 to an assault weapon.

Perhaps you don't own a gun, but do you own the fear and sense of separation from others that perpetuates the manifestation of guns? Do you distrust others based on prejudice and fear?

Sometimes it seems that we automatically suspect certain social, economic, or ethnic groups of wrongdoing, that we're afraid to reach out to *them* because they're not like *us*, and that we're so stiff and frozen by fear that we've lost the spontaneity and free-flowing interaction that Love inspires. "Our faith destroys all fear. We awake from the dream of fear to the vision of Reality, where there is no shadow of which to be afraid."[11]

## FEAR IS A SHADOW

Fear is the great impostor. It is not the Great Power. Fear looms in our consciousness and claims to have the might and potency to keep us from loving ourselves and each other. But fear is shadow, not substance. It cannot create a solid barrier to our joy and happiness or separate us from each other if we don't allow it to. If we are willing to move through its growing darkness, we shall find that it is nothing at all. The Light that is Present in every moment is the Power that dissipates the shadows. As we trust in the Allness of God as the only True Presence in every event, we'll find that the "living daylights" within us grow stronger and brighter, and that no one and nothing will be able to scare them out of us again.

*Process Sheet Twenty-Five*

# Scared Stiff

*INDIVIDUAL*
What fears from the past do you bring to this moment?

_____

_____

_____

What anxieties about the future do you hold in this moment?

_____

_____

_____

Write an affirmative statement of Truth that includes the word
NOW and that allows you to release the fears from the past and
anxieties about the future that you have listed above. (Example:
*"I release all fear of hereditary disease, knowing that Spirit is creating
my health and wholeness NOW."*)

_____

_____

_____

*GROUP*
Discussion of Lesson.

**Activity:** (*Materials: two shoeboxes with tops, one marked "PAST"
the other "FUTURE"; also if possible, a shovel and an area nearby
with soft dirt for burying the boxes. If no area is available, ask for a
volunteer from the group to bury the boxes later.*) After completing
the Individual process, each member of the group places his or her
"fears" in the appropriate box. If an area for burying the boxes is

available, the entire group should assist in burying the boxes and then hold hands as the facilitator reads the meditative prayer that follows. (If the boxes are to be buried later, the group can stand in a circle with the boxes in the middle of the circle and hold hands for the following meditative prayer.)

**Meditative Prayer:** (*Facilitator: read slowly with restful music in background, if desired.*) The Spirit of Goodness, Perfection, Wisdom, and Love is All there is in this moment…Spirit is All there is *to* this moment…say within yourself, "I bury all fear from the past…I understand that the past is like a carpet rolled up behind me…I no longer need to tread upon it…the past has no power over me and cannot repeat itself without my permission… I no longer give the past entrance to the moment in which I dwell…I dwell in the Eternal Moment of Spirit…I bury all anxiety about the future…I understand that it is within the Presence of Spirit and out of the Creative Power of Spirit that my future unfolds…I do not fear what Spirit creates, and Spirit is creating my life in this moment…I accept this moment as a Holy Moment in which there is only the Presence of Spirit within, through, around, and as me…I open my consciousness–my mind and my heart–to the Light of Spirit and allow the Light to dissipate the darkness of fear…the past is behind me…the future unfolds in harmony before me…and I dwell in the Light of the Presence forever…and so it is…Amen.

1. SOM 404:4.  2. Dan Greenburg and Marcia Jacobs, *How to Make Yourself Miserable,* (Random House), p. 6.  3. SOM 156:4.  4. SOM 411:2.  5. SOM 471:4.  6. SOM 404:3.
7. SOM 187:1.  8. SOM 335:1.  9. SOM 404:2.  10. Matthew 28:20 (Lamsa).
11. SOM 560:2.

## Opening Ourselves to Greater Responsibilities

*When you talk to yourself, do you "respect" yourself as a spiritual being or do you give yourself a hard time? Is your conversation with others* about spiritual health and wholeness or is it about the flu that's going around the office or your latest ache or pain? Do you respond to others from a loving sense of unity with them or do you react from a feeling of separateness and self-protection? Are you consciously aware that there is a Power within you that can do anything or do you spend your time thinking and talking about what you cannot do and have not done?

It is easy for us to get wrapped up in the physical world with its ups and downs, and to empower the downs with our thoughts and words. We must consciously and consistently remind ourselves that there is more to life than material form. There is a spiritual wonderment awaiting our perception. When we believe that "we're *only* human," we cannot experience the *spiritual* being that resides simultaneously with our human being.

## ARE WE "ONLY HUMAN"?

When we forget that we are capable of expressing the positive qualities of Spirit any time we choose, we begin to believe that all of our behavior–no matter how reactive, limited, unloving, and ungodlike it may be–is justified by our mortal condition. After all, we're only human! And the human world is unpredictable, filled with people and events that demand our human reactions. How will the guy who cut us off on the highway know that he's erred if we don't give him a "sign"? How will the salesclerk know that she's moving too slow if we don't show her through our impatience? How will our mate know how wrong he or she was if we're nice to them *before* they apologize?

However, if our conscious desire is to experience something beyond the flesh, then, like St. Francis of Assisi, we could choose to be an "instrument" of Spirit. We would consider (before we reacted) which of our potential spiritual responses would best reflect Love, Pardon, Faith, Hope, Light, and Joy. We would remind ourselves to seek to console before being consoled, to understand before being understood, and to love before being loved. We would look within before acting without, and in the process we would become an "agent" for the Almighty.

If we were to stop to consider *this* life as a part of something Wonderful–a Universe that functions in beautiful harmony within Itself–then we would take every opportunity to discover more of our true nature within that Universe. When we believe that our identity comes from our position and condition in the world, our concern and focus is often on how much money we make and how much we spend, how much influence we have over others and how powerful we appear. Rather than being an "instrument" of Spirit, we become a "tool" of the world. Our life becomes more about earning a living than expressing Life, more about losing weight than gaining Lightness of being, more about needing to be right than expressing Righteousness, and more about controlling others than expressing Freedom. We spend our time *manipulating* materially and not *manifesting* spiritually.

"Life manifests Itself through the individual. Therefore,

when one manifests goodness and purity, he is revealing the Father."[1] Each of us has the capacity to express goodness and purity every moment. Everyone has the potential to reveal Love, Pardon, Faith, Hope, Light, and Joy in any situation or experience. But we must be willing to be "used" by the Divine Presence within us.

## WANT TO BE USED?

For most of us, the idea of being "used" has a negative connotation, especially when we think of being used by another person. None of us wants to be exploited by others. We want to know that the good that we do is appreciated rather than taken for granted; that the love and friendship we give is reciprocal; and that we are loved in return for our love. We want to believe that our *selflessness* is not met with *selfishness*.

In order for us to give of ourselves–to share what we have without feeling used–there must be an element of trust. We must trust that the one to whom we are giving cares about us. We want *requited* love, *reciprocated* love. If we feel that our love is returned, we are willing to do anything for the one we love: "Tell me what you want; tell me what I can do for you." In other words, "*Use* me." When we love and feel loved in return, we WANT to be used.

If our criterion for allowing ourselves to be used is reciprocal love, then it should be easy for us to allow Spirit to use us. In the Bible we read of God's Love: "I have loved thee with an everlasting love: therefore with lovingkindness have I drawn thee."[2] We are not only loved, but we have been "sketched" by Love–designed by Love. Love is in, through, and around us, and resides as the very origin of our being. We are loved eternally. But are we willing to surrender *our position* for *Love's intention*, particularly in situations where we feel we have been wronged, or when we desire a certain outcome in a situation?

Often if it doesn't include our getting what we want, we find it difficult to *let* ourselves be used for the greater good of a situation. Most of the time we are open only to the outcome that we can see, and we don't trust the vastness and goodness of what lies beyond our vision. We don't trust that if we are *used* by Good, the result will necessarily include our good. Rather than our seeking to find how we can be an agent for Good, it seems that we want to hold Spirit captive in our mind like a genie in a magic lamp so that we can give specific instructions on how we can be served.

## WE LIVE IN A SPIRITUAL SYSTEM[3]

It is not what we do materially in life that brings about fulfillment, but the qualities we bring to what we do. The greatest earthly success is meaningless if the qualities of Spirit are missing. Our spiritual experience in every event is all that is meaningful or lasting. We can spend our life making sure that we don't go out on a spiritual limb–never apologizing when we're right, never forgiving when we're wronged, and portioning out our love, compassion, and understanding only to those who deserve it or at least can appreciate it–and in the process we shall miss out on the meaning of Life and our being meaningful in Life.

Within us is a Love that is Unconditional even though we may not feel It and even though we condition Its appearance with our limited perceptions. Within us is a Power that can and would do anything for us even though we don't allow It to. Within us is an Intelligence that can guide our every step even though we "plug our ears and hum" so that we can't hear It whisper, "Use me!"

"The Love of God is the Divine givingness: the eternal outpouring of Spirit through Its creation."[4] Why do we fear that if we surrender control of life's events, relinquish our opinion of how things should happen, don't watch where our love, compassion, and good intentions go, that it all might end up in the wrong hands? What comes from Love goes to Love: "For I was hungry, and you gave me food; I was thirsty, and you gave me drink; I was a stranger and you took me in; I was naked, and you clothed me; I was sick, and you visited me; I was in prison, and you came to me....Inasmuch as you have done it to one of the least of these my brethren, you did it to me."[5] The gift we give comes from Spirit and is given to Spirit. We are enriched as we are used by God; we're never depleted.

When we care more about loving than about being loved, and more about Righteousness than being right, it is easier for us to surrender to Spirit. When we LET GO OF THE LITTLE EGO we discover the Magnificence awaiting expression in our life. When I was in ministerial school there was a certain teacher who seemed to "get under my skin" no matter how hard I tried to prevent it (which, of course, made the problem worse!). It occurred to me on several occasions that the real solution would be for me to love this person, but it also seemed that every time I came to class with that intention in mind, the teacher would single me out for what I perceived to be humiliation and emotional abuse. Looking back now, I can see that what she did was a necessary part of my training, but at the time I wondered how I could ever put on the vestments of a minister with so much loathing in my heart.

One evening before class I was feeling exceptionally vulnerable, and I was wallowing miserably in self-pity when it occurred to me that even though "I" might not be able to love this person, God was already loving her. All I needed to do was to "get my bloated nothingness out of the way" so that Love could flow through. So during class, no matter what occurred, I affirmed that Love was present doing what (I thought) I couldn't do. It didn't take long for me to notice that as Love came to the fore in me, I could feel It, too. The "I" that was loving the teacher was one and the same! "I am that which thou art; thou art that which I am."[6]

When we allow ourselves to be "used" by Spirit, our "self" grows and expands into a greater awareness of our true spiritual nature. When we "choose to be used" in a particular situation, the Presence of Spirit permeates other areas of our life simultaneously, and other healings occur. That evening after class as I got ready for bed, I noticed that several warts on my hands that had caused me considerable embarrassment had (inexplicably?) disappeared! As we surrender to a Self that is higher, we animate the Spirit within, and It rushes forth to heal our sense of separateness. When we seek to be a blessing wherever we are–with the intention to just be a blessing and desiring nothing in return–we are blessed. We become an open space–a holy place for Spirit to pour more of Itself into the world.

## WILL *YOU* BE USED BY GOD?

Are you willing to be an instrument of the Peace of Spirit? Are you willing to be used by God? Are you willing to sow love within yourself where hate wants to grow? Are you willing to forgive when you've been injured? Are you willing to increase your faith when you are tempted to doubt the outcome of the spiritual process? Are you willing to allow the Truth at the core of your being to turn despair into hope, and hope into understanding? Will you turn from the darkness and look into the light? And, through it all, are you willing to forego sorrow and self-pity, and let the joy of the Indwelling Spirit spring forth from your being no matter what the circumstances may be? If so, you will be an "instrument" whose tone and quality are unequaled in all the Universe.

We must echo the Voice at the core of our being as It whispers, "Use me!" "For it is in Giving that we receive; It is in Pardoning that we are pardoned; And it is in Dying that we are born to Eternal Life."[7]

## *Process Sheet Twenty-Six*

# "Use Me!"

### *INDIVIDUAL*
Is there an area of your life where you have been withholding
Love, Pardon, Faith, Hope, Light, and Joy until something in the
outer world changed to justify your expression of these qualities?

_____

_____

_____

_____

_____

We must echo the Voice at the core of our being as It whispers,
"Use me!" if we are ever to experience our true spiritual nature.
Close your eyes and open your mind and heart to the Indwelling
Presence that can and *will* use you to bring Love, Pardon, Faith,
Hope, Light, and Joy into the world. Spend as much time as is
necessary in quiet contemplation of the Spirit within you until
you feel yourself surrender to Its Presence. Then commit yourself
to being used for Good in the areas that you have listed above.

### *GROUP*
Discussion of Lesson.

**Activity:** Same as for Individual.

**Meditation:** Make Me an Instrument of Thy Peace

(*Facilitator: read slowly with restful music in background, if desired.
Begin with one of the Relaxation Techniques on pages 299-300.*)

You have the capacity to express goodness and purity every moment...you have the potential to reveal Love...Pardon... Faith...Hope...Light...and Joy...in any situation or experience in life...but you must be willing to be "used" by the Divine Presence within you...are you willing to be an instrument of the Peace of Spirit?...are you willing to be used by God?...are you willing to surrender to Love within yourself rather than holding onto hate, resentment, anger, or guilt?...are you willing to forgive where you have been injured?...are you willing to increase your faith in those areas where you are tempted to doubt the outcome of the spiritual process?...are you willing to allow the Truth at the core of your being to turn confusion and distrust into understanding?...will you turn from the darkness and look into the Light and let the Joy of the Indwelling Spirit spring forth from your being no matter what the circumstances may be?...will you surrender the lesser for the greater?...will you be used for the greater good of your own experience and the greater good of the world?...Spirit has no other outlet but you...Love has no other instrument on which to play Its Love Song but you...Wisdom and Peace have no other mouth with which to speak but yours...surrender whatever you believe you know to the Great Unknown...let that Mind be in you that has no boundaries, limitations, accusations, or excuses..."For it is in Giving that we receive....It is in Pardoning that we are pardoned....And it is in Dying that we are born to Eternal Life"... And so It is...Amen.

1. SOM 480:2.   2. Jeremiah 31:3 (KJV).   3. See SOM 313:3.   4. SOM 460:6.
5. Matthew 25:35-36, 40 (Lamsa).   6. SOM 423:3.   7. Prayer of St. Francis of Assisi.

# Relaxation Techniques

*For Use in Preparation for,
and in Conjunction with,
Guided Meditations*

1. Sitting comfortably, with eyes closed, begin to breathe slowly and deeply...concentrating on each breath...in...and...out...in...and...out...with each breath feel yourself becoming lighter...and lighter...as if your physical body were becoming less dense...more transparent as you breath...in...and...out...with each breath your body seems to be disappearing...feeling as light as air... as wispy as a cloud...as transparent as mist...there is just your breath moving in...and...out...and as you breathe, feel yourself moving deeper within your consciousness...deeper within your mind...moving into the darkness...

2. Sitting comfortably, with eyes closed, breathe in and out very slowly...focus on your breathing...inhaling relaxation into your body...exhaling any tension...in... and...out...in...and...out...allow any thoughts to drift slowly in your mind like leaves falling from a tree...slowly down...and down...until they come to rest softly and silently at the "bottom" of your mind...let your mind relax... become clear...free of thought...at peace...

3. Sitting comfortably, with eyes closed, imagine that the room is filled with a beautiful white light...a light filled with the pure essence of peace and serenity...imagine that with every breath, you are inhaling peace and serenity... breathe it all the way down into your toes, your feet, your

legs...feel them relax...breathing the light into your torso...your arms...feel them relax...breathe the light into your neck and head...feel calmness and relaxation in your whole body...feeling more peaceful, more serene with every breath...in and out...very slowly...in...and...out...in...and...out...allow your thoughts to dissolve or drift away...until there is just a peaceful stillness in your mind...moving further into your own consciousness...into the safety and security within...leaving the outer world behind...